Creative Personnel Practices:

New Ideas for Local Government

John Matzer, Jr.

International City Management Association

PRACTICAL MANAGEMENT SERIES
Barbara H. Moore, Editor

Creative Personnel Practices
Capital Financing Strategies for Local Governments
The Entrepreneur in Local Government
Human Services on a Limited Budget
Microcomputers in Local Government
Telecommunications for Local Government

Library of Congress Cataloging in Publication Data
Matzer, John, 1934–
  Creative personnel practices.
  (Practical management series)
  Bibliography: p.
  1. Local government—Personnel management. I. Title.
II. Series.
JS148.M37 1984   352′.0051   83-22822
ISBN 0-87326-041-4

Printed in the United States of America.
12345 • 90898887868584

Foreword

Lean budgets, office automation, federal regulations, and a changing work force—all are affecting local government personnel systems and presenting new challenges to management. One of the responsibilities of personnel directors and other managers is to keep abreast of these and other changes and respond effectively to them.

Creative Personnel Practices: New Ideas for Local Government shows what local governments have done and can do to meet the challenge of change in this rapidly evolving field. Collecting insights from both the public and the private sector, this book provides guidance for evaluating personnel activities to gauge their effectiveness, creating a sound performance appraisal system, improving employee motivation through innovative and flexible incentives, bargaining in hard times, and responding intelligently to such emerging issues as sexual harassment and comparable worth.

This is the sixth book in ICMA's Practical Management Series, devoted to serving local officials' needs for timely information on current issues and problems.

We appreciate the outstanding work of John Matzer, Jr., city administrator of San Bernardino, California, in pulling this book together and the cooperation of the organizations that granted permission to reprint their material. David S. Arnold, Editor, ICMA, was of great help in planning for this book and for the entire Practical Management Series.

William H. Hansell, Jr.
Executive Director
International City
   Management Association

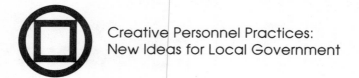

Creative Personnel Practices:
New Ideas for Local Government

The International City Management Association is the professional and educational organization for chief appointed management executives in local government. The purposes of ICMA are to strengthen the quality of local government through professional management and to develop and disseminate new approaches to management through training programs, information services, and publications.

Managers, carrying a wide range of titles, serve cities, towns, counties, and councils of governments in all parts of the United States and Canada. These managers serve at the direction of elected councils and governing boards. ICMA serves these managers and local governments through many programs that aim at improving the manager's professional competence and strengthening the quality of all local governments.

The International City Management Association was founded in 1914; adopted its City Management Code of Ethics in 1924; and established its Institute for Training in Municipal Administration in 1934. The Institute, in turn, provided the basis for the Municipal Management Series, generally termed the "ICMA Green Books."

ICMA's interests and activities include public management education; standards of ethics for members; the *Municipal Year Book* and other data services; urban research; and newsletters, a monthly magazine, *Public Management*, and other publications. ICMA's efforts for the improvement of local government management—as represented by this book—are offered for all local governments and educational institutions.

About the Editor and Authors

John Matzer, Jr., is City Administrator, San Bernardino, California. He was previously Distinguished Visiting Professor, California State University—Long Beach, where he now teaches graduate courses in public personnel management and collective bargaining. Mr. Matzer has served as Deputy Assistant Director, U.S. Office of Personnel Management; City Manager, Beverly Hills, California; Village Manager, Skokie, Illinois; and City Administrator, Trenton, New Jersey. He received B.A. and M.A. degrees from Rutgers University, New Brunswick, New Jersey, and he has taught at a number of universities over the years.

Following are the affiliations of the other contributors to *Creative Personnel Practices* at the time of writing.

David Alonso, Management Analyst, Office of Disaster Operations, Small Business Administration.

Vincent R. Ceriello, President, VRC Consulting Group, Los Altos, California.

Mark Lincoln Chadwin, Professor of Management, Old Dominion University, Norfolk, Virginia.

Paul J. Champagne, Professor of Management, Old Dominion University, Norfolk, Virginia.

Albert Cole, Jr., Benefit Consultant, Buck Consultants, Inc., New York, New York.

Debbie Cutchin, Assistant Professor, Political Science Department, University of Georgia, Athens, Georgia.

Philip A. Davis, Manager—Employee Relations, Memphis lamp plant, General Electric Company.

Basil S. Deming, Manager of Human Resources, Bendix Communications Division, Baltimore, Maryland.

John W. Falahee, President, John W. Falahee and Associates.

W. Maureen Godsey, Associate Director, ICMA Training Institute, Washington, D.C.

Philip C. Grant, Head, Department of Business Administration, Husson College, Bangor, Maine.

J. Peter Graves, President, Strategic Decision Data, Inc., Redlands, California.

John M. Greiner, Senior Research Associate, The Urban Institute, Washington, D.C.

Sud Ingle, General Manager, Quality Control, Mercury Marine, Fond Du Lac, Wisconsin.

Sally E. Ketchum, Managing Editor, *Medicine and Computer* magazine, White Plains, New York.

Edward Lawler, Professor of Psychology, Institute for Social Research, University of Michigan, and Professor of Organizational Behavior, University of Southern California.

John Liebert, Liebert, Cassidy, and Frierson, employee management law firm, Los Angeles, California.

Gerald M. Pauly, Director of Personnel Management, Sacramento County, California.

Donald L. Prescott, Technician, British Columbia Provincial Museum, Victoria, B.C., Canada.

Richel Raines, Project Leader, Sexual Issues in the Workplace Program, San Diego, California.

Joyce D. Ross, Associate Professor, School of Public Administration and Urban Studies, San Diego State University, San Diego, California.

Ruth D. Salinger, Employee Development Specialist, U.S. Office of Personnel Management, Washington, D.C.

Harold T. Smith, C.A.M., Professor of Information Management, Brigham Young University, Provo, Utah.

Trudy Sopp, Organization Development Specialist, San Diego, California.

Paul D. Staudohar, Professor of Business Administration, California State University, Hayward, California.

William M. Timmins, Brigham Young University, Provo, Utah.

William G. Wagner, formerly associated with the Western Electric Hawthorne project.

Yvonne Williams, Coordinator of Citywide Training, San Diego, California.

Dale Yoder, Professor Emeritus at the Graduate School of Business, Stanford University, and California State University, Long Beach, California.

Contents

Introduction

John Matzer, Jr.

Social, technical, and economic forces are significantly affecting local government personnel systems. Current challenges include a
changing work force, federal legislation and regulations, the financial crisis, legal requirements, technological advances, the evolution
of collective bargaining, and public demand for improved productivity and responsiveness. Work force demographics, attitudes, and
expectations are changing. Today's employees are concerned with
the humanization of the work environment. Workers question authority, seek interesting and satisfying work, want to participate in
decisions affecting them, and place more value on time for leisure
and personal affairs. Office automation is having a substantial effect on the quality of working life. A new consciousness is being fostered by court rulings that a job is an individual's most important
property right, and these court decisions are causing employees to
become increasingly litigious.

Personnel patterns are in a state of transition due to shifts in
traditional employment relationships, and local governments are
recognizing the need for personnel system reform. The personnel
function is being expanded to human resources management, which
matches the organization's needs with each individual's need for
personal growth and development. Public managers are developing
systems to measure the effectiveness of personnel activities. Performance appraisal systems are becoming more objective and job-
related. Merit pay plans are replacing fixed-rate and longevity pay
increase programs. Assessment centers are assuming an important
role in selection and career development. Affirmative action requirements are changing selection techniques.

Employee motivation, a perennial concern, is being approached
through new incentives, alternative work schedules, employee assis-

tance programs, job enlargement and enrichment, flexible benefit plans, and quality circles and other forms of participative management. Labor-management relationships are being altered by such new developments as concession bargaining, productivity bargaining, and labor-management committees. Critical local government personnel issues include comparable worth, sexual harassment and other forms of unlawful discrimination, the impact of technology on human resources, and computerized personnel information systems.

Since personnel costs are a major portion of local government budgets, local officials must keep abreast of new personnel techniques and complex issues. This collection of articles provides an overview of new developments, practices, and issues in personnel management. The articles review the state of the art in practical and nontechnical terms. A primary objective of this book is to highlight the evolution that is occurring in local government personnel management and the importance of these new issues and techniques to effective management.

Increasing personnel system effectiveness

Traditional personnel systems are being redefined, restructured, and realigned to make them more efficient, effective, and responsive to contemporary personnel issues. Part 1 reviews recent trends in human resources management, personnel management reform, and the evaluation of personnel activities.

Personnel management is shifting from a control orientation to an approach focusing on planning, development, and utilization of human resources. Human resources management reflects an effort to deal more effectively with the new social and individual values in the workplace. Particular attention is placed on forecasting skills that will be needed in the future and on personal career planning and development. Joyce Ross's article, "A Definition of Human Resources Management," examines the forces that are redirecting and expanding the role of the personnel function. She describes the relationship of human resources management to personnel and the significant components of a human resources management system.

Civil service reform is directed at improving personnel systems in accordance with common merit principles. Personnel reform is a growing trend among federal, state, and local governments. During the past decade every state and many local governments have implemented or studied some aspect of civil service reform. "Perspectives on Civil Service Reform" points out that common themes in these reform efforts include the creation of centralized management personnel systems separated from quasi-judicial activities; decentralization of such personnel activities as recruiting, examining, and position classification; development of objective job-related performance evaluation and merit pay systems; establishment of career executive programs; protection for whistleblowers, and establishment of broad job classes. The article goes on to describe the reasons for civil service reform and its benefits and implementation.

Another area receiving considerable attention is the development of evaluative methods to assess the effectiveness of personnel activities. Management requires an objective measurement system in order to evaluate and monitor the effectiveness of personnel activities. Efforts to evaluate have been restricted by professional resistance, lack of experience with measurement methodology, and the limited availability of appropriate performance criteria. Some progress, however, has been made in the development of evaluative systems. The U.S. Office of Personnel Management has designed a prototype measurement system described in *An Approach to the Measurement of Common Administrative Services: Productivity Measurement of Operating Personnel Offices* (February 1980).

Another publication, *Assessing Personnel Management: Objectives and Performance Indicators* (1977), prepared by the Public Services Laboratory of Georgetown University, is a guide for local officials in reviewing personnel management performance. Among the articles in this section is a self-audit of subobjectives and performance indicators for the basic personnel activities. Use of the indicators over time can provide the information needed to evaluate the effectiveness of the personnel function.

In "Practical Strategies for Evaluating Training," Ruth D. Salinger and Basil S. Deming discuss practical ways of using six different evaluation strategies to determine the extent to which training produces appropriate learning, the degree to which learning is transferred to the job, the degree to which the knowledge or skill is maintained over time, and the extent to which the value of improved performance meets or exceeds the cost of training. In "Auditing the Labor Relations Function," Dale Yoder and Paul D. Staudohar present a method for measuring the effectiveness of collective bargaining and grievance arbitration procedures.

Improving employee performance

Few personnel topics receive more attention than methods of improving employee performance. This section addresses important performance issues, including performance appraisal, merit pay, and assessment centers.

Performance appraisal systems are a means of improving productivity, avoiding discrimination complaints, and motivating employees. Poorly designed systems can have a negative impact on employee performance and offer the potential for being the litigation issue of the 1980s. Court decisions have stressed the need for valid and reliable job-related appraisal systems. Properly constructed evaluation systems are valuable in making pay, promotion, training, discipline, and other important personnel decisions. Substantial experimentation is occurring to replace subjective appraisal methods with objective, job-related systems. Performance measures have been established and tested for many local government services, and these measures can be used to design evaluation systems. Research indicates that an effective appraisal system involves supervisors; is standardized and formalized; stresses objective, job-related factors; and provides adequate training, an appeal process, and employee feedback. The article by J. Peter Graves describes the various appraisal techniques and their strengths and weaknesses. A case is made for a method that meets management's need for performance data and the employee's need for meaningful performance feedback.

Closely related to the performance issue is merit pay or pay for performance. Effective merit pay systems must be based on an objective measure of performance. Merit pay is an emotional issue. Many employees consider merit pay to be a myth. Some local governments that have tried merit pay systems have encountered serious problems. A recent evaluation of the federal merit pay experiment found it to be flawed. The report noted that, although merit pay is politically and ideologically attractive, it is costly, difficult to implement, and doesn't have many benefits. Despite the controversy surrounding merit pay, it is viewed as a motivational, equity, cost control, and productivity tool. Merit pay linked to performance is replacing automatic pay increases. Objective, job-related appraisal systems are an essential ingredient in successful merit pay programs. Problems associated with establishing a merit pay program include inflation, absence of a job-related appraisal system, growth of fringe benefits, supervisory resistance, and legal factors. Edward Lawler's article, "Performance Appraisal and Merit Pay," discusses problems associated with relating pay to performance and the conditions needed to make a system work.

Assessment centers are another useful tool for improving performance. Management selection and development have been aided by assessment centers that identify and measure behaviors and skills that are important to successful job performance. An assessment center consists of a formal procedure for incorporating group and individual exercises aimed at predicting the elements of managerial success. Assessment centers possess a high degree of validity and acceptance by the courts and participants. Basic steps involved in establishing an assessment center include job analysis, design of exercises, selection and training of assessors, observation, evaluation feedback, and validation. Minimum requirements for an assessment center are set forth in *Standards and Ethical Considerations for Assessment Center Operations* (1975) developed by the Third International Congress on the Assessment Center Method. Problems associated with assessment centers are cost, poor administration, inadequate assessor training, and poorly designed exercises. "Solving Personnel Problems through the Assessment Center" by Debbie Cutchin and David Alonso explores the assessment center process, its major elements and how to implement them, and some of the issues involved in conducting centers.

Motivating employees

Employee motivation is one of the most difficult challenges confronting local governments. Much time and effort have been spent reexamining how employees are motivated and experimenting with motivational strategies. The character of today's work force creates a need to find new ways to blend organizational and employee needs. Changing work values, a disappearing work ethic, more guaranteed wages and benefits, decreased employee loyalty, rising income, and diluted management authority have been cited as some of the causes of declining motivation. Employee surveys attribute worker dissatisfaction to changing attitudes, demeaning and inept supervision, an authoritarian atmosphere, poor communication, organizational policies, and the nature of work itself. The effects of job dissatisfaction are seen in increased turnover, absenteeism, accidents, grievances, and disciplinary actions, which result in increased costs and reduced productivity. This part of the book examines the issue of motivation and some of the techniques being employed to improve motivation and job satisfaction.

Local governments have recognized the importance of developing systems that identify dissatisfaction, analyze why it exists, and provide corrective action. Public managers are responding to changing worker attitudes and expectations by using monetary and nonmonetary incentive programs, job enlargement and enrichment, employee attitude surveys, alternative work schedules, quality circles, and improved compensation and benefit plans. These techniques serve as a means of providing for employee participation and making jobs more exciting and meaningful.

Although much research has been done on motivation, many supervisors understand very little about how and why their employees become motivated. There is considerable evidence that employees are motivated by various factors such as money, achievement, recognition, and power. Motivational strategies must be tailored to the individual's wants, needs, and purposes and cannot remain static. In "Motivation: Myths and Misnomers," Philip C. Grant helps put the motivation issue into perspective by exposing several myths about employee motivation and providing a better understanding of how managers can increase productivity.

Diverse monetary and nonmonetary incentive programs are available to reward employees on the basis of performance. Many times incentive programs fail because they do not meet employee needs and priorities and are poorly designed and administered. Obstacles to sound incentive programs include legal prohibitions, restrictive labor agreements, and administrative, fiscal, and political constraints. The cost and benefits of incentive programs should be carefully evaluated. Among the elements of a successful incentive program are objective measures of work performance, employee involvement in design and implementation, regular and frequent rewards, administrative simplicity, and appropriate monitoring and appeal provisions. John Greiner examines monetary incentives, performance targeting, and job enrichment as promising approaches for improving employee motivation.

Another motivational technique is alternative work schedules. Flextime, compressed workweek, and other forms of alternative work schedules increase employee satisfaction by enabling them to meet their individual needs and preferences. Donald L. Prescott describes work-hour models that can be used to evaluate work schedules and discusses the strengths and limitations of the standard workweek, extended workweek, staggered work hours, flextime, and compressed workweek.

Flexible or cafeteria benefit plans have emerged as another motivational technique. Such plans permit employees to select benefits most appropriate to their lifestyles and individual needs. Traditional benefit plans have proven less effective because of changes in the work force, rising medical and hospital costs, and inflation. Public employers must understand the difficulties associated with establishing flexible benefit plans. The plans can be expensive and have specialized accounting, data processing, counseling, and employee communication requirements. There may be union opposition and legal restrictions. Albert Cole, Jr., discusses cafeteria plans, including how they work, reasons for their creation, administrative requirements, plan designs, and major issues to consider in their development.

Employee interest in participating in decisions that affect their jobs has led to considerable interest in participatory management. Quality of work life programs, although limited in the public sector, reflect the concern about the impact of work on people and the organization. Quality circles, job enrichment, autonomous work groups, team building, and labor-management committees are representative of quality of work life efforts. These programs provide for employee participation and are based on the theory that involved employees are better motivated. While potentially beneficial, participative management can be time-consuming and marked by conflict and mediocre decisions. Philip A. Davis offers valuable tips on how to implement and operate successful participative systems.

A form of participative problem solving is the quality circle—a small group of employees and their supervisor from the same work area who voluntarily meet regularly to identify and recommend solutions to work-related problems. Quality circles can improve communications and reduce conflict and costs. Union resistance, lack of management support, failure to focus on important problems, and lack of participation are some of the problems associated with quality circles. In "How to Avoid Quality Circle Failure," Sud Ingle describes the reasons for such failures and outlines the secrets of a successful program. "An Overview of Useful Quality Circle Techniques" provides a brief introduction to some of the techniques used by circles to analyze and solve problems, and two case studies describe the use of quality circles in Dallas, Texas, and Fort Collins, Colorado.

Employee motivation, performance, and productivity can be seriously affected by personal problems, and public employers have an obligation to assist employees troubled with such problems. Personal problems can lead to low morale, reduced productivity, poor performance, turnover, increased costs, staff conflict, absenteeism, accidents, increased medical and other insurance costs, work disruption, and disciplinary problems. An effective approach to dealing with troubled employees is the establishment of an employee assistance program. These programs offer early intervention and treatment to employees with drug, alcohol, financial, legal, marital, and psychological problems. It has been estimated that employee assistance programs can return ten dollars for every one dollar invested. Successful employee assistance programs require written policies and procedures, confidentiality, early intervention, supervisor training, broad program coverage, professional administration, management and union support, and followup. William G. Wagner describes the employee assistance program operated by the city of Phoenix, discussing how the program was established, how it differs from other programs, and the basic elements of the program.

New labor–management ventures

The traditional collective bargaining pattern in the public sector is being altered by changes in the bargaining environment due to the financial crisis, citizen attitudes regarding unions, and modifications in the respective roles of labor and management. Local governments are expanding the scope of bargaining, seeking concessions, bargaining for productivity improvements, and joining labor in using cooperative approaches to solving problems. This section examines some of these new developments in labor–management relations.

Limited financial resources have stimulated public employer interest in concession bargaining. Concession bargaining consists of reopening and renegotiating existing contracts and requesting unions to make wage, benefit, and work rule changes. In exchange for granting concessions, unions seek job security, no-layoff pledges, contracting restrictions, severance pay, and training for laid-off employees. Unions also expect access to financial and confidential information and equality of sacrifice for management and nonunion employees. John W. Falahee's article examines the special considerations and techniques of concession bargaining and likely outcomes. John Liebert focuses on concession bargaining in the public sector and strategies that can be used at the bargaining table to reduce future personnel costs.

Productivity bargaining is another nontraditional bargaining technique receiving considerable attention because of its potential for cost reduction and productivity improvement. Bilateral negotiations are used in productivity bargaining to achieve changes in work rules and practices to increase productivity in exchange for a sharing of the gains with the workers. Productivity bargaining goes beyond wages, hours, and working conditions. Negotiations focus on work schedules and methods, workload, staffing levels, work quotas, job content, and other work rules. Employees share in the savings and benefits through job security, bonuses, wage and benefit increases, and greater involvement in management decision making and access to specialized information.

Another approach to improving labor–management cooperation is the labor–management committee. Such committees are formal advisory bodies created through collective bargaining to resolve mutual problems not covered by the written agreement. Among the subjects typically handled by labor–management committees are work scheduling, safety, training, productivity, merit pay, and housekeeping matters. The committees do not deal with negotiable issues or grievances. An excellent discussion of how to establish, develop, maintain, and evaluate labor–management committees is found in *A Guide to Labor-Management Committees in State and Local Government* by Gerald I. Susman (Public Technology, Inc., 1980). The guide points to the importance of an equal number of labor and management participants, defined membership terms, regularly scheduled meetings, a set agenda, minutes, dissemination of progress reports, and follow-up as essential ingredients to effective committees. Paul J. Champagne and Mark Lincoln Chadwin discuss labor–management committees, their structure and scope, costs, benefits, uses, and conditions favoring success.

Emerging personnel issues

Although local governments are confronted with many complex personnel issues, a few are particularly current. Part 5 examines four of these: comparable worth, the impact of automation on human resources, sexual harassment, and physical fitness.

Comparable worth is a major personnel issue of the 1980s. Women's organizations and some labor unions are clamoring for recognition of the issue. They point out that many jobs filled by women have been traditionally underpaid due to institutionalized sex discrimination. Comparable worth deals with equal pay for work of comparable value to the employer. The concept provides for equal salaries for jobs that require similar responsibilities, knowledge, skills, effort, and working conditions. Seventeen states have passed laws with comparable worth implications. Cities and counties are faced with finding ways of balancing the issue of equity with the realities of the marketplace, which has historically been used to set salaries. No completely reliable method has been found to compare the value of different jobs. If one could be found, employers would still be confronted with finding the money to remedy the problem. Comparable worth has emphasized the importance of a well-constructed and -documented job evaluation system as a way of correcting and overcoming pay disparities. Gerald M. Pauly reviews the comparable worth concept and why it is not a practical theory for public policy. The article examines the premise for comparable worth, job evaluation systems, and the use of prevailing rates to set pay scales.

Automation is another critical issue with significant human resources implications. Many studies have documented the hostility of employees to the introduction of automated systems. Automation sometimes leads to increased absenteeism, extended breaks and lunch hours, increased turnover, and other problems related to employee feelings of anxiety, concern about routinization of jobs, and fears of loss of job security and self-esteem. Human values and needs are often in conflict with technological advancement. Local governments are being challenged to coordinate and integrate people, the work environment, and the new technology. Public managers must understand the changes taking place and the potential human resource problems being created by automation. Harold T. Smith summarizes the findings of a research report that offers solutions to managing the office of the future. Sally Ketchum discusses the importance of human factors in the implementation of office automation. Vincent R. Ceriello provides helpful advice on computerizing a human resources management system.

Sexual harassment has become a sensitive and complex personnel issue. As a result of Equal Employment Opportunity Commission rules and court decisions, sexual harassment is a discriminatory employment practice that violates federal and state laws. Increasing numbers of sexual harassment complaints have been filed with state civil rights agencies and courts. Public employers need to distinguish between acceptable and unacceptable sexually oriented behavior in the workplace. If employers do not develop adequate corrective programs they risk violating the law and alienating a large portion of the work force. The burden is on the employer to prevent sexual harassment. Prevention and awareness are key elements of an effective program. Such a program should include a formal policy recognizing and prohibiting sexual harassment, training programs that foster an awareness of the policy and remedies, and an appeal process that provides for corrective action. "Sex and Power in the Work Place" by Richel Raines, Trudy Sopp, and Yvonne Williams discusses examples of sexual harassment and useful guidelines for the victim and harasser.

Another issue of considerable interest to local governments is employee physical fitness. Both public and private organizations have recognized that physical fitness programs pay. Improved health and well-being are reflected in better performance and reduced health insurance and workers compensation costs. Turnover and loss of personnel through premature death can also be reduced. Employee physical fitness programs are gaining popularity. Analyses of fitness programs show that to be successful they should be voluntary and provide medical exams, incentives, fitness testing, and monitoring. William M. Timmins describes employee physical fitness programs, reviews their use and success in the public sector.

Summary

Public personnel management is undergoing radical changes. A traditional approach to personnel is no longer adequate to respond to the social, economic, legal, and technological forces reshaping the management of human resources. Effective local government management requires personnel systems that are responsive to changing human needs and issues. Thus, local officials need to:

1. Keep informed of new personnel techniques and issues.
2. Closely monitor federal and state laws and regulations and court decisions affecting personnel.
3. Assess on a regular basis the effectiveness of the personnel organizational framework and activities.
4. Assign personnel a major role in the decision-making process.
5. Expand the personnel function to include human resources management.
6. Extend the search for solutions to personnel problems to the private sector.
7. Exhibit a willingness to innovate.
8. Challenge basic assumptions and perceptions.
9. Experiment with new approaches to achieving labor–management cooperation.
10. Examine the motivational aspects of personnel policies and practices and design programs that meet employee needs and expectations.
11. Recognize the human resource problems associated with automation and implement workable solutions.
12. Orient supervisory and management personnel to the changing role of personnel.
13. Support research on personnel problems and issues.

PART 1

Increasing Personnel System Effectiveness

A Definition of Human Resources Management

— Joyce D. Ross

The term "human resources management" is being heard increasingly around the halls of today's major corporations and frequently appears on organization charts as a legitimate corporate function. Yet little agreement exists on what human resources management is or what it should be. Because of the popular usage of the term and the lack of understanding on the part of practitioners and academicians as to its scope, human resources management has been used synonymously with personnel administration, industrial relations, employee development, training, employee relations and the like.

A definition of the field remains elusive. It is important to begin to define human resources management, for the way we label various phenomena determines to a large extent the way we think about them and subsequently act. When a new field or movement begins to mean all things to all people, it loses its appropriateness of use. As a result, the new movement oftentimes falls in disrepute, as happened with the sensitivity training movement. Thus, it appears in some areas that human resources management is becoming the catch-all phrase for all people-related activities in the organization, without the acknowledgment of human resources management's underlying values and specific differences from traditional personnel management.

It is feared that this confusion of labels will detract from the great potential human resources management has to offer to today's organizations. Therefore, the intent of this article is to define human resources management and indicate how it differs from the traditional practice of personnel.

Some background

Peter Drucker, preeminent among management writers and philosophers, has written extensively over the years about the notion of viewing people as human resources. All businesses, he has stated, depend on three factors of production: the human resource, the capital resource and the physical resource. If the organization is to survive, these resources have to be employed productively. In considering any resource, it is important to take into account supply, conservation, protection from exploitation, utilization and development. The only resource which can have an output greater than the sum of its parts is the human resource.

When an organization views its present and future employees as resources rather than purchased services, then it has begun a process of human resource development. Employees are thus considered investments—investments which yield varying results depending upon how the investment is treated. Human resources management represents a change in attitude on the part of management toward the workforce, a move away from seeing employees as a necessary expense of doing business to a critical investment in the organization's current performance and future growth. This philosophy underlies human resources management programs and reflects management's attitude toward the management of people at work.

Recent influences

The '70s brought about an increasing awareness of the effects of various social, technical and environmental forces on organizational and personnel requirements, which has extended into the '80s. The milieu in which organizations operate has become quite complex. Pressures for change are being generated by federal and state rules and regulations, advancing technology, special interest groups, and changing values and trends in the workforce.

Today's organizations are faced with new problems and new challenges created by these changes. Of particular importance is the impact of technology. Researchers have documented the ways in which the introduction into an organization of newer information-processing technologies brings about a complex series of problems for the personnel system. Too often the organization's personnel department would recognize only recruiting problems and would be unaware of other emerging personnel issues—such as increased dependence on staff support, conflicts between staff, and personnel obsolescence. Preoccupation with functional and technological details often excludes consideration of the human factor. While some companies anticipate the impact of technology on their workforce, few companies engage in any anticipatory human resource planning or implement programs to deal with the inevitable consequences of major technological change.

Changing attitudes and values toward work have also created internal and external pressures on the corporation. While much has been written about the "new" values toward work, it appears certain that work values will change with each generation. Certain trends are evident from demographic data projected into the '80s. The workforce will be younger, more diverse in terms of sex and race, and possess more years of schooling. These groups bring with them a concern for equal rights, upward mobility and "meaningful work." For those whose work does not seem meaningful, money becomes more important, for money can buy the leisure activities that substitute for meaningful work. The new members of the workforce appear to possess less organizational commitment but they do want to influence decisions affecting them and their work. Organizations need to be aware of these changes and respond to them, for they significantly affect motivation and productivity. The interaction of these various forces brings about a need for a more responsive and individualistic work environment.

Changing role for personnel

These trends on the contemporary scene necessitate an expansion of the traditional personnel role, for personnel is fundamentally affected by social, technical and environmental forces. Yet as one currently assesses most personnel departments, they often lack the ability to respond to these pressures.

In many organizations, personnel policies are based upon an assumption of a homogeneous workforce, i.e., a workforce where everyone possesses the same values, attitudes, backgrounds, sex and color. This situation is obviously no longer in existence, yet many personnel departments still design programs, such as benefit packages and training programs, for a workforce which existed in the '40s—white, male, head of household. These personnel policies do not fit the individualistic nature of today's workforce. While these policies may have been developed out of organizational convenience, they have continued because of tradition and inertia.

This is not to say that personnel is still being relegated to a position of lesser importance in the organization. Instead, the opposite is true. Personnel has received increased attention in the last few years, but for the wrong reasons. Legalistic requirements and federal and state regulations, combined with the financial penalties for failure to comply, have forced many organizations to recognize the importance of personnel. Yet the attitude many companies project is one of desiring to be kept out of trouble with the government rather than actively working toward the utilization of employees' skills and strengths. The emphasis on compliance continues to put personnel in a reactive mode. It is necessary to move beyond the strictly operational aspects of personnel administration and to re-analyze the priorities of the personnel function.

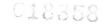

Relationship to personnel

Human resources management has redefined the personnel function and expanded its role from a control-oriented supplier of employees to an overall human resource planning, development and utilization approach. While human resources management has a major anchor in the discipline of personnel, it goes beyond this area because it seeks to achieve coordination and integration with overall planning and other managerial functions. Human resources management is a more comprehensive approach to the management of people at work.

With a base in the behavorial sciences, the field of human resources management is concerned about the motivation and development of the individual employee and the performance and productivity of the organization. A major factor differentiating human resources management from personnel is human resources management's special contribution to the organization's strategic planning. Before the recognition of the importance of human resources management, strategic decisions made in the corporation were essentially made on the basis of economic scenarios. Today, social development and workforce scenarios have gradually become equally important in planning for the future. The acknowledgment of the mutual dependence between traditional personnel functions, technology, organization structure, job design and people encourages the growth of the human resources management focus.

While variations will exist from organization to organization, a human resources department should consist of the following areas:

Human resources planning and forecasting which identifies future human resources needs and the designing strategies necessary to assure the meeting of these needs.

Individual motivation and organizational analysis that senses and acts upon employees' motivational development and work redesign. Attention should also be paid to designing jobs which meet individual and organizational requirements.

Personnel development plans which provide those opportunities employees need to achieve skills, and pursue growth and development through training, career development, career pathing and alternative work schedules.

Personnel utilization which maintains the human resource system through those functions which have been the basic underpinning for personnel in the past, i.e., recruitment, selection, appraisal, compensation, and collective bargaining.

These four areas cannot be considered as separate entities. Each area is highly interrelated; a change in one area will significantly affect the other areas. Thus, it becomes essential that human resource activities are designed as a whole system rather than a set of distinctive activities. What ties these functions together is a belief in the value and potential productivity of the American worker, otherwise known as the organization's human resources. It is this managerial philosophy which causes human resource management programs and policies to be carried out in a vigorous and productive manner. Human resources management attempts to meet the challenges of the '80s by anticipating present demands, planning for the future, and designing personnel systems to match those realities. Given this responsibility, it is no wonder that human resources management has become a critical organizational function.

In conclusion, perhaps we in personnel should have been listening more closely to Peter Drucker, who, in 1954, noted that it is no longer a question of whether we want to develop our human resources or even whether we should. It is now a matter of survival for society. We're pushing our physical resources to their limits. It is now the human area that shows the greatest potential for growth and organizational effectiveness. Twenty-six years later, Peter Drucker's words are being heard and understood.

Perspectives on Civil Service Reform

John Matzer, Jr.

Civil service reform is a growing trend among federal, state, and local governments. Its purpose is to make civil service/personnel systems more responsive to management and the public and to emphasize the need for common merit principles. The traditional role and responsibility of the civil service board or commission has been changed by the trends toward more public unionism and collective bargaining, equal employment opportunity requirements, professionalism, and increased public awareness through the media and interest groups. These trends have helped reduce the danger of political patronage, which was the primary basis of many existing merit systems.

The National Civil Service League, numerous state commissions, and the Committee for Economic Development, an independent research and education organization of 200 business executives and educators, all have recommended the overhauling of public personnel systems. With the adoption of the Civil Service Reform Act in 1978, civil service reform was implemented by the federal government. At least thirty-two states and many cities and counties have under study or are implementing some aspect of civil service reform.

A critical theme of civil service reform is the departure from the traditional commission-headed personnel agency. The National Civil Service League noted in a 1975 survey that half the large governments in the United States had abandoned the commission form of government for personnel management. A key element in civil service reform is to make the personnel system more directly responsible to management and to remove a possible conflict of interest resulting from a combination of judicial and executive functions.

The importance of separating the policy-making responsibilities from the appeals hearing authority of the typical civil service board is emphasized in a report published by the United States Office of Personnel Management and the Council of State Governments, which stated that "it may be difficult for those civil service boards which are vested with appeals hearing authority and policy-making authority to act objectively when hearing appeals concerning policies they may have made."[1]

Components of civil service reform

Much civil service reform activity among federal, state, and local governments has been directed at improving the responsiveness of civil service personnel to management and the general public. Examples of topics covered by civil service reform include reorganization, decentralization, revision of job titles, establishment of a career executive service, and linking pay to performance.

Reorganization   Reform may include reorganizing the personnel function to separate personnel administration activities from quasi-judicial or merit protection activities and placing them under the control of the chief executive officer. The basic purpose of the reorganization is to separate the conflicting responsibilities of the traditional civil service board for developing positive pesonnel policies and for hearing appeals. Such a separation is needed in order to avoid having a single body pass judgment on its own actions. The reorganization efforts implemented by the federal government; New York City; Montgomery County, Maryland; Contra Costa County, California, and other states and cities have centralized personnel management responsibility in the personnel agency under the administrative officer and established personnel or merit review boards with responsibility for safeguarding both the merit system and individual employees against abuses and unfair personnel actions.

The boards are not administrative bodies and are not responsible for the actions of the personnel agency. Instead, the boards focus on maintaining the integrity of the personnel system from political patronage and discrimination. The boards have the power to hold hearings on patronage, discrimination, and disciplinary appeal cases. Under an integrated personnel structure there is no delay in actions until a part-time civil service commission can meet.

Decentralization   Certain functions normally performed by a central personnel agency such as recruiting, examining, training, and position classification often become decentralized. The central personnel agency usually retains responsibility for the preparation of interagency class specifications and examination material and post-audits personnel actions relating to the decentralized functions. Decentralization is designed to place more decision-making authority in the hands of line managers commensurate with their accountability to the public. The primary objective of decentralization is to reduce the turnaround time between the appearance of a vacant position and the filling of the position.

Revision of job titles   Reform also may result in reduction in the overspecialization of job titles and the proliferation of levels within occupational areas through the establishment of broad job classes to provide increased management flexibility.

Establishment of a career executive service   In a career executive service the assignment, selection, and advancement of personnel are based solely on performance. The executive service provides a structure for selecting, assigning, developing, and managing top management personnel.

Linking pay to performance   Reform efforts also focus on the development of a system for linking compensation to performance. Recent achievements in the development of results-oriented evaluation systems promise to bring about notable improvements in the area of performance appraisal.

Many of the changes implemented by federal, state, and local governments are based on the Model Public Personnel Administration Law issued by the National Civil Service League.

Reasons for civil service reform

A basic reason for considering civil service reform is the fact that the external and internal environments in which many local personnel systems function has changed substantially over the years. Some of these changes include:

1. Substantial growth in the number and diversity of employees
2. Legal requirements that the city meet and confer with representatives of its employees and the evolution of collective bargaining systems separate from statutory civil service systems
3. State and federal laws and court decisions that specify the rights of employees, including "property rights" to retain their positions
4. Affirmative action requirements designed to improve the representation for minorities and women.

Many existing personnel systems are premised on public personnel principles established to serve and meet the needs and goals of another era. The systems are overly concerned with emphasizing the negative rather than the positive aspects of public personnel administration. A principal objective of such systems has been to ensure the integrity of the public service by protecting it from the excesses of the spoils system. Internal and external changes in personnel issues have created increased conflict within the systems and restricted the ability of local governments to respond to new demands in the future.

Following are some additional reasons for civil service reform:

1. Many existing systems serve as a disincentive rather than an incentive for performance improvement.
2. There may be a lack of management accountability for personnel actions because management has little discretion regarding hiring and firing decisions.
3. The system may involve a rigid and cumbersome set of procedures that cause excessive delays.
4. The system may not facilitate productivity improvement efforts.
5. The system may discourage the retention of the highest-quality employees by rewarding longevity rather than performance.
6. Safeguards designed to prevent political abuse of employees can result in severe constraints on the ability to correct situations where employees are not sufficiently productive or effective in their current positions.
7. In many current systems the existence of unions and memorandums of understanding have created two separate personnel systems.

Benefits of civil service reform

A public personnel system grounded on a positive personnel policy offers the following benefits:

1. Centralizes management responsibility for personnel activities with elected officials
2. Provides public managers with greater discretion in the selection, rewarding, assignment, and removal of employees
3. Assures that personnel resources are providing effective and efficient services to the public and are responsive to the citizens
4. Provides a more effective way for holding managers accountable for their performance by linking pay to performance
5. Improves labor–management relations
6. Recognizes the importance of affirmative action programs
7. Consolidates in a single body the responsibilities for personnel management with a separate board independent of that

authority performing appeals and investigatory functions to ensure that merit principles are upheld and employee rights are protected
8. Streamlines city personnel procedures and facilitates quick and decisive action
9. Strengthens the protection of employee rights.

Objectives of civil service reform

It is important that any improvement in the civil service system be based on the following merit principles, which are an integral part of civil service reform:

1. Recruiting, selecting, and advancing employees on the basis of their relative ability, knowledge, skills, and performance, including but not limited to open consideration of qualified applicants for initial appointment
2. Establishing equitable and adequate compensation
3. Training employees, as needed, to encourage high-quality performance and to facilitate career advancement
4. Retaining employees on the basis of the adequacy of their performance, correcting inadequate performance, and separating employees whose inadequate performance cannot be corrected
5. Assuring fair treatment of applicants and employees in the administration of personnel practices without regard to political affiliation or opinions, union activities, race, color, national origin, sex, age, handicap, or religious creed and with proper regard for their privacy and constitutional rights
6. Assuring that employees are protected against coercion for partisan political purposes and are prohibited from using their official authority for the purpose of interfering with or affecting the result of an election or a nomination for office.

In addition to conformance with basic merit principles, it is important that the civil service reform effort be directed at achieving the following objectives:

1. Provide personnel management services in the most efficient and cost-effective manner possible
2. Recognize the dynamic nature of local government and the need for flexibility and adaptability
3. Recognize the important role and changing requirements of the employee relations process
4. Ensure that the personnel system is equitable and understandable to both those who use the system to fill positions and those seeking employment or promotion

5. Recognize that employees are motivated by different incentives and perform at different levels
6. Strengthen the protection of employee rights and provide safeguards from political abuse
7. Improve management flexibility, creativity, initiative, and accountability for performance.

Implementation and strategy

Since civil service reform is a sensitive and sometimes controversial effort, it is important that considerable planning go into its implementation. Many local governments have personnel systems that have been in existence for a long time. Any effort to modernize them must be based on careful study with adequate opportunity for all affected parties to provide input. There are several ways that civil service reform can be initiated, including the establishment of a civil service or personnel reform task force, the retention of an independent consultant, and staff analysis and recommendations.

Civil service reform task force   The most prevalent method used to initiate civil service reform is through establishment of a civil service or personnel reform task force. The task force could consist of 7 or 9 members. A major advantage of this approach is the broad-based composition of the task force and its independence from the formal governmental structure. Task force members can be citizens or a combination of citizens and employees. For example, a task force could be composed of a representative from the League of Women Voters, the civil service board, the Chamber of Commerce, middle management, affiliated labor, and unaffiliated labor, plus a department head and a citizen at large.

The task force is assigned to review the civil service system with the objective of modernizing it to emphasize merit, performance, productivity, and affirmative action. Procedurally the task force reviews reports of civil service reform, interviews local officials, union leaders, employees, and other interested parties, conducts public hearings, and drafts proposals. Some task forces are assisted by a consultant, while others are supported by government staff. The task force is given a specific date to submit its report.

Consultant   Another method used to initiate civil service reform is to retain an experienced consultant, usually supplemented by a citizen task force. This method has the advantage of providing independent expert analysis because of the consultant's experience, but it has the disadvantage of being expensive. A consultant conducts an in-depth review of the existing personnel system and makes rec-

ommendations for improvements, including specific charter and ordinance changes.

Staff analysis   A third approach is to use existing staff to under-
take the analysis. Staff can work independently or with a citizen
task force. An advantage of the staff approach is the lower cost.
There are, however, several disadvantages. One is the potential
charge by citizens that the effort is rigged and is an attempt to return to the spoils system. Citizens may be concerned that there will
not be proper citizen oversight of the merit system. Employees may
fear that their employment rights will be in jeopardy and that they
will not be adequately protected against political patronage and
discrimination. Some management personnel may be opposed because of the threat of increased accountability. A lack of knowledge
about civil service reform could be another disadvantage of the staff
approach. Although many of these pitfalls are also associated with
the other approaches to civil service reform, they are particularly
significant in the case of the staff approach. More credibility tends
to be associated with the civil service reform effort if it is initiated
by a broad-based task force. Citizens, employees, and labor all feel
less threatened.

Scope of study   Following are some of the topics that could be addressed in the civil service reform study:

1. Structure of the local personnel system, including the role of
    the civil service board and the personnel director
2. Position classification policies, including expanded use of
    broad job descriptions
3. Creation of a separate management service and management
    compensation plan
4. Development of a pay for performance plan
5. Review of the appeal processes for all grievances and disci-
    plinary appeals
6. Review of the examination, selection, and appointment pro-
    cess, including the use of veteran's preference.

The final product of a civil service reform study would include:

1. A statement of basic personnel policy, including a definition
    of merit principles
2. Proposed organizational changes, including the establishment
    of a new personnel appeals and merit system monitoring
    body and personnel management structure
3. Description of various responsibilities and authority
4. Proposed charter and ordinance changes.

Conclusion

Modernization of local personnel systems is critical if local governments are to respond adequately to the era of limited resources, the public's demand for more and improved services, new technology that significantly alters the manner in which work is performed, the demand to increase productivity and accountability, and the increasing growth of collective bargaining. There is a need to shift the focus from rule making and a defensive posture to problem solving and a positive posture. Reform of the personnel system offers the potential for achieving increased managerial flexibility, improved productivity, better employee-management relations, and increased accountability.

1. *Analyses of Baseline Data Survey on Personnel Practices for States, Counties, Cities* (Washington, D.C.: U.S. Office of Personnel Management and the Council of State Governments, 1979), p. 52.

Self-Audit: Measuring Your Organization's Productivity

There are several major functions performed by public personnel managers: classification and staffing; recruitment and selection; compensation, including fringe benefits; performance appraisal and promotion, firing and transfers; employee development; employee-employer relations; and EEO/affirmative action. Each function requires a separate effort, but is highly interrelated with the others.

Tracking the following indicators related to each of the functional areas over time can provide you with the information needed to judge the productivity of your department. The exercise can help you identify areas where improvement can be made and functions that are being performed efficiently and effectively. Most of the data required to respond to the indicators should be readily available. The indicators will yield data that reflect the goals of your organization and, over time, progress toward meeting those goals.

Classification and staffing levels

Subobjective To maintain an accurate and up-to-date inventory of the kinds and levels of jobs in the government and establish appropriate staffing levels.

Adapted from material appearing as "Illustrative Subobjectives of Personnel Management and Indicators of Progress Toward Their Achievement," in *Assessing Personnel Management: Objectives and Performance Indicators*, by Selma J. Mushkin, Frank H. Sandifer, and Charles R. Warren (Washington, D.C.: Public Services Laboratory, George Washington University), 1977. The material also appears in: George J. Washnis, editor, *Productivity Improvement Handbook for State & Local Government* (New York: John Wiley & Sons), copyright © 1980 by the National Academy of Public Administration. Used with permission.

Indicators

1. Forecasts of staffing levels by occupation and classification.
2. Percentage of positions covered in the classification plan.
3. Percentage of job classes capable of being described in terms of the kinds of outputs produced by the employees; and percentage actually described in that way (e.g., number of persons served; number of treatments provided; tons of trash collected, etc.).
4. Percentage of jobs and job classes which have been subject to complete job analysis within the past three years.
5. Number and percentage of agency requests for reclassification met within a specified time.

Subobjective   To outline career progressions (ladders) in order to encourage employees to strive for high performance.

Indicators

1. Number and percentage of employees (at specified classes) who are upgraded on the basis of job performance.
2. Percentage of employees within sample job classes who progressed to higher level jobs in a 6 month (12 month) period.
3. Average length of time employees remain in the same job, by job class.
4. Extent to which class specifications identify clear career progression within each class (review of class specifications).
5. Number and percentage of employees who complain about lack of advancement to selected personnel managers.

Subobjective   To identify the knowledge, skills, and abilities needed to perform each kind and level of job for recruitment, training, and pay purposes.

Indicators

1. Percentage of job class specifications used as a basis for personnel actions (recruitment, training, pay review).
2. Number of employees taking courses to develop specified skills.
3. Percentage of employees trained in specific skills who report use of new skills on job.
4. Measured success in terms of output or performance of training programs that train for knowledge, skills, and abilities identified in job classifications.

Subobjective   To provide an accurate basis for review, analysis, and evaluation of organization, functions, work flow, work methods, and staff/equipment utilization.

Indicators

1.   Number of instances in last 12 months in which job descriptions have been used as data source in management analyses of organizations, programs, or functions.
2.   Number of instances in last 12 months in which management analysis led to changes in job classifications.

Recruitment and selection

Subobjective   To hire employees in order to reach and maintain a staffing level (numbers and qualifications) sufficient to meet public service requirements.

Indicators

1.   Percentage of agency requests met within specified time.
2.   Average period of time budgeted jobs remain vacant after recruitment request has been made.
3.   Number of "successful" employees selected, as measured by (a) production data (quality, quantity), (b) job knowledge tests, (c) supervisory or peer ratings.
4.   Cost and percentage of personnel staff engaged in recruitment and selection per new hire.
5.   Percentage of new employees who fail probation.
6.   Percentage of new employees who voluntarily leave within the first 12 months.
7.   Percentage of new employees who successfully complete the first 12 months.
8.   Percentage of new employees who earn promotions within the first 18 months (24 months).

Subobjective   To facilitate the hiring of well qualified employees by assuring that potential candidates have the opportunity of being considered for employment.

Indicators

1.   Length of time between examinations.
2.   Number and accessibility of examination sites (average travel time for selected examinees, by grade level).
3.   Extent to which announcement of examinations are publicized.
4.   Number of complaints concerning hours and days in which examinations are given.

Compensation, including fringe benefits

Subobjective   To motivate employees to maintain a high level of performance through adequate and equitable compensation.

Indicators

1. Comparison of pay in government for selected occupations (total salary and value of fringe benefits) with that of other public and private employers in the labor market.
2. Comparison of pay for different occupations in selected agencies or departments (total remuneration, as above).
3. Number and percentage of employees working under incentive pay plans.
4. Number and percentage of employees receiving pay increases for superior performance.

Performance appraisal and promotion, firing, and transfers

Subobjective   To identify (for employees, supervisors, and managers) specific employee performance weaknesses to be corrected and strengths to be enhanced and best utilized.

Indicators

1. Percentage of employees whose performance is evaluated periodically against established standards or objectives.
2. Percentage of performance appraisals that directly prompt the following types of actions: (a) promotions, (b) terminations, (c) reassignments, (d) step increases or bonus pay, (e) reclassifications, (f) training and development.
3. Number and percentage of jobs that lend themselves to output measurement for evaluation purposes.
4. Number and percentage of jobs in which supervisory (or peer) review suggests superior performance to achieve unit mission.

Subobjective   To encourage employees to strive for higher performance and overall excellence.

Indicators

1. Types of merit programs offered by the government (which formally recognize superior performance).
2. Number of employee proposals (innovations, inventions, suggestions) considered by supervisors, and percentage of employees given recognition for proposals.

Employee development

Subobjective   To assure that employees have and maintain the skills and attitudes needed to perform their jobs.

Indicators

1. Number and percentage of employees who: (a) understand agency mission and their role in that mission (requires instrumentation), (b) have participated in education or training programs, academic or vocational, during the past 12 months.
2. Number and types of sponsored training and development programs provided.
3. Proportion of employees, by department and agency, offered (or eligible for) training and development programs.
4. Changes in average test scores of examinations given at the completion of training programs or examinations given for promotion purposes.
5. Changes in available output data or performance measurements (by individual or work unit) following the completion of training programs.
6. Changes (decline or increase) in average test scores of new employees on entrance examinations during the past year (2 years).
7. Percentage of senior positions filled from within, and percentage by new hires.

Employee-employer relations

Subobjective   To enhance job satisfaction and motivation of employees.

Indicators

1. Job turnover rates, by major occupation.
2. Absenteeism rates—average days lost from work.
3. Accident rates on the job, by major occupation.
4. Job satisfaction and work self-fulfillment and self-esteem measurement.

Subobjective   To improve workforce effectiveness through (a) recognition of organizations or unions chosen by employees to represent them and (b) negotiating with employees collectively through their bargaining units.

Indicators

1. Number of separate bargaining units; number of employees per unit.

2. Average length of time to negotiate labor agreements, selected bargaining units.
3. Number of employee grievances.
4. Average length of time required to resolve grievances.
5. Number of employees covered by productivity bargaining contract provisions.
6. Percentage of negotiated labor agreements that contain productivity provisions.
7. Number of labor negotiations that include productivity as a bargaining issue.

EEO/affirmative action

Subobjective   To increase the responsiveness of government through attainment of a more nearly representative workforce.

Indicators

1. Number and percentage of minority group members in workforce compared to population of the jurisdiction (population of the employment region).
2. Number and frequency of EEO complaints and appeals.
3. Changes during a specified period in the proportion of management-level positions held by target group members.
4. Changes in the distribution of target group members among pay grades and classifications.
5. Changes in the percentage of new hirings of target group members.
6. Changes in the number of promotions obtained by target group members.
7. Changes in the percentage of market group employees subjected to adverse personnel action.
8. Response of non-minority members to EEO/affirmative action programs.

Practical Strategies for Evaluating Training

Ruth D. Salinger and Basil S. Deming

When you get down to the basics of training evaluation, you are faced with a few critical questions. The first is quite elementary: *What do you want to know about the training?*

The answer to that question embodies second-order questions which give the basic outline to any evaluation effort.

Suppose your answer to the first question is simply, "I want to know if participants think the training was well taught." That implies a second-order question: *Do participants judge the training to have been well taught?*

From this question, the evaluator can begin to plan the evaluation activity—in this case, probably some sort of participant reactionnaire to the instructor's style and choice of methodology and media.

Beyond asking whether participants judge some training event as well taught (or well organized), four questions encompass most of the reasons for conducting training evaluation:

1. To what degree does the training produce appropriate learning?
2. To what degree is learning transferred to the job?
3. To what degree is the knowledge or skill level maintained over time?
4. Does the value of participants' improved performance meet or exceed the cost of training?

Our purpose is to describe practical ways of answering these critical questions, particularly in training settings with inevitable

Evaluation question	Evaluation strategy
1. To what degree does the training produce appropriate learning?	Delayed-treatment control group
2. To what degree is learning transferred to the job?	Modified critical incident method
	Over-the-shoulder evaluation
	Performance analysis
3. To what degree is the knowledge or skill level maintained over time?	Time-series evaluation
4. Does the value of participants' improved performance meet or exceed the cost of training?	Cost-benefit analysis

Figure 1.

constraints on time, resources and access to personnel. Most of our suggestions stem from actual experience in evaluating training courses and programs in federal agency settings. These strategies, however, should be applicable in any training situation. Figure 1 indicates the relevance of each strategy to be discussed for each critical question.

Does training produce appropriate learning?

Whether training produces appropriate learning is particularly difficult to discuss in executive development programs. One reason is the existence of what experimental researchers call the "halo" effect. The halo exists in the eyes of the beholder, formed as a result of a prior belief about a person or a prior experience which revealed the person as talented or "good" in some significant way.

For example, let's suppose Robert Redman has just been selected as the top company salesperson of the year. Greta Gray, company president, is rightly impressed with Redman's achievement. Coincidentally, Gray needs to fill an open sales manager position. She promotes Redman to the position despite the fact that he has no previous managerial experience or training. Gray's decision may prove to be fortuitous, but if Redman has no supervisory skills, Gray may rue her decision in the long run. In effect, Gray has projected a halo over Redman's head. Whether the halo becomes tarnished is a matter of time, talent and fortune.

How does the halo effect work in an executive development program? In most organizations, individuals are selected or at least rated by seniors who currently fill executive positions. Rarely can an individual self-select into such a program. The selection process, whether rigorous or somewhat arbitrary, labels a relatively small number of managers as "good bets." In effect, the organization wagers that these managers will become the executives who run the show, and it is willing to nurture their development as managers with high executive potential.

The halo effect can make evaluation problematic. Since managerial skills and abilities are extremely difficult to quantify, self-ratings and ratings by supervisors are most commonly used in assessment of professional development. These ratings are highly subjective, no matter how well defined the ratings scales are. Thus, they are extremely susceptible to the halo effect.

Robert Redman might fail to develop any significant skills or knowledges through his company's executive development program, but his supervisor, impressed with his executive potential, may tend to perceive him in a more positive light than if he did not possess this potential. Thus the growth—the professional development—like the halo, may exist only in the eyes of the beholder. One might achieve the same effect by simply rating potential executives and publishing the results, rather than treating these managers to lengthy and expensive development programs. In the meantime, things like productivity and work effectiveness can remain unchanged, despite the constant nurturing of managerial talent.

It is virtually impossible to keep people from projecting halos onto those who have been labeled as having high potential for success. There is a way, however, to neutralize the effect for purposes of evaluation. It consists of forming two groups from a pool of chosen candidates. One group is earmarked for immediate entry into the program; the other is required to wait through a full cycle of the program before starting. The groups must be formed by random selection from the candidate pool so that no distinction is given to those who begin immediately.

This "delayed-treatment" design has the virtue of a control group which is not only equivalent to the experimental group but which is perceived by others as equivalent—thus neutralizing the halo effect. The price paid is delay for those selected as controls. But, delay is better than denial, and the advantage of unbiased evaluation which this design affords is considerable. An equivalent control group also provides a way of accounting for other factors which may contribute to real or perceived growth. In the case of the executive development program, they may be factors such as maturity over time, continuing workshops and other training activities not identified as part of the program, or even a general shift in organizational perceptions of what constitutes successful executive performance.

The delayed-treatment design would look like this:

	Group A	Group B
Treatment *(cycle 1)*	X	
Assessment	X	X
Treatment *(cycle 2)*		X
Assessment		X

There is yet another advantage to using a delayed-treatment design with an equivalent control group regardless of the nature of the training. Once the follow-up assessment is made on both experimental and control groups, control group participants enter the next cycle of training. During this second cycle, any changes made in the program as a result of the first cycle evaluation can be assessed. Because the first and second cycle participants were essentially equivalent, specific differences in subsequent performance ratings may be traced to program changes. In essence, the control group becomes the second experimental group.

Let's suppose, as in our executive development program example, that a participant questionnaire administered after the first cycle reveals that many participants believe they received inadequate guidance in making choices of training opportunities and developmental work assignments. Program administrators may decide to add a new dimension to the program in its second cycle, such as using selected executives as "mentors," with one mentor for each participant. Because the two groups are essentially equivalent, one can reasonably argue that improvement, evidenced in ratings of the second group, resulted from the new program dimension.

Is learning transferred to the job?

Information about participants' change in job behavior resulting from training is an important part of determining the ultimate impact that training has on the organization. Yet, practical problems may exist which limit the trainer's ability to assess the effect of training on job performance:

1. The timing of the evaluation is such that the trainer cannot collect pre-course data; for example, the request for evaluating a program's effectiveness may come *after* the training session has been conducted.
2. The nature of the training or the job is such that the trainer cannot collect work samples or observe the work-in-progress in order to measure the effects of training.

Under such circumstances, the trainer can still find out about participant changes caused by attending a training program through a "modified critical incident" method. Professor James N.

Mosel of George Washington University originally developed the modified critical incident approach for use as a training evaluation tool. In general, the method entails talking with participants after they have been back on the job to ask about behavioral change and to obtain specific examples of any change cited. Data on the impact of training can be summarized for the group of trainees, along with information on obstacles encountered by participants in attempting change.

Specifically, the evaluator contacts participants after the end of training. The time might be one month later for training that can be applied fairly soon, or four to six months later for training where occasions for use may not arise immediately or where the skill learned has to be used over time to produce measurable results.

The evaluator can first ask trainees (by letter) to participate in an evaluation of the training program they attended, telling them they will be contacted shortly for an interview appointment. The evaluator can then call the trainees a week or so later to arrange a time for the interview; the interviews can be done either by telephone or in person. We found the preliminary contact with trainees and the arrangement for interview time increases the likelihood that the trainees will set aside enough time for the interview (usually 30-60 minutes) and will cooperate in the effort.

The interviews require certain types of questions and degrees of probing in order to produce data about behavioral change due to training. (See Figure 2 for a sample of questions and probes.) For instance, because you are relying on the participants' self-reports, it is essential that you ask for specific examples of change (hence the relation to the "critical incident" approach) and that you feel reasonably confident that the change was a result of the person's training. (How is this different from before training?) You can also ask about the impact of behavior change on the person's work environment and about difficulties encountered with attempting change.

The evaluator can analyze the data collected using this process:

1. Write each separate behavior change that participants describe on individual index cards.
2. Sort the cards (behaviors) either by the course module or instructional objective the behavior relates to, or by some "natural" grouping to which you can then apply a label (an example of a "communications" behavior might involve a manager being more direct with subordinates and peers, talking out problems rather than avoiding them, especially if they involve misunderstanding).
3. Determine how many *behaviors* occurred (the "depth" of change for the class) and how many *participants* changed in some way (the "breadth" of the course's influence).

1. Since you completed the _____ course, is there anything in the way you go about your job which is different from your former way, and which you feel results, directly or indirectly, from your experience in the course?

   Probes:
   a. Could you tell me more about that? What was the result?
   b. Could you give me an example of that? What was the result?
   c. How did you carry that out? Who was involved? What was the result?
   d. How is that different from before attending the course?
   e. Have you done that more than once? Any difference each time?
   f. Were there any problems in carrying that out? What?
   g. Will you continue to do this? Foresee any problems?

2. Anything else you can think of? (Use probes; repeat as needed)

3. As a result of their experience in the course, some participants got ideas for new things or changes in the way to approach their jobs—but they have not tried them out yet. Has this happened to you?

   Probes:
   a. What is it?
   b. Do you think you'll be able to do this? If not, what would stand in the way?

4. Were there any new things or changes you tried in your job as a result of your experience in the course that didn't work out?

   Probes:
   a. What was it?
   b. Why didn't it work out?
   c. Still interested in doing this? If so, how do you think you can make it happen?

5. Is there any way you think the course should be changed to make it more useful on your job?

   Probes:
   a. What are they?
   b. Anything in the course you would have left out?
   c. Anything not in the course that should be there?

Figure 2. Sample questions and probes.

4. If desired, list the actual behaviors cited in each category.
5. Describe any other data collected, such as: the impact of the change on the work environment (What happened? Was the effect positive or negative?); obstacles encountered in attempting change; and non-behavioral changes cited, such as changes in knowledges or attitudes, or changes planned but not yet implemented.

Since the modified critical incident approach does not require pre-course measures and can be applied after completion of training, it is particularly practical for occasions when the evaluator has had little time or opportunity to construct and implement a more elaborate evaluation design. Its versatility allows it to be applied to a wide variety of training courses and programs.

"Over-the-shoulder" evaluation

Frequently, managers ask for evaluation results before the transfer of learning to the job can be adequately measured (such assessment might require weeks or months between end-of-course and on-the-job measures). Rather than sacrifice valuable follow-up data, you may be able to take advantage of fortuitous circumstances in your organization—especially if the course being evaluated has already been given in the past six months.

For example, suppose you evaluate a week-long course in basic management techniques, taking both in-course and post-course on-the-job measures. For the latter, you think you should wait three months or more before interviewing managers to find out about their use of course learnings on the job. Management, however, wants the evaluation completed in six weeks.

Assuming this is a popular course, offered quarterly for example, you can follow up with participants from the earlier session to measure extent of behavioral change and take whatever in-course measures you had planned during this session:

Session:

#1 (Feb.) You can follow up with trainees from this session.

#2 (May) You are asked to evaluate this session.

#3 (Aug.) This session may be changed based on your findings.

Note several cautions:

1. Make sure the sessions are the same, or highly similar, in terms of instructors, materials, content, etc. If there are important differences, these can be noted and taken into account during your data gathering and analysis efforts.
2. Compare whatever trainee characteristics for the two sessions you feel are relevant. In an evaluation of a course for scientists, for instance, we looked at the number of Ph.D.s versus M.D.s in each session. We found that the make-up of the two sessions for this variable was comparable. We then attempted to select our interview sample to represent, among other variables, the proportion of Ph.D.s and M.D.s in the course. Again, consider any important differences between

sessions in participant characteristics when you make your conclusions and recommendations.

3. While you need to wait an appropriate amount of time before doing a follow-up, if you wait too long (more than six months), at least two problems occur: influences on behavior change other than the training may play a major role (i.e., on-the-job learning); and, if you use interviews to obtain the data, people tend to forget what they have done differently on the job as a result of training.

Performance analysis

Performance analysis is a method used to determine the causes for employee performance not meeting expected levels and to suggest solutions for increasing or changing performance. For instance, an analyst may find that employees do not know how to do the job (lack of skills/knowledges), and may suggest that employees be trained. Or, the analysis may show that machinery is frequently broken or important information does not reach employees (lack of organizational/environmental support) or that employees have few incentives (payoffs) to perform as expected (inappropriate reward system).

Ideally, the trainer uses performance analysis to find out if a training program is an appropriate solution to a performance problem and if other solutions should be implemented instead of, or in addition to, training. This approach helps ensure that training is given when needed and will have the biggest impact possible. (See Figure 3.)

However, as a trainer, you may find yourself in a situation in which you are not able to, or choose not to, conduct a performance analysis before providing training:

1. The problem may not be worth devoting time to a formal analysis;
2. Resources are not available to do the analysis;
3. You may be trying to get a foot in the door as a consultant to managers and need to gradually build up trust in your services; conducting a performance analysis might not be the best move at this time.

Still, the method of performance analysis may prove useful not only before training but also during the evaluation of a training program. When determining how well participant learning has transferred to the job, you may find that even though participants show they are proficient in a skill or possess an acceptable amount of knowledge at the end of training, not much performance change has taken place on the job. If this is the case, you can use the perfor-

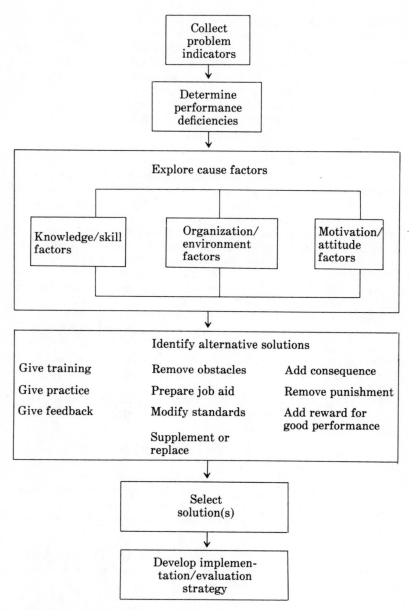

Source: Adapted from *Performance Appraisal—Analyzing Performance Deficiencies,* Personnel Management Training Center, U.S. Office of Personnel Management, Washington, D.C.

Figure 3. Performance analysis model.

mance analysis approach to determine what might be preventing expected changes.

For instance, consider an actual organization which employs scientists, engineers and other professionals. These individuals travel frequently in their work and thus need travel vouchers prepared when they have completed their trips. After the travelers' secretaries prepare the vouchers, a central finance office reviews and processes the vouchers. A training course on travel regulations for secretaries has recently been instituted.

In evaluating the course, we concluded that while the course was effective in producing learning, organizational factors worked against the training's impact on the job. For instance, although the organization processes a high volume of travel vouchers, any one secretary may handle them infrequently. Figure 4 summarizes the findings of the post-training performance analysis. From such an analysis, the trainer can recommend efforts in addition to training which will increase the likelihood that training will have a reasonable chance of "sticking" and being effective. For instance, job aids for secretaries might be useful for the infrequently performed task of preparing vouchers. Ensuring that all those who work with vouchers have updated copies of the regulations is another step.

Changing incentives for secretaries to apply what they have learned and to take the time to construct a proper voucher would require more complex actions and would involve coordination across organizational units. The trainer as analyst and evaluator can at least present evidence on what influences performance and make recommendations for cooperative efforts for improving performance.

Is the knowledge or skill level maintained over time?

Access to trainees before and after training can be difficult for the evaluator. We consider ourselves fortunate to have trainees long enough to pretest and posttest them. Yet, in many cases we should ask not only if trainees have transferred their learning to the job, but if new or improved skills have been maintained over time.

An effective way of assessing learning transfer and retention is with a *time-series evaluation* design:

$$\text{Pretest}$$
$$T_1 \quad T_2 \quad T_3$$
$$\text{Treatment}$$
$$X$$
$$\text{Posttest}$$
$$T_4 \quad T_5 \quad T_6$$

Obviously, it is rarely feasible to formally test trainees several times before and after training. But a "test" may be nothing more

General cause of performance problems

1. Skill/knowledge (including: ability to do the job; frequency of use of skills; feedback on performance)

2. Organizational/ environmental

3. Motivational

Specific problems found

a. Individual secretaries fill out vouchers infrequently and may forget travel rules.

b. Secretaries do not receive immediate feedback on how well they have prepared the vouchers. They usually only see the vouchers after the central finance office has reviewed them and readied them for payment. Most vouchers submitted with errors are corrected in the finance office. Corrections frequently do not include the reason for changes made.

a. Secretaries may not have all the information from the traveler needed to complete the voucher.

b. Updated travel regulations are not consistently available to all who need them.

c. Work on vouchers is interrupted for higher priority tasks.

a. Evaluation of secretaries' job performance does not include evaluating preparation of travel vouchers.

b. Overall, there are no negative consequences to secretaries if they submit incorrect vouchers.

c. There may be positive consequences for secretaries who do not take the time needed to correctly fill out vouchers and instead devote the time to higher priority tasks.

Figure 4. Summary of post-training performance analysis.

than a sample of work involving the knowledge of skills the training conveys, and samples can be taken without disrupting work. This principle may be applied anywhere tasks are relatively unchanging and directly measurable, like voucher preparation, photocopy composition or mail sorting.

The time-series design, while more demanding than a simple pretest/posttest design, provides more control over potential sources of invalidity than the latter. If no difference appears in the first three test scores, a difference between the third and fourth test scores would not be interpreted to be a result of maturation, testing or regression (common threats to internal validity).

In addition, repeated assessments after the fourth test show whether or not the effects of the training diminished over time. Empirical observation and experimentation have documented the effect of time on learning which is not reinforced. Typically, most forgetting occurs rapidly, followed by a more gradual loss until the learner retains only a small fraction of information. In the evaluation of the "travel regulations" course discussed earlier, a pretest/posttest comparison immediately before and after the classroom session revealed that substantial learning had occurred. Structured interviews with course participants prompted us to speculate that information learned or reinforced during the course was subsequently forgotten or confused with other information of a similar nature (such as slightly modified voucher formats or subtle changes in travel regulations).

While loss of information retrieval is a common occurrence, repeated posttesting (or sampling) does not always produce a decline in performance. We noted in an evaluation of a keyboard skills course for photocomposition operators that speed and error rates of several trainees improved markedly from the immediate course posttest to the follow-up work sample taken three to five weeks later.

The key difference between the secretaries who prepared vouchers and the photocomposition operators was the element of continued practice. Most secretaries prepared vouchers only occasionally. Several reported they had not prepared one voucher within a month's time after the course. By contrast, the photocomposition operators were able to exercise the techniques learned in their course immediately and continuously.

In sum, the time-series design allows the evaluator to determine not only whether knowledge or skill was transferred to the job, but also whether knowledge or skill was sufficiently mastered to resist performance deterioration over time.

Does the value of participants' improved performance meet or exceed the cost of training?

A *cost-benefit analysis* of training may be considered the ultimate assessment. Management expects training programs not only to have positive effects on the organization's accomplishments, but also not to cost more than those improvements are worth. For a given time period, the *value* of improvements resulting from train-

ing should be *greater* than the *cost* of conducting the training.
Methods currently exist for determining:

1. The cost of training;
2. The value of training for jobs whose outputs—products or services—are repetitive and can be counted;
3. The value of training for managerial jobs.

These models enable the evaluator to translate benefits from training into dollars and to make informed decisions about the future of the training. We described a situation in which secretaries prepare travel vouchers which are reviewed in a central finance office. Training in travel regulations had been instituted for the secretarial staff. The evaluation of the course included measuring the effectiveness of the training in producing learning and in determining factors which were influencing performance, beyond possession of appropriate skills and knowledges. Another part of the evaluation involved a cost-benefit analysis of the training.

The original evaluation plan called for examining the impact of the training on voucher error rates by secretaries. We planned to use a non-randomized pretest-posttest design:

	Experimental group	Control group
Pretest	T_1	T_1
Treatment	X	
Posttest	T_2	T_2

The "treatment" was to be training, and the measure taken at two different times (T_1 and T_2) was to be number of errors in vouchers. With such a design, we could determine the effectiveness of the training in reducing errors. The control group was to consist of those secretaries who had not been trained through this particular course and who submitted vouchers.

After determining the number of vouchers with errors for the trained and untrained groups, we discovered that the time period in which we worked did not contain enough trainee vouchers to be useful for the analysis (and we could not change the time period). Rather than drop the idea of a cost-benefit analysis, we did a "theoretical value of training" analysis. This entailed determining the *potential maximum cost savings* to the organization if *all* errors were eliminated. Figure 5 summarizes the factors and calculations required.

The time period in question was four weeks. We then translated figures into a one-year base. The salary costs associated with vouchers in error were developed by looking at the extra time devoted to these vouchers by each individual in the finance office.

Some assumptions were made in producing the cost-benefit analysis, e.g., that training all the secretaries who submitted vouch-

A: Extra time spent by finance office to process vouchers with errors	B: Total number of vouchers with errors submitted in 4-week period	C: Total extra time (4-week period)	D: Total extra time per year
16 minutes/ voucher	195	1,170 minutes = 52 hours	676 hours

E: Yearly salary costs of examiners to process vouchers with errors	F: Cost to train 15 secretaries (1 class) (includes secretary and instructor salaries, materials, course development)	G: Cost to train 150* secretaries (10 classes) *No. of secretaries submitting vouchers with errors
$4,300	$3,600	$36,000

Figure 5. Theoretical value of training analysis.

ers with errors would eliminate all the errors. This was not likely to be the case, since the training course did not address arithmetic skills, therefore arithmetic errors occurred in the vouchers. We had hints that the training might not be cost-effective and we wanted to give the training program every chance to prove itself. Since an extreme difference still exists between the cost of training (Figure 5, col. G) and the value of the errors reduced (Figure 5, col. E), even with such assumptions, we concluded that the training does not pay for itself.

In sum, we used available information and a general cost-benefit scheme to produce an estimate of the value of training to the organization, despite the roadblocks and detours encountered. Assumptions were clearly stated for the user of the information and recommendations made concerning the future of the training.

Conclusion

The six evaluation strategies discussed above are not the only ones available to the evaluator in answering the four critical evaluation questions. Moreover, the appropriateness of each strategy depends on the characteristics of the training course or program under study and on evaluation resources and constraints. Obviously, the more resources and fewer constraints, the greater and more satisfactory will be the choices of evaluation strategies.

Nevertheless, effective evaluation can be conducted under far from ideal conditions ... the kinds of conditions evaluators normally face in their organizations.

Auditing the Labor Relations Function

Dale Yoder and Paul D. Staudohar

Formal audits of personnel administration and industrial relations (PAIR) have achieved wide and growing acceptance—and logically so: Management needs more detailed feedback with which to pinpoint, measure, and compare operational performance. PAIR audits test and refine theories, identify and evaluate improved measures of individual and organizational performance, and suggest new policies and programs for improved human resources management.

This article examines the auditing of a key PAIR function: labor relations. Subtopics include (1) the need for PAIR auditing in general; (2) the extent of labor relations auditing; (3) changes in the environment of labor relations that justify additional auditing attention; and (4) questions for reviewing collective bargaining, grievances, and arbitration as major components of the labor relations function.

Need for auditing

In earlier periods, some managers opposed attempts at formal appraisals of employment relations. They argued that the essence of PAIR success is maintenance of an intangible tone and atmosphere in employment, that the most important accomplishments in the management of people defy evaluation and measurement. They resented efforts to establish standards and yardsticks for assessing the value of PAIR programs. Many managers argued that the contributions of their efforts had to be accepted on faith as self-evident.

Reprinted by permission of the publisher from *Personnel*, May–June 1983. © 1983 by Periodicals Division, American Management Associations, New York. All rights reserved. Some of this article has been adapted from Dale Yoder and Paul D. Staudohar's *Personnel Management and Industrial Relations*, seventh edition, © 1982 by Prentice-Hall, Inc.

Several changes have influenced increased recognition of the need for formal PAIR audits. Alert managers know that managerial philosophy and theory have changed, particularly in terms of awareness of the importance of employee participation in establishing and accomplishing organizational goals. At the same time, wider responsibility has been given PAIR departments for assuring organizational effectiveness. And the fluctuating economic climate, with periods of high inflation, unemployment, declining productivity rates, and international competition have spurred reassessment of how effectively PAIR managers are accomplishing their assigned functions.

Attempts at auditing PAIR have leaned heavily on attitude surveys and questionnaires evaluating the overall effectiveness of PAIR functions. Some evaluative information reports the results of programs on such "bottom line" indicators as profits, productivity, turnover, and absenteeism. Few evaluations of specialized PAIR functions are described in the literature. More can be expected as managers continue to realize the importance of tailoring their audits to individual programs.

Extent of labor relations auditing

Labor relations as a PAIR function involves group relationships with unionized and nonunionized employees. Principal areas include collective bargaining, contract administration, grievance handling, arbitration of grievances, and compliance with labor relations law. Emphasis on areas varies among firms, especially with respect to whether they are unionized or not. Nonunion firms spend more time on union avoidance and preparing for representation elections, and less time on negotiations and grievance procedures.

A recent study of 523 firms by Audrey Freedman at The Conference Board indicates that proportionately few firms formally evaluate their labor relations performance. The survey found that 20 percent of the unionized firms had no evaluation of labor relations at all; another 60 percent conducted informal evaluations periodically; and only 20 percent had a formal procedure for evaluating labor relations performance. Among nonunion companies, 42 percent did not evaluate labor relations, 45 percent had informal evaluations, and 13 percent had formal evaluations.

Unionized firms that conducted formal and informal evaluations were asked about the relative importance attached to different aspects of labor relations. Regarded as the most important factor by a majority of the respondents was the effect of negotiations on labor cost. Also consistently ranked high in importance was "employee attitudes and morale." Interestingly, avoidance of strikes was not generally considered of high importance. But since this study was conducted, some important changes have taken place.

Changing patterns of labor relations

In 1982, a new "concessionary" mood in labor relations became evident in the United States. Unions approached the bargaining table with unusually modest demands, beginning with the Teamster negotiations early in the year. As unemployment worsened to the highest levels in over four decades, some unions allowed reopened discussions on existing contracts, permitting reduced wages and fringe benefits in exchange for greater job security. This was done in the landmark Ford/United Automobile Workers agreement, followed shortly thereafter by a similar agreement between General Motors and the UAW.

Givebacks or takeaways—reductions in terms of rewards previously negotiated by unions—became increasingly common in several other industries. Givebacks to avoid plant closings or layoffs were negotiated by firms in the airline, meatpacking, rubber, and steel industries. The practice of pattern bargaining, whereby the union contract with a target firm is followed on overall economic concessions by other firms in the industry, has been weakened considerably. This is because, in almost every major U.S. industry, one or more large firms have been unwilling to match a generous pattern of wage and fringe benefits.

A parallel trend involves increased cooperation between labor and management in some industries toward improving productivity and quality of work life. In many unionized firms, the parties have been hard at work to create a climate for increased organizational effectiveness. A spirit of cooperation is growing and, in some cases, may actually replace the traditional adversary relationship.

These changes in the economic and work environment justify careful examination of the labor relations function. Auditing provides information to show not only how well programs are doing in achieving objectives, but also to evaluate the rationale of these objectives and the theories and policies on which they are based. Auditing thus provides assessments of the effectiveness of current practices and suggests ways of adapting them.

The next two sections of this article discuss auditing the labor relations function in the areas of (1) collective bargaining and (2) grievances and arbitration. These inquiries are not meant to be answered with a simple "yes" or "no" response. Instead, they are intended to stimulate a probe of the crucial dimensions of labor relations. From the audit and the probe, it is to be hoped that useful recommendations will emerge, leading to constructive changes in labor relations policies and programs.

Collective bargaining

Items in this category are divided generally into three areas: attitudes, processes, and outcomes. These areas are interrelated; that is, it can be hypothesized that an appropriate structuring of attitudes and judicious attention to the processes of negotiations will lead to improved outcomes. For example, an aggressive posture by management on takeaways tends to influence attitudes and bargaining outcomes in one direction. Cooperative proposals for productivity improvement, on the other hand, tend to lead to a different kind of attitudinal response.

The following questionnaire is designed especially for completion by members of the management negotiating team. Its purpose is not to provide a numerical score, but rather to serve as a spark for discussions between managers and negotiators about evaluating bargaining effectiveness and suggesting ways to improve future negotiations. (No attempt has been made to leave space for answers on the printed pages here.)

Attitudes

1. How would you characterize the tenor of negotiations?
   _____ adversary relationship
   _____ joint problem solving
   _____ some adversary and some elements of cooperation and accommodation
2. Why did you/did you not experience significant feelings of trust toward the union negotiators?
3. Why did you/did you not feel a high level of respect for the union negotiators?
4. Describe your behavior toward the union—for example, friendly, hostile, or other.
5. Describe the behavior of the union negotiators toward you—for example, friendly, hostile, or other.

Process

6. In retrospect, do you think you engaged in enough research toward preparing for negotiations? Why or why not?
7. Specify areas in which greater preparation for negotiations was needed.
8. Did members of the bargaining team have clearly assigned and understood roles? What changes would you suggest for this role assignment?
9. Indicate the five most important provisions, in rank order (a through e), that you sought to have included in the new contract.
10. In what areas, if any, did you seek to negotiate takeaways, or removal of union rights contained in the previous contract?

Compensation: fringe benefits, cost-of-living allowance, premium pay, other

Hours, shifts, vacations, and so forth: length of the workday, shift scheduling, overtime scheduling, other

Individual job rights: seniority, posting of vacancies, discipline for cause, other

Union security: union shop, agency shop, dues checkoff, other

Methods for enforcing the contract: grievance procedure, grievance arbitration, other

11. Do you feel you had adequate support from members of your bargaining team? Why or why not?
12. Describe any unusual pressures placed on you as a negotiator by management personnel who were not directly involved in negotiations.
13. Were methods for costing-out union proposals made during negotiations—for example, present value formula, discounted cash-flow model, roll-up (total cost of old wages divided by total cost of old fringe benefits to calculate increased cost of current benefits as a result of any wage increase)?
14. Describe proposals made in negotiations for improving productivity and/or the quality of work life.
15. In what ways was mediation helpful in reaching agreement?
16. If you did not use mediation, do you feel in retrospect that it would have been useful? Why or why not?

Outcome

17. On the issues you indicated in question 9, how successful were you in achieving your objective to get them included in the contract?

	Totally	Partially	Not at all
Issue *a*	_____	_____	_____
Issue *b*	_____	_____	_____
Issue *c*	_____	_____	_____
Issue *d*	_____	_____	_____
Issue *e*	_____	_____	_____

18. In which of the areas in question 10 were you successful through negotiations in altering previous contractual arrangements in your favor? What factors led to this success?
19. If there was a strike, how might it have been avoided through improved negotiating methods?
20. List the issues that presented the most difficulty in reaching agreement in negotiations.
21. Identify and describe the specific ways in which contract provisions are expected to improve productivity and the quality of work life.

Grievances and arbitration

Grievance procedures provide a mechanism for prompt resolution of work-related problems. The principal objectives that grievance procedures promote include:

1. An orderly channel for reducing pressures and anxieties of employees.
2. A mechanism for equitable, just interpretation and application of negotiated terms.
3. A force preventing arbitrary, capricious, and unreasonable actions against employees.

Grievance arbitration is the final step in nearly all collective bargaining agreements in private industry. However, only a small percentage of all grievances result in arbitration. Most are settled at earlier stages of the grievance procedure. Generally speaking, a sign of an effective grievance procedure is the resolution of a high proportion of grievances at the first step (usually an informal discussion between the employee and his or her supervisor).

Precise measures of the effectiveness of grievance procedures are difficult to obtain. Organizational characteristics, levels of technology utilized, age of the parties' relationship, environmental forces, behavioral patterns, and other variables may affect outcomes. The following questions suggest points that may justify close examination in the auditing. They are divided into two areas: grievance procedures and grievance arbitration.

Grievance procedures

1. What types of disputes is the grievance procedure designed to handle? What types are excluded? Why?
2. What has been done to ensure that all grievances are investigated to get pertinent facts?
3. Does a device exist (perhaps in written form) for gathering information about grievances? If so, how can this device be improved? If not, would there be value in creating such a device?
4. Are supervisors adequately trained to handle grievances? Why or why not?
5. Are time limits placed on the initial filing of grievances to prevent stale claims and to permit the expeditious processing of grievances through the steps of the procedure? Do these time limits work?
6. In what ways is grievance processing encumbered by lack of trust, respect, or cooperation?
7. Are any agreements—made with individuals on grievances— inconsistent with the collective bargaining agreements? What has been done to prevent such an inconsistency?

8. Is a high proportion of grievances resolved in the early stages of the grievance procedure? If not, what can be done to encourage early grievance settlement?
9. If there is a grievance committee, with equal numbers of management and labor representatives, are partisan positions invariably taken regardless of the merits of individual grievances? How can this problem be avoided?
10. What are the results of grievances that were resolved short of arbitration?

    _____ number of grievances in which management's position was followed

    _____ number of grievances in which the union's position was followed

    _____ number of grievances in which a compromise was adopted between these positions

Grievance arbitration

11. Is arbitration limited to matters involving the "interpretation or application of the agreement" to prevent the union from obtaining rights not gained in negotiations?
12. Was research conducted on the history of collective bargaining (from minutes, notes, or tapes) that strengthen your position in arbitration? How has such research been beneficial to your results in arbitration?
13. Has laxity in enforcement of contract provisions given rise to past practices that forfeit management's contract rights in arbitration? What can be done to prevent this?
14. Are the past decisions of prospective arbitrators studied in determining choice of an arbitrator? Describe your rationale in utilizing this information.
15. Was arbitral precedent studied for supporting views in preparing your arguments in arbitration cases? Illustrate how this precedent was used and why it was effective or not.
16. Are there certain grievances for which expedited arbitration might be used? If so, what particular cases?
17. What have been the results of arbitrated grievances?

    _____ number of decisions for management

    _____ number of decisions for the union

    _____ number of split decisions

Concluding thoughts

The purpose of questions for audit such as those provided in this article is to help PAIR practitioners act effectively on the labor relations function. As a practitioner responsible for designing a questionnaire, you may wish to delete or modify some questions and add others, depending on the circumstances of your organization and the environment in which it operates.

Whatever questions you choose for the audit, they should be asked of a broad range of participants in collective bargaining and grievances. Thorough responses should be encouraged. The time and effort spent can be worthwhile in causing reevaluation of what is being done, and in coming up with recommendations for a more effective labor relations function in the future.

PART 2

Improving Employee Performance

Let's Put Appraisal Back in Performance Appraisal

J. Peter Graves

Maybe it sounds funny to suggest that we need to put appraisal back in performance appraisal. But, in fact, over the last 20 years, we have seen a systematic trend away from appraisal in performance appraisal.

In most articles, seminars and advertisements on the subject, performance appraisal is described as something that a manager "conducts," like a meeting. The focus is usually on the way to "conduct an appraisal" in a manner that is forward-looking, motivating, encouraging, and so on. Great emphasis is placed on the manager's interpersonal and counseling skills, such as active listening, empathy and openness. Further, it is universally suggested that such "appraisals" be conducted more frequently than once a year—preferably on an ongoing basis.

All this attention on the interaction between manager and subordinate on performance issues is fine, but it is not performance appraisal. What is needed is a clear distinction between performance appraisal and discussions about performance. "Appraisal" is defined by Webster's as "to judge the quality or worth of." Performance appraisal is a judgmental process of evaluating the performance of another. If and when the appraiser chooses to share the evaluation with the person evaluated, then we have a performance discussion or a feedback session.

Discussion and doubletalk

Most of the current interest under the topic of performance appraisal is really about the performance discussion—its timing, frequency, content, the role of the manager and subordinate, etc. The effect of this interest and attention has been two-fold. The first effect is that we now know how to much better conduct such a discussion, and practitioners are developing innovative programs for training managers in talking about performance with their subordinates.

The second result, however, is that far less attention is being placed on the appraisal process itself. In some instances, the process of evaluating performance is viewed as incompatible or inconsistent with good performance discussions. Since our understanding of the effective performance discussion is of relatively recent origin, compared with evaluation techniques, it is sometimes even assumed that frequent discussion is the new way to do appraisals, while rankings, ratings and forms represent the old way to appraise performance.

Some organizations, in their eagerness to appear to be up-to-date on the issue of performance appraisal, will avow that, "We only use performance appraisals for development in our organization," or "We don't rank or compare people around here." These kinds of statements ignore a fact of organizational life—organizations will always comparatively evaluate the performance of their members. Said another way, organizations will always rate the performance of their members from good to poor, and compare performance from better to worse.

Whenever the organization makes a personnel decision—a promotion, transfer, layoff, merit increase or demotion—a comparative, evaluative decision has been made. Since decisions are seldom made without information, one wonders where the data are coming from in organizations that only use appraisals "for development."

Our current infatuation with the performance discussion is causing increasing disparity between what organizations are doing about performance appraisals and what they say they are doing. To be sure, there is nothing out of the ordinary in discrepancies of this sort, except that in this particular situation, it can get the organization in trouble.

Federal guidelines are clear

The principal reason for reconsidering the appraisal now is that the EEOC's uniform guidelines on selection and testing view performance appraisals to be as much a test as the paper-and-pencil variety. Organizations today must be able to defend the basis for personnel decisions. The weight of proving that a decision is job-related and not unfairly biased rests squarely on the performance data that are used.

Because of the attention being focused on personnel actions by EEO concerns, the rules of the game have changed. Organizations can no longer afford the luxury of an appraisal process that is merely compatible with their climate and management philosophy. When required, an organization must also be able to retrace the entire decision process that resulted in a promotion, layoff or other such action. For decisions like these, that benefit some and not others (these are called zero-sum situations), managers need comparative data. Such information clearly identifies the high and low performers on the important criteria. Appraisals must demonstrably comply with the federal guidelines in two important respects: reliability and validity.

But is it reliable?   Personnel specialists are adept at throwing about the words "reliability and validity" as if they were roughly synonymous—like "fuel economy and estimated highway mileage" when describing an automobile. But these appraisal words are not the same because they describe two very different aspects of evaluation or appraisal. To continue the automobile analogy, they are about as similar as "good fuel economy" and "impressive to the folks in Toledo." One is a characteristic of the automobile, the other of the setting in which it is used. The same is true of the reliability and validity of performance appraisal. Reliability is a characteristic of the method being used to gather data. The validity of a system is not a property of the method used, but of the setting in which it is used.

While there are many technical definitions of reliability, an easy way to judge the reliability of any evaluation is to answer a few simple questions, like the following:

1. Would you expect the ratings to be the same whether they were going to be used in feedback sessions or kept for confidential management use?
2. Would you expect the evaluations to look the same whether performed by a "Theory X" task-oriented rater, or a "Theory Y" people-oriented rater?
3. Would you expect the ratings to look the same whether performed by a manager trained in evaluation or one untrained?
4. Would you expect the ratings to be the same whether the appraisal was performed on Monday morning or Wednesday afternoon?

If you can answer "yes" to such questions, then the evaluations are reliable. If you have to answer "no"—that is, if situational factors, rater differences, or the confidentiality of the data can affect the ratings themselves—then the rating process is not very reliable.

Those validity issues   Note that we haven't said anything about which criteria to use for evaluation, who should evaluate, nor how frequently the evaluations should be conducted. These issues all relate to the validity of an evaluation. These validity issues are currently very popular topics in articles and seminars on performance appraisal. We seem to know all the right questions to ask about validity, but we don't know when to ask them. Validity issues are meaningless without reliability, because an appraisal process must first be reliable before it can be valid. But reliability does not guarantee validity either.

For years we have been accustomed to questioning the reliability and validity of tests and measurements because psychologists have been producing generalized aptitude and intelligence tests with reliability and validity built in. Even today, tests designed for the general population, such as college entrance exams, must demonstrate both reliability and validity. But appraisal validity is job-related, and a valid appraisal is one that measures the right criteria to determine performance.

Since the issuance of the EEOC guidelines, it has become clear that only in the rarest instances can the validity of a general test or battery suffice for job-related validity in the legal sense. Job-relatedness also means situation specific, so no appraisal can be said to be validated unless reference is made to some specific job situation. What all this means is that an organization must be prepared to demonstrate that its appraisal system is reliable and valid for each job.

Noncomparative methods

At first glance, there appear to be many alternative methodologies for appraisals. But as each one is considered in light of the requirements for legal and meaningful appraisal, the number of realistic alternatives narrows considerably. As each technique is discussed, the focus will be not on how to use them, but rather on their strengths and weaknesses relating to reliability and validity. Following customary practice, the various approaches will be considered in two categories: noncomparative and comparative.

Noncomparative methods are so called because they consider the performance of an individual with little or no reference to the performance of others. In most cases, these procedures evaluate an individual's performance with reference to job requirements, job standards or negotiated expectations. Some approaches described in this section are not appraisal methods at all, but are included simply because the lore of contemporary performance appraisal usually includes them.

Management by objectives   Management by Objectives (MBO) was suggested by Douglas McGregor as an alternative to traditional appraisal. After 25 years of attempting to substitute MBO for appraisal, however, most organizations still view performance appraisal uneasily. It is not that MBO has failed; it is that MBO simply is not performance appraisal.

The many features of MBO have received exhaustive attention elsewhere, but a few points are distinct advantages pertaining to performance appraisal. First, it is a powerful means of clarifying job requirements and documenting those shared expectations. These documents then serve as the logical starting point for a later review of performance. Regardless of whether the philosophy of MBO is ever fully integrated in the organization, the process of systemizing previously informal expectations is a tremendous addition to discussions about performance. For this reason, MBO has been a favorite among the proponents of the performance discussion.

MBO is not appraisal because it is not evaluative. Nor is it intended to be; it is contrary to the philosophy of MBO for individuals to be compared or evaluated. The accomplishment of a stated objective is no more than that—just an accomplished objective. Before the accomplishment can be useful for management decision making, the accomplishment must be evaluated or appraised.

We are all familiar with the difficulty of trying to compare a challenging objective almost attained to the overattainment of an easy objective. The resolution of such a situation is a judgmental one. Such judgments must always follow MBO so managers will have the information they need for making decisions. That MBO itself provides none of this necessary information is its major weakness as an appraisal method.

Critical incidents   Some organizations make a practice of recording in detail specific instances of on-the-job performance for later review. If done properly, the critical incidents are recorded and discussed descriptively rather than evaluatively.

Because it is not evaluative, and describes specific actions and behaviors, the critical incident method is a powerful support to the performance discussion. The manager and subordinate are then able to discuss the actual behaviors the subordinate engaged in when faced with problem situations. By discussing the critical incidents descriptively, the potential for defensiveness and disagreement is greatly reduced. Unlike Management by Objectives, the critical incidents are retrospective only, and provide little or no stimulus for discussing future performance.

While the critical incident approach provides the basis for a good performance discussion, somebody ultimately has to determine whether the subordinate performed effectively or not. If decisions on salary or promotion are pending, someone has to determine whether the subordinate performed better or worse than others. So another appraisal is necessary to translate the critical incidents into usable data for decision making.

In a very real sense, the MBO and critical incident methods are just formalized means of documenting performance expectations and outcomes, rather than appraisals. This documentation is invaluable when discussing performance, but is inadequate when making and defending comparative decisions.

Narrative appraisal   Narrative appraisal is the first approach that can realistically be considered an appraisal, because it is evaluative as well as descriptive. The appraiser writes a narrative description of the individual's performance, using specific incidents where necessary, but also containing adjectives like "excellent," "unsatisfactory" and so on.

As mentioned above, critical incidents and objectives must first be evaluated before becoming useful for decision making. But, because the narrative appraisal is evaluative, it may, by itself, form the basis for noncomparative decisions. For example, if an individual must be terminated because of poor performance, a narrative appraisal may provide the necessary basis for the decision.

Compared to more structured methods to be described below, the narrative appraisal is much more flexible for the appraisers. Generally, they are free to write as much or as little as they desire. Given that appraiser attitude toward the appraisal process can be an important factor in the quality of results, this flexibility is an important asset.

One disadvantage is that the evaluative words in the narrative appraisal take on tremendous meaning to those who read the appraisal. Unfortunately, the real meaning of such adjectives is usually not available within a single narrative appraisal. An engineer who believed he was getting reasonably good performance reviews suddenly found himself caught in a 5% reduction in force. It turned out that the phrase he had been seeing in his appraisals—"quite good"—was just about the worst that the engineers in his organization were ever told about their performance.

Like many others, the engineer simply didn't understand how easily a code can develop among appraisers. The code words are much like the "giant," "economy" and "family" designations that food manufacturers use in their packaging. As long as you know the code, or can see the different sizes lined up together, each adjective has real and consistent meaning. Lacking such comparison, however, the reader understandably believes exactly what he reads.

To the extent that no serious action needs to be taken, many managers see nothing wrong in all this. With a bit of contorted logic, they can even persuade themselves that it is helpful to the subordinate. "What would happen," they reason, "if these lower performers were to learn where they really stand? It would be so demoralizing that it would render them useless."

While written narrative adds the evaluative dimension, it provides no comparative information. A termination for poor performance, mentioned earlier, is a noncomparative decision. But, if a person must be laid off because of budget cutbacks, we have a very different situation. Even though the same individual may be involved in each case, the layoff decision is a comparative one because the poor performer must be shown to be the poorest performer. For decisions that require a knowledge of who has performed better than others, more information than is provided by the narrative appraisal must somehow be obtained.

Rating scales   By far the most widely used appraisal method is the rating scale. Judgments about performance are recorded on a graphic scale, usually consisting of five to seven points, from low to high.

Sometimes, adjectives are used to define each scale point, such as: outstanding, very good, satisfactory, marginal or unsatisfactory. The scales are generally used for more than one dimension or criterion of performance. Thus, an appraisal form may have many different scales to complete, each representing a different facet of job-related performance.

These scales are easy to construct and score, easy to understand, and require minimal time for appraisers to complete. Because rating scales can be used with multiple criteria, instead of a single, global evaluation, the appraisal can be more carefully matched to the job description.

The principal weakness of the rating scale is its unreliability. Because it is simple and straightforward, raters check any point on the scale they wish. While this should mean that the evaluation will be sensitive and meaningful, it can also mean some or all of the following:

1.   All persons could be rated outstanding when they really are not.
2.   Raters can give higher ratings when they know that ratees will be shown the appraisals. (Research has shown this to be almost universally the case.)

3. A harsh rater can rate everyone lower than an average or lenient rater would.
4. If a salary decision has already been made, the ratings can easily be made to justify the salary action.

The control game   This list of possibilities can go on and on. There is an equally long list of controls to prevent them from happening. Some organizations, to prevent all ratees from being rated high, establish minimum and maximum percentages for the number of ratings in each category. They may, for example allow only 5% in the outstanding category, or require at least 2% in the bottom category. That would be fine, unless you had only 1% outstanding. Another 4% would be rated higher to fill a quota. Or what if you had a highly qualified group with 10% who are really outstanding? Such a rule would permit only half of the best performers to be accurately rated. This cure can be worse than the disease.

To overcome leniency and central tendency errors, some organizations have elaborate rater-training programs. Sometimes appraisals are required to be completed and filed before salary discussions begin, to prevent the decision from driving the appraisal.

The above are all examples of the way organizations typically try to control the lack of reliability inherent in the rating scale technique. But notice that they are all external controls—none of them are modifications of the rating scale itself to increase reliability. They add an expensive and burdensome mechanism to the administration of the rating process. All of the benefits of a simple, straightforward process would be eaten up by the control mechanisms; and you still wouldn't know if your efforts had improved the reliability; you could only hope they had.

Behaviorally anchored rating scales   The behaviorally anchored rating scale (BARS) is an approach to the rating scale that attempts to address some of the reliability problems mentioned above, but from the inside of the appraisal process—rather than with an external rule or constraint. The BARS uses the rating scale, but instead of adjectives at each scale point, behavioral anchors related to the criterion being measured are used. Figure 1 is an example of a BARS used to measure "perseverence" in a computer programmer's job.

By using observable behaviors instead of adjectives, the meaning of each point on the scale is clarified. The raters don't need to imagine what outstanding performance is—they can see an actual example in the behavioral anchor. BARS is also a boon to the performance discussion. Because behaviors are much easier to discuss than adjectives, the performance discussion can deal with specific activities that need attention.

How perseverent is the employee?

_____ Could be expected to keep working until a difficult job is completed.

_____ Could be expected to continue working on a difficult job past normal quitting time rather than let it go until the next day.

_____ Could be expected to continue working on a difficult job until an opportunity arises to work on another task.

_____ Could be expected to need frequent admonitions to continue working on a difficult job.

_____ Could be expected to ask for a new assignment when faced with a difficult job.

_____ Could be expected to stop work on a hard job at the first sign of difficulty.

Figure 1. Behaviorally anchored rating scale (BARS).

The most glaring disadvantage of the BARS is the time and resources needed to develop meaningful behavioral anchors. After a careful job analysis has identified the dimensions of a job that should be evaluated, a complete set of behavioral anchors must be written for each dimension (and five to 10 dimensions for a single job are not uncommon). This task cannot be accomplished without the participation of the most important people—the high performing job incumbents and their managers. Also, since the job analysis performed for one job is not valid for another, the entire process must be repeated for every single job.

A rose is a rose?

Even if the organization can muster the resources to develop the behavioral anchors, they quickly encounter a more disturbing problem. Some performance dimensions, they discover, cannot be reduced to specific behaviors. This is especially true with professional or managerial positions, where the exercise of judgment and discretion is required.

Suppose, for example, that a job analysis identified "evaluating the performance of subordinates" as an important dimension of a supervisor's job. It is hard to imagine what the behavioral anchors for this dimension might look like. "Evaluating" is a cognitive, judgmental task, not an observable behavior. (Note again that we are not talking about conducting a performance discussion.)

This dilemma is even more likely to occur as you move up the ladder of responsibility to senior managers and top professionals. The logic for this is unavoidable: If we could reduce the contribution of these valuable people to a set of behaviors, the task of executive and professional development could likewise be reduced to merely training a set of behaviors. Such is obviously not the case.

But there is an even more fundamental disadvantage. The argument that behaviors are better than adjectives is a strong one, but only if the behaviors are actually observed. Because it cannot be assumed that the person being appraised has exhibited one of the behaviors described in the anchors, they are frequently written not as behaviors, but in the form, "Could be expected to . . ." If no such behavior has ever been seen, then the raters are recording their expectations about behaviors that might occur if conditions were right. It can hardly be argued that guesses about possible behaviors are any more reliable than adjectives about past performance.

Despite these weaknesses of the behaviorally anchored rating scale method, it is a strong favorite among personnel professionals and writers on the subject.

Comparative methods

Arguments for a comparative approach are simple and powerful. The simple part of it is that organizations do it anyway, all the time. Whenever personnel decisions are made, the performance of the individuals being considered is ranked and compared. People are not promoted because they achieve their objectives, but rather because they achieve their objectives *better* than others. Most personnel decisions are zero-sum in nature and do not involve just a single person. A single person may be promoted, but others are considered and not promoted. It is also clear from court tests of appraisal systems that evidence for not promoting a person is just as important as evidence to promote.

To make these comparative decisions, managers need comparative data on performance, which they will get from the formal appraisal system or somewhere else. Even in organizations that roundly proclaim that ranking and comparisons destroy teamwork and self-esteem, the managers will have all the comparative data they need to make personnel decisions. We'd like to hope (and so would the federal government) that the comparative evaluations used by these organizations are reliable and valid, but they are more likely to be informal and undocumented.

If the formal appraisal system fails to provide managers with the data they need, they will use informal methods. The real question is not whether the organization rates or ranks the performance of its members, but whether they will be open and explicit—or obscure and subtle—about the methods and criteria used. The real irony is that organizations that enthusiastically embrace MBO-type "appraisals," because they are "developmental," are only pushing the comparative appraisals into the smoke-filled rooms and the informal bull sessions.

The second reason (the powerful one) for using comparative as opposed to noncomparative methods is that they are far more reliable. This is because reliability is controlled by the rating process itself, not by rules, policies, and other external constraints. If an appraiser using a noncomparative method wishes to avoid controversy, or lies, or misunderstands the instructions, or simply can't think straight, this will all affect the appraisal, but there is no way to know that this is happening.

If comparative methods are used, some or even all of these sources of unreliability can be completely controlled. The comparative approach simply requires raters to make remarks about one person's performance that are consistent with what they are saying about another's.

Comparative ranking   Ranking is the most widely used method of comparative evaluation. All individuals in a given category are ranked from highest to lowest based on their performance. Such an evaluation can be done by a single individual, but is usually done by a group of raters.

One advantage is that ranking is obviously a simple and straightforward procedure. It takes little formal instruction and capitalizes on the natural tendency to rank individual performance from highest to lowest. The direct result is exactly the type of comparative data needed for personnel decision making. No extrapolation or intermediate calculations are necessary to arrive at a consistent picture of relative performance. (As we shall see, this gives rise to a major weakness, too.) The only limitation on the numbers of individuals who can be ranked is simply the number of individuals supervised by the rater.

Because ranking directly produces the complete comparative picture, it can be manipulated very easily. If a rater wants a ratee to look different than his or her performance actually warrants, the rater need only move the ratee's name up or down the ranking. When more than a single rater is used, this manipulation often takes the form of social or political pressure as the raters assemble their judgments into a consensus.

Another weakness is that it is usually possible to use only a single, global criterion of performance. This raises serious validity questions because it reduces performance to a single index. Job analyses, on the other hand, almost always identify multiple dimensions of performance.

Another disadvantage is that rank-order data reveals little about the intervals between the individuals listed in the ranking. Can you realistically assume that everyone is equally spaced from the highest performers to the lowest? It is often surprising, and not a little unsettling, what compensation specialists do with simple, rank-order data. Percentiles are quickly calculated and quartile groups are delineated as if the difference between persons seven and eight were exactly the same as between 21 and 22.

Serious problems can also result when rankings are combined. Frequently, rankings from small groups are combined into departmental rankings, which may be further combined with other departments. (Even if this is not done explicitly, changing rank data into percentiles and then equating percentile scores achieves exactly the same thing.) There are no acceptable means to do this without making unwarranted assumptions about the performance of various groups. There are obvious political overtones as well, when rankings are merged across organizational boundaries. Conscious manipulation of ranking data is commonplace, for example, when departments jockey for shares of a limited salary increase pool.

Paired comparisons   With this method, the rater compares the performance of a pair of individuals. The rater's task is to choose the individual whose performance is better on a particular quality or dimension. Every possible combination of everyone being rated is presented to the rater. The relative position of the ratees in the final ranking is determined by the number of times one individual is preferred over another.

The principal advantage of the paired comparison over the straight ranking is that the consistency of the raters' judgments will be visible. For example, when a rater says that Person A's performance is better than Person B's, B is better than C. When the rater adds that C is better than A, the rater is doing more than recording a preference; the rater is also documenting an inconsistency. The practical value of this process is that the paired comparison is far more difficult to manipulate. This is especially the case as the number of ratees increases. Most raters quickly realize that being honest and candid is the safest way to maintain the consistency of their decisions with the paired comparison.

Another advantage of the paired comparison is that every comparison between ratees is actually made. Pairwise decisions are implied by the straight ranking method, but, in practice, those in the middle of a rank order often do not receive the attention given those on the top and bottom. The paired comparison assures equal attention to all ratees and increases the overall reliability of the evaluations.

A main disadvantage involves the number of ratees included. As the number of ratees increases, the number of possible pairs increases very fast. With 10 ratees, the rater is faced with 45 pairs, but with 20 ratees, the combinations jump to 190. At 30 ratees, not by any means an unusual size group to be evaluated, a rater would have to complete 435 pairs. The unreliability caused by fatigue and boredom would quickly erase any benefits of using the paired comparison.

Another weakness surfaces when the pairings are scored. While the paired comparison can be effectively used with multiple raters, every rater must know and evaluate each ratee to avoid a serious flaw in the way the paired comparisons are scored. When raters are only able to evaluate a subset of the total ratees, the scoring procedure is biased toward the better-known ratees. Well-known, above-average ratees are ranked higher than less well-known peers of equal performance. Well-known, below-average ratees are ranked lower than their less well-known equals. This bias toward notoriety is an artifact of the scoring procedure for the paired comparison, and is not "washed out" with a large sample of sizes.

The forced-choice nature of the paired comparison does not allow for an "equals" decision. The rater is forced to choose one or the other, even when the two appear equal in the rater's mind. Further, the rater has no way of recording the degree of difference between ratees. Sometimes there will be large differences in the performance of the two ratees; other times there will be slight, but meaningful differences. With the paired comparison, the rater will have an either-or choice. Because of this inflexibility, the final ranking will only show ordinal position, and will provide no information on the differences between individual performances. Thus, paired comparisons will suffer the same weaknesses mentioned earlier about the intervals in the straight ranking method.

The scaled comparison   The scaled comparison is an entirely new methodology for appraisal. Also known under the commercial name of the Objective Judgment Quotient (OJQ), the scaled comparison has been in use for more than 10 years in the public and private sectors. The scaled comparison represents the first really new technology in evaluation since the introduction of the Likert-type scales more than 40 years ago.

Like the paired comparison, the scaled comparison requires the rater to compare the performance of two individuals on a certain criterion. But there the similarity ends because moderate differences can be noted on the rating form used for this method. For instance, if the rater thought A's performance was much better than B's, the space on the rating form nearest A's name would be checked. If B's performance was seen as much better than A's, then the space nearest B's name would be checked. If they were seen as equal, a middle space would be checked. Moderate differences could be indicated with the intermediate spaces.

Unlike other comparative methods, the scaled comparison is not limited to a single global criterion of effectiveness. Every important dimension of a job can be separately measured and weighed if some criteria are more important than others; a one-to-one match between the job analysis and the appraisal can be made.

Another advantage is that because multiple criteria are usually employed, the ratings will not result in a single number. This makes it possible to speak of strengths and weaknesses in performance instead of a position in a one-dimensional rank order. Also, the scaled comparison is not restricted by large numbers as is the paired comparison. Groups as large as 2,800 individuals have been evaluated at the same time without the process becoming burdensome to raters.

The scaled comparison does not require that one rater know all or even most of the individuals to be evaluated. Many raters, each familiar with but a subset of the total group of ratees, may participate. All of the evaluations from the various raters are combined into a consensus that shows the relative position of all ratees. Small groups of ratees are combined computationally into larger groups without the difficult, and often political, merging of rankings across divisions or departments.

In addition, the scaled comparison uses multiple raters. This is viewed as an advantage, but it can also be a disadvantage as well. Multiple raters are required because the scaled comparison is a means of consensual data gathering. Thus, the result is not the opinion of a single rater, but rather is the consensus of five to 10 raters who know the individual being evaluated.

The consensus also offers greater control over bias and manipulation than even the paired comparison. As mentioned earlier, the paired comparison allows the evaluation of the raters' decisions by "comparing them to themselves"—that is, by seeing whether raters are being logically consistent form one decision to the next. In addition, the scaled comparison allows the comparison of an individual rater's judgments to the consensus, to see how that rater's views differ from those of the other raters. This represents increased control over appraisal manipulation, and, more importantly, it permits the discovery of unique viewpoints at the same time that a consensus is obtained.

Finally, the scoring of the scaled comparison does not just result in a rank order on each criterion. Rather, the data show intervals between ratees as well as rank position. If two ratees were judged to be equal by the raters, they would appear equal in the results. If the highest performer were "head and shoulders" above the second best, the scaled comparison would preserve that perceived difference. The practical value of interval data over ordinal (rank) data is that they reflect the real distribution of performance—whether normal (bell-shaped), skewed, flat, or bimodal.

Some disadvantages   While mentioned above as an advantage, the requirement for multiple raters may also be a disadvantage. In organizations in which the immediate supervisor has traditionally been the only appraiser, management might feel that nobody else knows as much about an individual's performance. Except under unusual circumstances, this is rarely the case. What is very likely, however, is that managers in this situation may be reluctant to share the job of evaluation with others. In the case of the scaled comparison, this reluctance is often softened as the raters begin to appreciate its control over manipulation and bias. But many organizations simply may not have the climate that permits multiple raters under any condition.

Another disadvantage is that the scaled comparison is not an appraisal "system"—it is just a data-gathering process. The organization using it must build the system around it, from the job analysis, which identifies the evaluation criteria, all the way to the performance discussion that logically follows the appraisal. Such a total system is a requirement for any valid appraisal, but it may come more neatly packaged with some methods discussed earlier.

Finally, management may not want strong comparative data about performance. Some organizations have definite, though probably unstated, policies that certain personnel decisions are to be made without respect to measured performance. Such unwritten expectations often apply to relatives of key executives, protected EEO groups, and situations where seniority counts more than performance. A valid, nonmanipulable appraisal method would simply get in the way, constraining managers to act contrary to their real intentions. While this might not be an attractive picture of organization decision making, it is reality in many organizations.

Performance appraisal and the performance discussion

Is the scaled comparison just a new tool for managers to get what they need from appraisals? If employees are uncomfortable finding out where they stand in a simple rank order, do they like it any better knowing the gaps between themselves and their co-workers? Does the scaled comparison really make it easier to talk to employees about their performance?

Much attention has been paid to the employee reaction to knowing where they stand relative to their peers. Blame for the apparent negative reaction has unfortunately been placed on the appraisal method, with the reasoning that using a noncomparative method would avoid the negative reaction. But it is not that simple, for we know that every organization uses some comparative process, either formally or informally. The real problem lies with the validity of the performance data and how those data are presented to employees.

It is important, first of all, to realize that negative reactions to appraisals do not just come from those being evaluated. Appraisers are cynical about their own methods, too, and are just as uncomfortable about defending the results as appraisees are about hearing them. It was this discomfort that McGregor said causes a manager to feel he is "playing God" with appraisals.

Experienced managers know that most appraisal methods work like the old shell game. Every appraiser, and most appraisees, knows that there is neither trick nor magic to making the pea appear under the right shell. Unless raters really enjoy such games, the forms and procedures quickly become a burden. Part of this burden is due to imperfect methodologies, as I have already discussed. But a significant part is due to basic differences in the reasons for performing appraisals.

In many respects, the reasons management needs performance appraisal are incompatible with why the individual employee needs it. Managers need (and the law now encourages) comparative performance data for making comparative decisions—decisions that are zero-sum in nature. Managers need these data in a form that clearly identifies the high, medium, and low performers.

What the employee needs

The individual, however, needs nothing of the sort. In fact, Thompson and Dalton have shown that when comparative or ranking data are too obvious, or "too public," it negatively affects the morale of all, even those at the top of the list. The emphasis here is not on whether the ranking information is known, but the degree of public knowledge about performance. (Some information, of course, will always be available by simply noting who gets promoted, let go, and so on.)

It is wrong to assume that the problem is that someone used a zero-sum appraisal method. That is analogous to saying that the reason you had an automobile accident is that you got out of bed that morning. Sure, you could have avoided the accident by not getting up. But you can't avoid getting out of bed any more than organizations can avoid comparing the performance of their employees. On the other hand, organizations can avoid mishandling the sensitive performance data they collect.

The individual employee needs information about his or her performance that clearly and realistically identifies strengths and weaknesses. In addition to being a review of past performance, the data should also stimulate a dialogue between manager and subordinate that looks forward to the next appraisal period, with an eye to growth and development.

But we know that if the review doesn't go well, the discussion of future performance won't go at all. And the review seldom goes well if the appraisal process is unreliable or invalid. Since most appraisal methods are both, it is not surprising that Meyer, Kay and French suggest that *two* discussions take place—one to review past performance and the other to consider future plans. Still others have suggested that past performance plays no role at all in a performance discussion; only future goals and objectives are important. These "solutions," however, simply create two separate processes—one for decision making and one for performance discussions.

One good system

We don't need two systems; we need one appraisal process that provides believable information about performance. So believable, in fact, that during the discussion, no time at all is spent asking who (did this to me), where (did these data come from), why (do we have to do this at all), how (were the results calculated) or when (can I talk to my lawyer). The only question ought to be, "How do those who know me on the job view my performance in all the different areas of my responsibility?"

Answering this question does not require that the individual be shown a ranking of his or her peer group. That would have the "too obvious" effect mentioned earlier, and would be demoralizing for even high performers. What is needed is a clear and credible statement of strengths and areas for needed improvement, not a single number or a bunch of numbers. And, at the same time, the confidentiality of everybody else's appraisals must be guarded. If the review of past performance meets these conditions, the discussion will smoothly lead to the next question, "Where do we go from here?"

A good comparative appraisal method can fill both management's need for performance data and the individual's need for meaningful performance feedback. Such is hardly the case even with the best of the noncomparative approaches. The scaled comparison represents a means of bridging the gap between comparative appraisals and the performance discussion in three ways:

1. The data can't be manipulated.
2. The data reflects a consensus rather than a single viewpoint.
3. The data measures all the meaningful criteria.
4. The data is also the same appraisal that management uses for decision making.

For many of the above reasons, the scaled comparison has been received favorably by collective bargaining units, and some employee groups have requested that management use it for their appraisals. When the scaled comparison is used, much of the skepticism surrounding the appraisal process begins to dissipate.

For their part, managers responsible for appraisals favor the scaled comparison for the following reasons:

1.   It can't be manipulated by raters to force a desired outcome.
2.   It achieves a consensus without political pressure.
3.   It permits rating of the raters on appraisal ability.
4.   It provides them with data for decision making and performance feedback.
5.   It doesn't require consultants or specialists.

As a result, the managers feel less like they are "playing God" when they appraise their employees. They also begin to view the appraisal as a powerful and essential tool, rather than a burdensome requirement.

References

Guion, R. M. *Personnel Testing* (New York: McGraw-Hill, 1965).

Kingstrom, Paul O., and Allen R. Bass. "A critical analysis of studies comparing behaviorally anchored rating scales (BARS) and other rating formats," *Personnel Psychology*, Vol. 34 (1981), pp. 263-289.

McGregor, Douglas. "An Uneasy Look at Performance Appraisal," *Harvard Business Review* (May-June 1957), pp. 89-94.

Meyer, H. H., E. Key, and J. R. P. French. "Split Roles in Performance Appraisal," *Harvard Business Review* (Jan.-Feb. 1965), pp. 125-129.

Thompson, Paul H., and Gene W. Dalton, "Performance Appraisal: Managers Beware," *Harvard Business Review* (Jan.-Feb. 1970), pp. 149-157.

"Uniform Guidelines on Employee Selection Procedures," Federal Register, Vol. 43, No. 166 (Aug. 25, 1982).

Performance Appraisal and Merit Pay

Edward Lawler

Despite considerable research, I don't think we can say we have perfected the area of performance appraisal and pay administration enough to call it a science. It is more art than science.

Further, we are finding out that the process side of the equation may be more important than the mechanics. By this I mean how people deal with each other, how they relate to each other, the kinds of interpersonal relationships may be more important than such things as the type of form used.

Why tie pay to performance?

Unless you appraise performance, unless you do it well, it is impossible to relate pay to performance, and I think there are three reasons to tie pay to performance.

One is that as a society we are committed to a sense of equity that says rewards and performance should be related. So if we are going to satisfy that sense of equity, we need to tie pay to performance.

Second, the research on motivation is quite clear; it shows that to be a motivator, pay must be clearly tied to performance. People have to see a clear relationship between pay and performance. If that does not exist, then pay is not a motivator.

Finally, if we tie pay to performance, we are ahead of the game in attracting and retaining the best people. A considerable amount of research shows that outstanding performers—people who are highly motivated—prefer to work in and remain in situations where pay and performance are related.

Reprinted from *Intergovernmental Personnel Notes*, May–June 1979.

Why so difficult?

Appraising performance and tying pay to it is an extremely emotional issue. It is an uncomfortable activity for both the superior and the subordinate. It is uncomfortable because it involves issues that are very important to people—not only the pay treatment, but people's self-esteem, how they perform, their competence.

Often, I think, we try to deny those emotional issues, or we tend to project the discomfort onto the subordinate, as if the superior is not uncomfortable. Research, however, shows that both are uncomfortable, each for different reasons.

An extremely high level of commitment is needed if performance appraisal is going to be done well. It is not something that is done easily because of the emotional issues, the other issues that I have mentioned before, and without a high level of commitment it is rarely done well. By high level of commitment, I mean the superior must spend hours and hours of time.

It is subjective, and any subjective process, particularly when it is an emotional one, is difficult to carry out. Tied into this is the fact that interpersonal skills are clearly needed, and are one of the important keys to making it go well.

One of the things that happens when you introduce a pay for performance system is that people begin to look at the system and say, "Okay, I have been told the rules have changed, now what I need to do is figure out how I can get the game to pay off for me, what behavior is needed." And they begin to look around and to develop hypotheses about, for example, if I do this I will get a larger than normal increase, or a bonus, or whatever it is. That is what you hope for. But if the system is not clear in demonstrating what is rewarded, doesn't have adequate performance appraisal, you find that people develop a wide range of very different perceptions of what pays off.

If you interview subordinates in an organization that has a "merit pay system" but has poor performance appraisal, you will find a wide range of opinion about whether the system works or not, and what it means to get a merit increase. Often the perceptions are very cynical, they are counterproductive, and indeed they are really not motivating anything except what we would properly call superstitious behavior.

Another concern I have when systems don't work is for the poor performer. When supervisors are uncomfortable in dealing with poor performers, they can become very dogmatic and very punitive because of their own discomfort, which does not help anyone.

How do you make it work?

I think there are some important preconditions that need to be in place if performance appraisal and merit pay are going to work. We always say, when we go into industrial organizations, you need support from the top. However, a serious concern [in the public sector] is whether that support will continue as administrations and political forces change. I think it's critical that you have support from the top throughout both the political sector and the career service sector. Performance appraisal and merit pay have to be administered from the top down. No one can be exempt from it. The people at the top need to model the process that should go on lower down. Without that modeling, the system does not work.

Another precondition is in the area of job design. This may be the trickiest one to bring into place so that performance appraisal can work effectively. Without adequately defined and designed jobs, it is impossible to do performance appraisal effectively. This means simply that if there is no job there, if there are no results that the person is responsible for, no turf or work area that is assigned to the individual, talking about performance appraisal is a waste of time. Performance appraisal is impossible because it becomes so subjective that it's more of a personal like-dislike than an outcomes-based process.

What are the mechanics?

Now let's look at the mechanics required to make the process go well. First, the appraisal must be based on behavior. Traits are simply an inadequate basis for appraising performance. They are guaranteed to produce defensiveness, rigidity on the part of subordinates, and inadequate feedback. I say this despite the fact that if you look at the private sector, something like 50 percent of the organizations in this country still appraise performance on the basis of traits. We know that this is ineffective, counterproductive, and should be eliminated. So whatever is done, it must be behavior-related and stated as well as possible in measurable, observable, behavioral dimensions.

If you are talking about reliability, for example, or dependability of a person, that has to be converted into behavior. What does it mean? Does it mean being there every day? Does it mean following through on instructions within a certain time period? That has to be defined if the process is going to be effective.

In addition, it is critical that the behavior-related measures developed have certain characteristics. For example, it is crucial that they include all the behaviors that you wish the subordinate to demonstrate.

All too often, appraisal systems latch on to one dimension. If areas like EEO appraisal of subordinates, and development of subordinates, are not part of the appraisal system, the supervisor ignores them. Therefore, it is critical that inclusive measures of performance be developed.

In addition, it is very desirable for the measures to be influenced by the behavior of the person being appraised. All too often we develop measures that are largely determined by decisions or actions taken above the person or by environmental events over which the one appraised has no control.

I have argued that the measures need to have certain characteristics—the need to be inclusive, behavior-related, and influenced by the subordinate's behavior—and finally I would argue that they need to be documented. There needs to be a written record. The written record imposes a certain rigor on the process that is not likely to be present otherwise, and, in addition, because of the concern we have about rights-consciousness, I think we need that written record to fall back on in case of challenge.

There also needs to be some way of checking to see whether appraisal has actually taken place; hence the argument for the written record. Unfortunately, if there is no check and balance to determine whether an appraisal has taken place, it often is not done.

Three sessions needed

In the mechanical area, I think timing is absolutely crucial to making appraisal go well. First, there has to be a preliminary session in which there is agreement on the behaviors to be measured and what is adequate performance in those behavior areas. I think it is also desirable at the same time to reach some decisions about what will happen in a pay area if performance levels are achieved. There needs to be agreement on what the job is, on what the performance is going to be, areas to be measured, and what constitutes outstanding, good, and adequate performance in those areas. That should be related to a promised or alluded-to pay action. This and only this can make clear the relationship between behavior and pay.

At the end of the year, superior and subordinate need to discuss the subordinate's performance and how that relates to the pay action. It is critical here that the subordinate be given a chance to present his/her performance case to the supervisor.

Finally, I think there needs to be a separate development session with the subordinate. My preference is that this take place sometime after the evaluation for the year, and that it be forward-looking, discussing the subordinate's development and training needs, and areas of weakness.

In sum, I am arguing for three sessions—a preliminary discussion session, a post-performance discussion session, and a development session. As you may note at this point, the time involved is beginning to build up. Each of these meetings may take an hour or more. This is why I said earlier that a significant commitment is required.

In the administrative process I think there needs to be some sort of appeal for the individual if he or she does not agree with the appraisal. That can be an appeal to an outside board or it can be an appeal one or two levels higher in management.

On the process side, I am arguing that it has to be an open process—open between the superior and the subordinate, and open generally within the organization. Tied into this is the importance of its being a two-way participative process. If subordinates feel that they can influence the type of goals, the type of measures being taken, and the judgment of the supervisor, then they tend to feel that the process is fair, that the appraisal is reasonable, even if they don't get a particularly favorable appraisal.

Finally, I think there is a critical need for training. Most supervisors cannot carry out a performance appraisal without training. There are some, but they are in the minority.

So if I were to leave you with a concluding thought, it is to train, train, train, and remember to be flexible in areas like job design and the preconditions that are needed to make it work.

Solving Personnel Problems through the Assessment Center

Debbie Cutchin and David Alonso

What is an assessment center?

The assessment center method "refers to a group-oriented, standardized series of activities which provide a basis for judgment or
predictions of human behavior believed or known to be relevant to
work performed in an organizational setting."[1] An assessment center, then, can be thought of as both a place and a process. It is a place
where people participate in a variety of measurement techniques
designed to identify their strengths and weaknesses for some specific purpose: placement, upgrading, or development. It is the process of bringing together the information from a variety of sources
and arriving at a summary recommendation and/or description of
the individual candidate being evaluated.

Those behaviors which have been determined through a job
analysis to be crucial to job success are at the core of the exercises
which make up an assessment center. The focus on job related
behaviors is important both professionally and legally. By centering
on behaviors, the predictive value of the assessment center method
is increased over traditional intelligence or psychological tests.[2]
This is because the behaviors that are displayed by a candidate during the exercises can be expected to be displayed by the candidate in
a similar situation on the job. Using behavior also forces both the
assessors of the exercise and the candidates to focus on "real data"
—data that is perceived during the course of the assessment center
itself. The assessor is less likely to project his or her motives or values on the candidates.

Reprinted with permission from Management Information Service Reports, vol. 13,
no. 2 (Washington, D.C.: International City Management Association, February
1981).

There are two approaches to evaluation and validity which can be used for an assessment center: criterion related validity approaches and content validity models.

Criterion related validity approaches address the question: "Is the assessment center predictive of success on the job?" Each of the three types of criterion validity models (classical predictive correlational, modified predictive correlational, and group comparison) share some of the same strengths and weaknesses. Each model allows the personnel department to evaluate over time the relative success of each employee based on behavioral measurement. These measurements can be used to update performance appraisal systems and forecast training and employment needs. The classical correlational study differs from the modified version in that the modified version allows feedback to the employee about his or her performance.

The problems with criterion related validity models are that they:

1. Cost a lot in follow up for measuring employee performance over time;
2. Require that the organization continually re-evaluate; and
3. Use experimental designs in which some employees go through the assessment center while others are excluded.

Although this method is considered most scientific, it has not been widely used, primarily because of the requirements for longitudinal data.

While criterion related models are difficult to establish, by standardizing the assessment center experience for each assessor and candidate, greater validity can be achieved. Assessor groups should be mixed by race and sex, and should all be on the same level of management within the organization. Ideally, assessors should be chosen from jurisdictions or organizations outside the immediate environment in order to minimize the effect of bias in assessors who know candidates. Care should be taken to recognize the "critical assessors" (those who are unable to distinguish between various traits or levels of performance) by monitoring the evaluation process so that initial evaluations of candidates are made on an individual basis. Time is allotted at the end of each exercise for individual comments and scoring by assessors. Group consensus is reached on each candidate at the end of the assessment center.

Interaction between the assessors and candidates should be kept to a minimum prior to or during the assessment center. The actual administration should be standardized by having each candidate have standard activity schedules and the same time limits for preparing and performing each exercise. Roles that are used during the role play exercises should be randomly passed out to the candidates. By adhering to the standardization goal, part of the problem of equal treatment and consideration will be alleviated.

The other primary form of validity, content validity, addresses the question: "Does the procedure accurately simulate the real job environment and the skills, knowledge, and abilities required?" Content validity models have been found to be legally valid by the Supreme Court in *Washington* v. *Davis* (1976).[3] Here the emphasis is on identifying the critical components of the job through on-the-job observation, traditional job analysis, incumbent questionnaires, and reference to the *Dictionary of Occupational Titles*.

Throughout each stage of development of the job analysis, the criterion and job dimensions are analyzed by knowledgeable persons for their relative importance to success on the job. Each dimension, then, is defined in behavioral terms from which the exercises are developed. The common rule of thumb is that at least two exercises should measure a representative sample of behaviors for each dimension. The exercises themselves should reflect both the content and the context of the job. John Haymaker, in his doctoral dissertation, outlines a complete step-by-step approach to this type of validation based on Mussio and Smith's work in content validity.[4]

For an assessment center to be valid and reliable, a set of minimum standards should be adhered to. These standards, developed by the Third International Congress on the Assessment Center

1. Multiple assessment techniques must be used. At least one of these techniques must be a simulation.
2. Multiple assessors must be used. These assessors must receive training prior to participating in a center.
3. Judgments resulting in an outcome (i.e., recommendation for promotion, specific training and development, or selection) must be based on pooling information from assessors and techniques.
4. An overall evaluation of behavior must be made by the assessors at a separate time from observation of the behavior.
5. Simulation exercises are used. These exercises are developed to tap a variety of predetermined behaviors. They have been pretested prior to use to insure that the techniques provide reliable, objective, and relevant behavioral information for the organization in question.
6. The dimensions, attributes, characteristics, or qualities evaluated by the assessment center are determined by an analysis of job behaviors.
7. The techniques used in the assessment center are designed to provide information which is used in evaluating the dimensions, attributes, or qualities previously determined.

Figure 1. Standards and ethical considerations for assessment center operation.

Method, should guide any unit of government which is considering using the assessment center method.[5] These are listed in Figure 1.

In summary, although a study over time is obviously the most important test, if the job analysis generates relevant and job-related information and can be documented, then content validity is ensured. However, each assessment center requires its own type of evaluation depending on the goal of the center—placement, promotion, or training and development. The important consideration is that managers must realize "why conducting job analysis is important, why [to] have assessor training, and why [to] document observations."[6]

The increasing use of assessment centers

Initially used by the military in World Wars I and II for the early identification of officer potential, the assessment center technology was brought to the civilian sector in 1956 by AT&T. Its Manager Progress Study has assessed more than 70,000 candidates for first level manager positions.[7] Candidates chosen by the assessment center method in this project "have been found to be two to three times more likely to be successful at higher management levels than those promoted on the basis of supervisory judgments."[8]

Using assessment center technology for selecting individuals to perform in managerial positions allows "the chance rate of picking a winner" to more than double over traditional methods such as paper and pencil exams or basing determinations on past experience, resumes, or references.[9] Since AT&T's introduction of assessment center processes, hundreds of companies such as IBM, Sears, General Electric, and J.C. Penney have come to recognize its potential. In recent years, the public sector has also utilized the assessment center approach. First used in the Internal Revenue Service, the assessment center method has also been utilized by the old Civil Service Commission, the Office of Management and Budget, the Federal Aviation Authority, and the Department of Housing and Urban Development. The Wisconsin and Illinois state governments have also used this method.[10]

Several local governments in Georgia (Rome, Athens, East Point, LaGrange, Valdosta, and Macon-Bibb County) are currently using the assessment center process. Primarily focusing on the selection and promotion of police and firefighters, these governments have found the assessment center process feasible, desirable, and an improvement in making individual personnel choices.

City officials in Athens stated that the approach is "viable and effective." Rome is pleased with its experience in selecting police and firefighters and is investigating its potential for placing transit operators and other employee groups. For these localities the problem of obtaining valid, unbiased selection and promotion procedures has been reduced through the utilization of this process.

The Department of Community Affairs for the state of Georgia has taken an active role in disseminating this technology to local government in Georgia. The long-range goals of this program include state monitoring and revisions of assessment centers to ensure validity and the establishment of regional assessment centers that can be used by local governments to share the costs.

The Department and the Institute of Government at the University of Georgia are developing plans for a Certified Assessor Program which would provide the pool of qualified assessors needed to implement a large scale regional center. Satisfied with their performance in the police and fire departments, many local governments in Georgia are studying the process for its potential to solve the many other crucial problems of personnel administration.

The rest of this report presents a discussion of the assessment center process, including its major elements and their implementation, in order to identify its various uses for local government. First, we will suggest a comprehensive model for the use of assessment centers in the personnel function. Then, we will focus on the components of an assessment center, and turn to the legal implications of the system. Finally, we will suggest how it can be used to develop a comprehensive personnel strategy. Throughout, we will refer to an assessment center simulation which we developed and ran May 12-15, 1980, to select an assistant city manager for a medium sized city in Georgia. (This was designed and implemented under a grant from the U.S. Department of Education within the Public Service Fellowship Program.)

A comprehensive personnel model for the use of assessment centers

Our model for the use of assessment centers as a comprehensive personnel tool is based on the following assumptions:

1. All of the personnel functions (selection, promotion, training and development, performance appraisals, AA/EEO, incentives, and wage and salary determination) require a clear understanding of the job requirements. This is typically provided through the use of job analysis.
2. In order to match people with appropriate jobs in organizations, some determination has to be made about the basic performance levels of the employee. This diagnosis can be accomplished through the use of valid assessment centers.
3. Because assessment centers are designed to measure an employee's performance of *behavioral components of a job*, the information generated during the process can be used to develop each of the areas of personnel administration.
4. Although assessment centers are in the short run an expensive technology, if the information generated in the center is

fully used the costs can be spread over the entire personnel function. Moreover, cost savings can be realized by choosing, rewarding, and developing employees throughout their organizational career in a systematic, comprehensive manner, reducing turnover and firing.

5. By using a comprehensive approach to the personnel function, which is based on the performance requirements of the job, organizations can raise productivity levels through the effective use of training and development opportunities and reward systems built on performance appraisals and feedback.

6. Assessment centers can be used as an evaluation device in order both to update the overall personnel practices of an organization or locality and to provide specific, behaviorally oriented feedback to employees.

A valid assessment center starts with a job analysis. This is used to develop the situation-specific exercises that measure the behavioral components of the job. At the core of this model is a single job analysis which has been developed with multiple uses in mind. Instead of having a separate job analysis designed for each of the personnel functions, by planning ahead the personnel department can utilize the information generated in the assessment center to more fully develop a coordinated system based on the behavioral dimensions of performance.

Traditionally, the information which has been gathered during the assessment center has been used only for selection/promotion or training and development. The emphasis has been on those with potential (i.e., those selected for entry, promotion, or training), rather than those not chosen. But the information can also be used to enhance other personnel programs which are legally required or desired by managers.

For instance, through the utilization of job related criteria which are validly measured by an assessment center, the legal obligations of EEO are met. This information can also be used to prepare a long term upward mobility program for minorities, women, and disadvantaged employees which is required by AA. Strengths and weaknesses can be identified in order to tailor training and development programs to specific employees in order to realize the maximum benefit for the dollar. Because assessment centers measure job relevant behaviors, determinations about wage and salary levels can be based on performance rather than solely on experience or seniority. Finally, the development of any successful performance appraisal system requires a determination of what is performance and how the employee is performing now, and the existence of a feedback system to the employee. All of these needs can be addressed by assessment centers.

The personnel administrator relies on these programs to help motivate the employee to be more productive. AA/EEO can be seen as a way to expand the market of potentially outstanding employees who would otherwise be overlooked due to racism or sexism. Using current performance as a base, appraisal systems are most effective if they are focused on moving employees to higher levels of productivity. This requires a diagnosis as a critical beginning step. Pay for performance, which provides the necessary reward for high productivity, can be made more effective when combined with incentive packages (e.g., time off, continued education, flextime, training opportunities) which have been tailored to the specific performance and needs of the employee. In short, by viewing personnel administration from a long term organizational perspective, greater efficiency can be realized both through the use of personnel information and the application of coherent practices which act as motivators.

Today local governments need employees and managers who understand such complex areas as budget control and analysis, cash management and investment, data processing, inventory and risk management, intergovernmental relations, grantsmanship, and labor relations. The jack of all trades manager is faced with an array of complex problems and conflicting demands. The need for expertise has never been greater, which makes the challenge of personnel administration a major part of any effort to enhance government productivity.

Since 1972 when state and local jurisdictions were brought under the anti-discrimination provision of the Civil Rights Act of 1964, the legal environment has significantly affected public personnel administration. The tests of business necessity and job relatedness for hiring and promotion decisions as well as affirmative action require standardization in personnel administration.[11] This standardization requires specific information which can only be produced through job analysis. Compliance with affirmative action not only demands an active recruitment program, but also the design and implementation of an upward mobility program through training and development and job counseling. Skills must be taught and updated. In order to incur the greatest efficiency in training and development dollars, there is first a need for accurate diagnosis and measurement of the employee's skills, abilities, and knowledge.

Local governments also face economic pressures. The demand for government services has increased while the financial resources necessary for their provision are under constant attack. Inflationary pressures not only affect the individual consumer, but also decrease the purchasing power of the tax dollar. Growing anti-tax sentiment creates the dilemma of satisfying an increased demand for services with less revenue. This makes issues of productivity paramount to local government.

Performance appraisal, "pay for performance," and the identification of unproductive employees are all seen as potential solutions to the conflict between the demand for government services and the cost of government services. These solutions require a personnel system that is professional, comprehensive, and responsive to an environment that demands information and solutions to problems. The need to maximize the personnel dollar has never been greater. Higher quality personnel, training and development programs to motivate employees, and incentives to keep valued employees are needed if local governments are to weather the storm.

Cutting personnel costs and wastes is also essential in the 1980s. Wages and salaries account for over 60 percent of local government operating costs. For some departments over 80 percent of the costs are personnel.[12] A personnel system that hires bad, ineffective, or inappropriate employees is costly. The cost of firing employees or absorbing the money invested in recruiting, selecting, and training employees who are unable to do the job can be avoided by having a system that hires competent people in the first place.

Since many local governments work under some form of civil service or merit system, the sunk costs of hiring an employee are not the only costs involved. The cost of removing a bad employee in these jurisdictions includes the time and expense of documenting the employee's poor performance and proving that removal is the appropriate penalty. Bad selection decisions are even more costly in the arena of supervisory and managerial personnel, where the consequences of poor performance may affect an entire department or organization in both reduced productivity and political embarrassment.

In summary, the assessment center, if viewed in a comprehensive perspective, can generate the type of information needed to solve the personnel problems of the 1980s. The assessment center can help select high producing employees and managers, train and develop staff, and serve as a starting point for performance appraisal and wage and salary determination. By providing the relevant and appropriate information about the organizational requirements for a job and the human potential for successful completion for each worker, the assessment center begins to integrate the personnel function. Productivity in this context means receiving the maximum level of performance from each employee, vis-à-vis a coordinated system of performance appraisal, training and development, and evaluation and feedback throughout the employee's career.

Elements of the assessment center

The job analysis.   The job analysis is the critical element of the assessment center. It is from the analysis that the appropriate skills and behavior, job characteristics or dimensions, and situational exercises are determined. The job analysis should discover the skills, knowledge, and abilities necessary to perform the job successfully, and include situations that are typical of the job routine. All of this is developed with the aid of a person(s) knowledgeable about job requirements.

This element of the assessment center process provides the basis for the relationship between assessment centers and AA/EEO, performance appraisal, wage and salary determination, and training and development programs. Each of these personnel functions relies on the job analysis to provide the framework to determine job relatedness, pay for performance, and the direction of development programs. The assessment of each employee's skills, knowledge, and abilities with relation to the specific job criterion can be used not only to select or promote an employee but also to:

1.   Set minimum standards and expectations for performance;
2.   Define the specific development needs and interests; and
3.   Enhance the personnel department's ability to meet the legal requirements of AA/EEO.

One of the techniques that was used in our analysis and that has proven helpful in other assessment centers is the incumbent interview questionnaire. By interviewing people who have served in the job, useful information about the necessary skills and behaviors for successful performance can be gathered. Our questionnaire was sent to all the city managers in Georgia. We asked them about the specific job requirements they would use if they were going to hire an assistant city manager. In addition, personal interviews were conducted with city managers and personnel directors familiar with the job of assistant city manager. The *Dictionary of Occupational Titles* was used in setting the parameters of the particular job category.

Essentially, the analysis should seek to obtain information from those who have previous experience in the job or who could be considered experts about the job requirements. This analysis must be comprehensive and documented. A list of job characteristics is then drawn and defined for the particular job that has been analyzed. Prior to use in the assessment center, these job dimensions should be discussed with the assessors to reach agreement and understanding about their meaning.

The exercises   There are several types of exercises that can be used in an assessment center. Which ones are used depends on the goals and the particular job being assessed. The crucial factors are that they be situation specific and that they measure the behavioral components of the job. The scoring forms should indicate the specific behaviors and skills that are important and should allow the assessor to grade those skills and behaviors using a standard scale. Each form should allow the assessor to place a number by a candidate's performance and a written comment for each job dimension.

Many centers use a paper and pencil test which examines special skills or knowledge and/or a standard psychological test. In addition, extended candidate interviews are conducted. Assessment centers are unique, however, among personnel tools in their use of the situation-specific exercise that seeks to simulate the job environment. Several traditional exercises were used in our assessment center:

Assigned role play (group discussion) had the candidates assume the role of city department heads. They had the job of allocating general revenue sharing funds in an allotted amount of time. The candidates were randomly assigned a role (or point of view) and instructed to sell to the other candidates their proposals. The candidates were encouraged to bargain aspects of their budget as they saw fit. The skills and behaviors that were examined included communication, analytical abilities, decision making, problem solving with professional knowledge, and the use of tact, political awareness, and leadership.

The *leaderless group discussion* (non-assigned role play) focused on three problems faced by many city governments: the control of budgeting funds, the use of government-owned facilities, and a sexual harassment problem. As a group, the candidates were directed to discuss each case study, reach a consensus, and make a recommendation to the city manager. The important skills and behaviors here were communication, problem solving, tact, self-confidence, creativity, ethics, loyalty, political awareness, leadership, and personal motivation.

The *in-basket* with memos, letters, messages, and problems to be organized addressed the problem of time management. The job of the candidate was to organize his or her in-basket according to the time requirements of the specific items. A form was completed by the candidates concerning the process they used to reach their decisions and justifications. Along with the management of time, the in-basket seeks to analyze a candidate's ability to make decisions, solve problems, organize, delegate authority, and demonstrate political awareness and public relations skills.

An *analysis problem* was designed as an individual exercise. It concerned the direction an airport development project should take. A great deal of information was provided about three options for the airport. Each candidate was directed to sift through the data, which included charts, tables, maps, and written information, identify the relevant material, and write an executive summary of each option for the city manager. Each candidate was asked to consider several constraints: economic, political, administrative, social, and environmental. The analysis required a concise, logical statement of each option and the ability to communicate in writing the appropriate data.

Our final exercise was the short presentation of a *speech*. The candidate was assigned to prepare a five minute speech to a group of public works employees who are within 10 percent of the number required to call for an election for a union. His or her job was to present the city's position in the hopes of stopping the unionization movement before it spread to the police and fire departments. In this exercise candidates were rated on their communication, analytic, and organizing skills, tact, self-confidence, political awareness, and public relations skills.

Physical arrangements   The physical arrangements of an assessment center depend on the type of assessment and the type of exercises used. If there is more than one group of candidates, then there should be enough rooms to separate each candidate group before and after the exercises. The assessors should also be separated from the candidates unless they are viewing one of the group situation exercises. In that case it is probably more manageable if you keep the assessors in one room and direct each candidate group into that room as necessary.

If the assessment center is also being used for training and development purposes, it would be appropriate to consider videotaping the situational exercises in order to give the candidates an opportunity for self-evaluation. Our assessment center videotaped the role play, leaderless discussion, and speech exercises through a two-way mirror. In order to ensure high quality tapes, we recommend using multiple microphones and a low-light camera.

The running of an assessment center will be much easier if standardized arrangements are made in advance and some thought is given to the movement of candidates and assessors throughout the day.

Training the assessors   An assessment center is only as good as its job analysis and its assessors. Assessors should be able to differentiate between different levels of behavior and skills. This skill can be analyzed through the use of several different psychological tests.[13] Assessors should have a thorough knowledge of the job that was gained through being in that position or supervising that position. In short, your assessors are the real "experts."

Research at IBM showed that those "assessment centers which have a well organized, full-day observer training program were much more effective than those centers which de-emphasized training."[14] The training should allow the assessor to practice observing and measuring behavior, to perform the in-basket exercise if used, and to participate in skill building sessions by viewing behavior and differentiating between good and bad behaviors. One tool which can be used was developed under the Intergovernmental Personnel Act by the Selection Consulting Center in Sacramento, California. It is a 45 minute film designed to train potential assessors.[15] The goal is that assessors understand why behaviors are important and be made to realize that only behavioral data will be measured.

A good assessor training program will also allow the assessors to study the exercises and the job dimensions so that group consensus and understanding can be reached concerning their meaning. It should be recognized that the assessment center is a developmental process which involves judgments on the part of the assessors. Being a good assessor, therefore, requires some practice. Assessors will improve as their experience with the method and types of exercises grows. Any training should include a review of the scoring sheets and the standard rules for assessors, as outlined earlier.

Because of the time factor involved in our project, our assessor training was limited to one-half of a day. All our assessors were familiar with the position of assistant city manager (they consisted of four city managers and one county commissioner), and most were familiar with the assessment center method and its use.

Candidate evaluation should be handled individually by each assessor until the end of the assessment center. It is at that time that assessors as a group should reach a consensus about each candidate. Feedback to candidates should come as close to the end of the assessment center as possible. The type of feedback will depend on the scope of the assessment center. If the results are used for initial placement into a job, then it may not be necessary to offer counseling to those candidates who were not selected. However, if the results are used for promotion, training and development, or the early identification of managerial skills, some form of comprehensive, relevant job counseling is necessary for those candidates who did not perform well in the center.

For validity purposes, evaluation and research should be conducted to determine the relationships between the assessment center results and future job performance. Candidate and assessor evaluation of the assessment center is important for providing information that can aid the design and implementation of other assessment centers and assessor training programs. Of course, the running of the assessment center itself should be documented and evaluated for future improvement of the center's performance.

Additional issues

There are several issues in conducting assessment centers which should be considered to ensure fair and equitable treatment of candidates not only for validity purposes but for psychological reasons.

Just as a paper and pencil test is stressful, so too is an assessment center. Performing badly in an assessment center can prove very damaging to candidates and every effort should be made to counsel them, even if training and development is not designed into the assessment center. Many people have problems with such openly competitive situations, and the stress caused by the exercises should be discussed with the assessors prior to the assessment center and with the candidates afterward. In our assessment center we found the speech exercise to be particularly stressful for most of our candidates, who were not experienced in speaking before a group of high-status people. The assessment center should serve to develop both the assessors and the candidates by using relevant, specific feedback.

The issue of competent assessors is critical. Every effort should be made to have an adequate and effective training program. Even though assessors may know the job intimately, efforts should be made to improve their observing and interviewing skills. Accordingly, the training program should be documented and continuously improved. Because the assessment center serves as a developmental process for the assessors, as assessors become more experienced their ability to observe and differentiate between good and bad behaviors will increase.[16] This is consistent with the goal of our comprehensive model of personnel based on assessment centers. Your supervisory personnel will also increase their ability not only to conduct their daily duties of management, but to better participate in performance appraisal systems.

EEO law and affirmative action regulations require that the selection and promotion method be standardized (or reliable) and valid. The court requires that the procedures comply with the job relatedness test; therefore the job analysis should be comprehensive, systematic, documented, and defensible. The job dimensions used in the assessment center should be weighted in terms of their relative importance to the particular job analyzed. While the assessment center process has been applauded for its ability to remain free of bias and prejudice, the method was challenged as a selection and promotion device in the city of Omaha.[17] In question was its reliability. The city of Omaha's assessment center process was ruled legal, but not before it was compared to the "Ethical Standards of Conduct of Assessment Centers" criteria used by the courts.[18] It appears then that the ethical standards should be used by local governments as a model for selecting assessment center packages.

Finally, one criticism of assessment centers is their costs in comparison to the traditional methods of job interviews or paper and pencil tests. While the initial costs are greater for the assessment center, the higher quality and amount of information generated through it are also greater. Assessment centers vary considerably in costs with one estimate ranging from $5.00 to $500.00 per person. It should be realized that the costs of an assessment center will vary greatly. One method of evaluating the usefulness of the assessment center for personnel functions is an informal cost/benefit analysis as suggested below.

Costs of a typical assessment center

Preparation of the assessment center package and assessor manual   This includes consultant fees. It is important to remember that if the consultant works with your personnel department in the development of the package and manual, this should be a one time only cost.

Assessor time   This includes time off the job during both training and the assessment center itself.

Materials   This includes xeroxing, printing, mail, paper, and pencils.

Candidate time   For selection, this may include the costs of bringing candidates in for the assessment center (depending on your government's particular policy on this matter); for promotion, this includes time off the job for both participation in the assessment center and any feedback and debriefing sessions.

Benefits of a typical assessment center

Compliance with the law   Assessment centers meet the requirements of business necessity and job relatedness which are required under Affirmative Action/Equal Employment law; the rise of valid selection and promotion procedures can save future legal costs.

Quality of personnel selected or promoted   If the person who scores highest in the job dimensions required for a particular job is selected or promoted, then the community will receive the maximum benefit for its personnel dollar.

Savings from firing   Following the same logic, the higher the quality of employee, the less likely will be the need for firing for nonperformance; included in the cost of firing are down-time between when the employee exits and a new employee is chosen, the recruitment, selection, and training of the new employee, and the loss of training taken with the fired employee.

Savings on other personnel costs   Referring to the comprehensive model suggested here, savings can be realized by more efficient utilization of all the personnel functions; for instance, by using the data generated in the assessment center to determine training needs, a greater return on appropriate training programs can be realized.

Repeated usage As with all valid, standardized personnel tools, benefits can be incurred through repeated use which will reduce the cost from a long term perspective.

Assessor skill enhancement Much of the literature supports the idea that skills gained by assessors in accurate observation and recording of work performance will also enhance the supervisor's ability to develop and implement performance appraisal systems, as well as provide more effective feedback to employees about their job performance.

Several methods could be used to reduce the costs of using assessment center technology. First, cost savings can be realized by taking a comprehensive perspective of the personnel function, and sharing information among specialists within an organization as suggested by our model. Second, this technology can be most effectively used for two types of positions: high level jobs where the political and financial costs of firing are high (e.g., city manager) or where there are multiple people in the same position (e.g., police captain). Third, costs can be greatly reduced if units of local government share the technology. In Georgia nine cities are sharing the police officer assessment center package and are also exchanging assessors.

In summary, while the initial costs of an assessment center may seem great, if the center is designed correctly, it can be used repeatedly, thereby stretching the costs over a period of time.

Summary

Assessment centers have been used for a number of years by many private organizations. Recently public organizations and local governments have been learning about the technique and its value as a personnel tool. If the assessment center and its elements are viewed from a long term organizational perspective, the process can be used for a variety of purposes: long-range organizational planning, goal setting, performance appraisal systems, job enrichment, upward mobility plans, improved training and development opportunities, and legal selection and promotion procedures.

All of these goals can be served by fully using the information generated by a comprehensive, valid assessment center. By viewing the assessment center process as a diagnostic tool, the personnel function, rather than being a problem, can begin to offer solutions to meet the future human resource needs of local governments.

Note: The authors thank Delmer Dunn, Harold Holtz, and Jerry Singer of the Institute of Government, and Bob Golembiewski of the Political Science Department, University of Georgia, for their comments and recommendations. Special appreciation goes to the many city managers of Georgia who contributed their time.

1. Robert B. Finkel, "Managerial Assessment Centers," in *Handbook of Industrial and Organizational Psychology*, ed. M. D. Dunnette (Chicago: Rand McNally, 1976), p. 861.
2. H.B. Wollowick and W. J. McNamara, "Relationship of the Components of an Assessment Center to Management Success," *Journal of Applied Psychology*, 1969, p. 350.
3. *Washington* v. *Davis*, 426 U.S. 229 (1976).
4. John C. Haymaker, *Development of a Model for Content Validation of Assessment Centers* (Athens, Georgia: University of Georgia, 1979). S. J. Mussio and M. K. Smith, *Content Validity: A Procedural Manual* (Washington, D.C.: International Personnel Management Association, 1973).
5. J. L. Moses et al., "Standards and Ethical Considerations for Assessment Center Operations," Task Force on Development of Assessment Center Standards, Third International Congress on the Assessment Center Method, Quebec, May 1975, p. 2.
6. Joyce D. Ross, "A Current Review of Public Sector Assessment Centers: A Cause for Concern," *Public Personnel Management*, January-February 1979, p. 45.
7. William C. Byham, "The Assessment Center as a Selection Technique," *Training and Development Journal*, December 1971, p. 86.
8. Ibid., p. 192.
9. Ross, "Public Sector Assessment Centers," p. 42.
10. Charles Wise, "Assessment Centers in the Public Sector," *Public Productivity Review*, Vol. 3, No. 4, Spring/Summer 1979, p. 84.
11. J.R. Heinricks and S. Haanpera, "Reliability of Measurement in Situation Exercises: Assessment of the Assessment Center Method," *Personnel Psychology*, Vol. 29, 1976, pp. 31-40.
12. Katherine C. Janka, "Municipal In-Service Training," in *The Municipal Year Book 1976* (Washington, D.C.: International City Management Association, 1976), p. 192.
13. For a discussion of the differentiation phenomenon, see: Abraham Pizam, "Social Differentiation—a New Psychological Barrier to Performance Appraisal," *Public Personnel Management*, Vol. 14, No. 4, July/August 1975, pp. 244-247; F. E. Fiedler's "least preferred person" technique in "Leader Attitudes, Group Climate, and Group Creativity," *Journal of Abnormal Social Psychology*, Vol. 65, No. 5 (1962); H. Schroder, M. Driver, S. Streufert, *Human Information Process* (New York: Holt Rinehart, 1967).
14. Ross, "Public Sector Assessment Centers," p. 45.
15. Contact John Klinefeller, Director, Selection Consulting Center, 5777 Madison Avenue, Suite 820, Sacramento, California 96841.
16. Byham, "Assessment Center as a Selection Technique," p. 88.
17. Ross, "Public Sector Assessment Centers," p. 44.
18. Ibid., p. 45.

PART 3

Motivating Employees

Motivation: Myths and Misnomers

— Philip C. Grant

No other subject in management is more ridden with mythology than employee motivation. This mythology has led, perhaps more than any other factor, to the misuse, abuse and lack of use of our human resources. Managers could substantially increase productivity if they knew the truth about motivation.

A motivated worker is a productive worker

A motivated worker may be a productive worker, but not necessarily. Motivation is usually a necessary, but not a sufficient, condition for high productivity.

A highly motivated worker can be quite unproductive because of a host of other factors. Lack of employee knowledge and skill, inefficient work methods, old equipment, faulty information and materials can cause low worker productivity, regardless of how highly motivated the employee is.

Motivated behavior can also be misdirected. An employee can exert much effort, but if it is not in line with organizational goals, performance is obviously unconstructive and he or she is unproductive.

People won't work as hard today as they used to

This misconception stems from managers' frustration in directing their employees. The implication is that people today are somehow inferior, when it comes to work, to the human beings of yesteryear —that something in people's nature has changed to make them poorer workers.

Reprinted from *Management World*, with permission from the Administrative Management Society (AMS), Willow Grove, PA 19090. Copyright 1982 AMS.

This is just not true. Employees will work just as hard today as ever. But they must be as motivated as before. And the evidence suggests that today's employees are not as motivated as their ancestors.

There are a number of reasons why, but two are most important.

First, employee needs and values have evolved. Economic issues no longer dominate. Workers now want opportunities to satisfy esteem, status and self-actualization needs.

But organizational reward structures have not kept pace. They have failed to provide the kinds of rewards most valued nowadays. Thus one of the critical requirements for motivation is not being met: incentives are not suitable for satisfying the most intense employee needs.

The second important factor contributing to lower motivation is reduction in the use of contingent reward systems. Yet it is incentive receipt, dependent on the level of employee effort, that is the other critical requirement for motivation.

Today, most companies guarantee more rewards than they once did. And where company guarantees leave off, government guarantees pick up: unemployment compensation, food stamps, etc.

If this statement were rephrased to "people *don't* work as hard today as they used to," it would no longer be a myth. However, it must be emphasized that they will work as hard as they used to, given the right conditions. The problem is that the right conditions do not exist.

Actually, present-day personnel probably have a greater capacity for production than did their predecessors. Workers are better educated, better trained and may even have superior physical and mental faculties.

Motivation is the culprit. Lack of it may be the largest factor contributing to the gross underutilization of human potential.

A happy worker is a motivated worker

This ingrained bit of folklore continues to permeate thinking, despite years of research that demonstrates little or no correlation between happiness and motivation. Satisfaction (happiness) and motivation do not consistently show a positive correlation.

For example, in one common situation, the value of all rewards (both intrinsic and extrinsic) received by an employee is perceived by that employee as essentially guaranteed or fixed. Rewards are seen as entitlements, independent of effort. The tenured, sixty-year-old, full professor may be a case in point.

As an employee increases on-the-job effort, the costs (stress, fatigue, boredom, etc.) also seem to increase. The employee will exert the amount of effort that provides the most satisfaction. In this case, maximum satisfaction results from a very low level of motivation.

A different, but nonetheless common situation is when both rewards and costs are contingent on effort expended. A piece rate worker, for instance, might well face such a reward-cost structure.

This employee still seeks to attain satisfaction. But in this case, it is achieved with a relatively high level of motivation. However, the maximum amount of satisfaction experienced by this employee will be little compared to the employee in the first case, because the motivation needed is so high.

Thus, it is apparent that a worker can be highly satisfied and unmotivated, in the first case, or highly motivated and very unhappy in case two.

Substantial advantages accrue from having workers both highly satisfied and highly motivated. In practice, however, achieving high satisfaction and motivation simultaneously may be the exception rather than the rule.

Motivation comes from within—you either have it or you don't

No employee is by nature motivated or unmotivated. Motivation is determined in part by internal needs—forces *within* the employee—and in part by forces *outside* the employee. These outside forces, called incentives, or rewards, are entirely within management's control.

By properly designing intrinsic and extrinsic reward structures, high levels of employee effort can be generated. The critical components in reward are suitable for satisfying the most intense employee needs (highly valued incentives); and incentive receipt, which is highly contingent on the level of employee effort.

Some employees, however, can be more easily motivated than others. Certain individuals can expend more effort than others. These employees are easier to motivate than those who experience high costs at relatively low levels of effort.

It is also true that some employees are easier to motivate than others because they respond to simpler, less expensive, or more manageable types of rewards. For example, praise may stimulate one worker, while another may require an elaborately enriched job design.

The greater the reward, the greater the motivation

Many organizations are suffering severe productivity problems because of this misconception. For decades, unions have been bargaining their way to ever-higher wages, better working conditions and greater fringes. Management has given in to these increasing union demands partly because we assume that higher rewards boost employee motivation and thus company productivity. Nothing could be further from the truth!

Higher rewards *will* increase worker satisfaction. But increases in the absolute level of rewards, even when the rewards are highly valued, will *not* increase employee motivation when those rewards are assured regardless of employee effort. In fact, a guaranteed reward, regardless of its size, will demotivate employees, resulting in low productivity.

Not tying rewards to performance in any meaningful way is one of the most serious mistakes made by many organizations in attempting to manage employees toward greater productivity.

Even though a given reward may be contingent on effort expended, it will lose its motivational force as larger and larger amounts of it are received. This is an old principle of economics—that of declining marginal utility.

As a worker becomes satiated with a given reward, additional increments of the reward begin to lose value. When a reward no longer is perceived by the employee to have value, it no longer can motivate.

Money motivates best

This is a misstatement for at least three reasons.

Studies have shown that most workers today value other types of rewards more than money. The average worker wants job security, interesting, challenging work, good relations with supervisors and peers, opportunities for advancement, and status and recognition in return for performance. All these are usually valued more than a paycheck.

A second reason why money should not be categorized as the best of incentives is because it is expensive. Other incentives, such as praise, challenging work and achievement opportunities, not only can provide higher motivation but can impose less of a financial burden on the organization.

Third, it is often impractical to make money rewards contingent on performance. For example, monetary payments can seldom be scheduled to rigorously coincide with employee performance changes. But unless payments can be timed to follow performance changes, those payments lose their motivational force.

In addition, it is frequently impractical to assess employee performance with great accuracy. Tying dollar payments to invalid performance assessments obviously can create undue financial hazards.

One final aspect of money's impracticality as a performance contingent incentive is that most employers must provide guaranteed minimum wages and salaries to attract and retain personnel. Employees insist on guaranteed minimal levels of satisfaction from income. Money's motivational "punch" must be compromised to achieve these desired levels of satisfaction.

Improving the quality of worklife will motivate

Though currently popular, this misguided belief may cause more damage in the next decade than any of the other myths.

Many companies are rushing headlong into upgrading the physical and social settings in which work takes place and into restructuring the very character of work through job-enrichment programs. This is reducing worker alienation, apathy, and on-the-job discontent—certainly worthy outcomes.

But improving worklife quality does little to help international competition. Those who see present worklife quality improvement programs as a way to respond to Japanese productivity are not recognizing the basic tenet of motivation: to motivate, rewards must be tied to worker effort. Worker job satisfaction is rising, but productivity is not and *will* not unless the employee's sense of heightened quality of worklife is made a function of effort expenditure.

Present evidence suggests that very few worklife improvement programs do incorporate these contingent reward designs. This is, at the least, disappointing. With slight modifications, many of the quality of worklife programs now being undertaken could encompass means for improving both satisfaction and motivation.

Motivate employees to the greatest degree possible

This argument may seem hard to dispute. Even renowned texts and articles on the subject assume that more motivation is better.

Writers and researchers, as well as managers concerned with motivation, seem obsessed with finding mechanisms to increase motivation. No one ever asks, "How much motivation is enough?"

It is possible to achieve *too much* employee motivation. People who exert too much effort will often experience emotional, physical and mental stress that eventually causes lower performance.

Long-term, excessive motivation can contribute to early "burn out." Prolonged periods of extreme effort, accompanied by physical and psychological stress, are the source of numerous neurophysical diseases.

The cost of motivation can also make it an unworthy goal. Rewards, monetary or otherwise, usually represent some kind of cost to the company. The value of the rewards required to boost employee effort may exceed the value of employee output.

Finally, increasing motivation frequently requires some trade-off with satisfaction. As discussed earlier, high satisfaction and high motivation, though both worthy objectives, may not be obtainable simultaneously. Motivation should sometimes be sacrificed in the interest of satisfaction.

Thousands of daily decisions regarding the management of employees are presently guided by these false beliefs. It is understandable why we are experiencing a decline in productivity when, clearly, the most expensive and valuable of our resources—the human being—is being wasted.

Motivating Improved Productivity: Three Promising Approaches

John M. Greiner

Productivity improvement efforts by local governments have often focused on ways to enhance the motivation of their personnel. Indeed, although more than sixty cents from every dollar of local government operating expenses goes towards employee salaries and benefits, many feel that government service is not conducive to maximum employee efficiency or effectiveness. Government personnel policies and civil service systems are frequently accused of stifling incentive and ignoring excellence. This can lead to alienation, frustration, poor morale, and low productivity.

Local governments have turned to a variety of motivational techniques on the assumption that improved motivation will encourage both management and nonmanagement employees to work harder, smarter, or both. The approaches tried include the "task systems" commonly used by sanitation departments (crews are allowed to leave work with a full day's pay as soon as they finish their scheduled routes), career development programs, and variations in working hours such as flextime or the four-day work week. Many governments provide various nonmonetary rewards (citations, plaques, pins, award dinners, or feature articles in the employee newsletter) to foster and recognize improved employee performance.

Three motivational techniques—monetary incentives, performance targeting, and job enrichment—appear especially promising for improving employee motivation and productivity. The remainder of this article focuses on these three approaches.[1]

Reprinted with permission from *Public Management* magazine, October 1979.

Monetary incentives

The classic approach to motivating employees is to provide cash rewards contingent on performance. Monetary incentives have long played an important role in the private sector. However, their use in the public sector has, with the exception of merit increases, been relatively limited. Nevertheless, the following types of monetary incentives have been tried by local governments.

Performance bonuses   These are one-time financial awards paid specifically for superior job performance.

Piecework bonuses   A piecework bonus is a special type of performance bonus that ties a worker's pay directly to the worker's production. Variations include payment of a specified amount of money for each unit of output produced, payment for each unit produced above a specified amount, and payment on the basis of engineered time standards for each unit produced.

Shared savings plans   Shared savings plans are monetary rewards for a group of workers based on cost savings achieved by the group within a given period. A specified portion of the savings is distributed (often as a bonus) among the employees who contributed to the cost reductions.

Performance-based wage increases   Permanent increases in wages or salaries may be given to reward outstanding performance as measured by output, efficiency, or work quality. Two variations of this approach are of special interest in the public sector.

Merit system increases   Under this variation, existing civil service or merit system procedures are used for awarding the increases. Of special interest from a motivational standpoint are those few programs that focus specifically on rewarding job performance—quantity and quality—measured in concrete terms.

Performance increases obtained through productivity bargaining
Two variations of productivity bargaining have been used by local governments to link higher pay to improved performance. One is the "buy-out," where in return for union approval of work rule changes likely to improve productivity, management agrees to provide a specified wage increase. The second variation—"gain sharing"—is designed to provide workers with monetary rewards only if productivity increases. Often the rewards must be funded out of savings generated by the workers.

Suggestion awards   Awards programs are designed to encourage employees to contribute ideas for decreasing costs, increasing quality, or otherwise improving operations. These programs often constitute a type of shared savings plan in that the size of the award is based on the magnitude of the cost savings produced by the suggestion in the first year it is implemented.

Safety awards   Monetary (or nonmonetary) rewards may go to encourage employees to improve their safety records.

Attendance incentives   Monetary rewards also are used to induce employees to improve their attendance records. For example, rewards could be awarded to reduce lateness or abuse of sick leave.

Educational incentives   Monetary rewards may be given to encourage employees to take certain types of training or to continue their formal education.

When based on *clear, objective, output-oriented measures* of employee performance, the first three of these techniques—performance bonuses, piecework bonuses, and shared savings progams—have shown considerable evidence of promoting significant improvements in local government productivity. Relatively few local governments have tried such incentives. Most have focused on services where performance is relatively easy to measure—sanitation, vehicle maintenance, keypunching, building maintenance, and meter repairs. However, performance bonuses—especially for managers—appear to be receiving increased attention from local governments, especially after their inclusion in federal civil service legislation.

Merit increases are, of course, common in local governments. Unfortunately, there appears to be little evidence that traditional merit increase procedures—where employee appraisals are based on subjective trait ratings by supervisors—encourage improved productivity. In fact, they may actually be counterproductive. True, there have been numerous efforts by local governments to "tinker" with existing merit system procedures to try to focus them more directly on actual job performance. Some, for instance, have provided special rewards for "outstanding performance," varying the size of the step increase depending on an employee's performance rating, limiting the number of increases which can be provided, or even eliminating step increases in favor of discretionary increases based on "performance."

The limited evidence available on these variations indicates that such tinkering is not enough. Indeed, the most promising merit increase programs appear to be in the few jurisdictions that have undertaken a complete overhaul of their systems to provide (1) objective, results-oriented performance measures focusing on work quantity and quality and its contribution to service efficiency and effectiveness, and (2) performance appraisal techniques that can make extensive use of such information. Without such fundamental changes, merit increases are unlikely to serve as much of an incentive.

The other types of monetary incentives focus less directly or comprehensively on motivating improved productivity. Productivity bargaining has reportedly been used by about one of ten local governments, but the proportion of those efforts that has resulted in gain sharing or other monetary rewards for employees is not known.[2] While large savings have been claimed in connection with some of these efforts, such programs do not generally focus directly on improving an employee's day-to-day motivation.

The same can be said for educational incentives, attendance incentives, and safety awards. Although some of these programs have been credited with generating overall improvements in productivity, their effectiveness in motivating improved employee performance has not been widely documented.

Performance targeting

The setting of performance targets—explicit statements of the desired performance of an individual or group (in quantitative terms, where possible)—is a management device that can potentially serve as a motivator in and of itself. In local governments, performance targeting usually occurs in connection with three types of efforts: management and budgeting procedures, employee performance appraisal processes, and work measurement programs. Correspondingly, performance targeting efforts in local governments usually take one of three forms.

Management-by-objectives (MBO) MBO is a system of management in which superior and subordinate managers jointly identify common goals, define each manager's major areas of responsibility in terms of expected results (targets), and use these expectations as guides to managing the organization.

Appraisal-by-objectives (ABO) ABO is the use of MBO procedures to specify performance targets in connection with appraisals of management and nonmanagement employees. Such appraisals are based, in part, on the degree to which the employee's performance targets have been achieved.

Work standards Work standards are precise specifications of the work to be accomplished by individual employees or groups of employees, generally in terms of the amount and type of work to be completed and the time allotted for it. These targets are often derived from engineered time standards.

The use of performance targeting is relatively widespread and appears to be growing. Surveys of local governments indicate that about 40 percent use some form of MBO, 20 percent use ABO, and 50 percent use work standards in at least one agency.[3] A few jurisdictions have linked target achievement to bonuses or wage increases. Although the targets have usually focused on work load to be processed and due dates to be met rather than service outcomes and productivity, a few cities have begun to base management performance targets on comprehensive systems of service effectiveness measures.

Unfortunately, there is little hard evidence on the impact of such programs on public employee motivation. Indeed, the potential motivational benefits of such techniques often appear to be overlooked by local governments which tend to concentrate on using the targets for planning, scheduling, and budgeting. Nevertheless, there is considerable evidence from private sector and laboratory studies that the setting of specific, reasonable, yet challenging performance targets can stimulate improved employee performance even without the use of monetary rewards.

Job enrichment

Job enrichment emphasizes motivating employees by making their work more intrinsically interesting and the work place a more challenging, humane, and satisfying place to be. Enrichment techniques alter the "content" of the job, usually by increasing the employee's autonomy and participation in decision making, the variety of the skills used or work assigned, the completeness (for example, lack of fragmentation) of the tasks performed, and/or the amount of direct feedback the employee receives on the results of his or her labors. Such efforts have taken a variety of forms in the public sector.

Team efforts   Team efforts are designed to bring employees performing diverse functions or working in different units together to work as a single group. The following kinds of teams have been used by local governments.

Operating teams   These are groups of employees who perform their day-to-day tasks as a team. Local government examples include team policing, custodial teams, and health-care teams.

Problem-oriented teams and task forces   These groups come together on a temporary or permanent basis to discuss and recommend solutions to specific problems. Participation on the team is not considered part of an employee's regular job but an addition to that job.

Management teams   These are groups of supervisory and management personnel who work together regularly to deal with operational problems, daily decisions, or objectives that fall between (or transcend) existing organizational boundaries.

Increased participation   Procedures may be established that give employees increased opportunities to contribute to the decision-making and problem-solving responsibilities customarily reserved for management. Several approaches have been used by local governments.

Joint labor-management committees   Such committees provide a formal but nonadversary process by which employee unions or associations can deal constructively with management on noncontractual items such as productivity, working conditions, and safety. The committees often include participation by rank-and-file employees.

Participative decision making   These techniques give line employees an opportunity to influence managerial decisions. The approaches used range from establishing an advisory role for employees (via informal meetings or opinion surveys) to allowing employees (or their representatives) to vote on—or even veto—managerial decisions. A few governments have included line employees in policymaking bodies; others have encouraged employees to work as a group to solve certain specific problems.

Job rotation   Job rotation is a procedure for systematically providing employees with experiences in different jobs on a regular basis. Rotation may occur within a department, between departments, or even between different jurisdictions. (Ad hoc rotations such as temporary assignments to cover for absentees, and rotation of new employees for training purposes, should probably not be considered a form of job enrichment.)

Job redesign   Job redesign encompasses comprehensive efforts to redefine a job in a manner that addresses all four principal objectives of job enrichment—greater responsibility for completing an entire task, greater control over how and when work is done, frequent feedback on performance, and more varied job responsibilities. Two major types of job redesign are particularly important in local governments.

Job enlargement   This involves increasing the number of tasks assigned to an employee without major increases in the employee's autonomy, decision-making authority, or skill level. Job enlargement tends to broaden the job rather than deepen the employee's responsibility for it. Local government examples include the use of public safety officers who handle both police and fire duties and generalized inspectors cross trained to conduct a variety of building (and other) inspections.

Job restructuring   This is a systematic effort to increase the depth of a job by building into it higher knowledge and skill requirements, greater autonomy, and increased responsibility for planning, directing, and controlling the work done. Local government examples include the use of "generalist" patrol officers responsible for conducting criminal investigations and doing whatever else is needed to deal with situations they encounter; the restructuring of nursing and social worker jobs to eliminate routine tasks and permit greater concentration on professional responsibilities; the redesign of jobs in municipal licensing and permit operations to provide complete responsibility for processing a specific kind of document; and the "broadbanding" of job classifications so that workers can be assigned to a variety of positions of similar complexity, responsibility, and experience requirements.

Over 300 examples of local government efforts involving job enrichment have been reported; more than half of these were for police personnel.[4] However, with the exception of team policing and public safety officers, most of these programs have involved only relatively minor job changes for small groups of employees.

Although there is little hard data on the impact of such efforts, the limited information available indicates that the most effective job enrichment approaches (in terms of improving productivity) are (1) programs which alter the nature of the employee's day-to-day job, such as operating teams and job redesign efforts, and (2) programs which increase participation by line employees in decisions affecting their work.

Surprisingly, none of these approaches have given consistent evidence of improving the job satisfaction of public employees. Since increased satisfaction is often regarded as the hallmark—and the principal benefit—of job enrichment, these results cast some doubt on whether the employees involved actually perceived the programs as enriching.

The most promising approaches

Local governments have been experimenting with a variety of approaches for enhancing the motivation and productivity of their employees. While there is a serious lack of systematic evaluative information on the impacts of most of these approaches, the limited information that is available indicates that monetary incentives based on objective, outcome-oriented performance criteria have had significant positive effects on productivity. Many of the successful monetary incentive programs have involved various forms of performance targeting; indeed, the introduction of target-setting procedures such as MBO or ABO appears to represent a fruitful first step toward improving the motivation of many types of public employees. Some types of job enrichment—the use of police teams, public safety officers, and (to a lesser extent) certain examples of job restructuring and increased decision participation by line employees—have also given evidence of improving productivity.

How should a local government proceed? Probably the first step should be to begin to develop employee appraisal procedures that utilize objective, results-oriented performance criteria, preferably incorporating performance targets.

In the meantime, governments desiring to improve productivity by enhancing employee motivation should probably focus on designing *management* or, for nonmanagement employees, *group* incentives tied to the performance of organizational units but not linked to existing employee performance appraisal procedures (given the usual inadequacies of the latter). The more promising job enrichment approaches noted above also deserve further testing and development. Of course, in undertaking any of these approaches, a government should ensure adequate training for supervisory and nonsupervisory employees, consultation and communication with employees and their unions concerning the procedures, and top level management commitment and support.

Although it will still be a while before the foregoing techniques can be accepted as reliable, effective tools for improving employee motivation and productivity, with continued interest and experimentation by local governments, that day will not be far off.

1. The results reported here are based on a recent study by The Urban Institute sponsored by the Office of Policy Development and Research of the U.S. Department of Housing and Urban Development. The findings from that study are described in a book, *Developing a Creative and Productive Government Work Force: An Examination of Programs for Improving the Motivation of State and Local Government Employees*, by John M. Greiner, Harry P. Hatry, Margo P. Koss, Annie P. Millar, and Jane P. Woodward (Washington, D.C.: The Urban Institute, 1980).

2. "The Status of Local Government Productivity," International City Management Association (Washington, D.C., March 1977).

3. See "The Status of Local Government Productivity" and the 1976 survey of member governments by the International Personnel Management Association.

4. Greiner et al., *Developing a Creative and Productive Government Work Force.*

Variations in the Scheduling of Work: A Look at Some of the Models

_____ Donald L. Prescott

Personnel management involves managing human resources in work organizations. The personnel manager must know the basic areas important in managing employees and the underlying motivational foundations and assumptions of each area. This includes such variables as: the motives and needs of every person working on a task; the motivational requirements of each task performed; the motives of the manager; and the internal and external environments of the organization. These variables reflect the needs of employees in the context of the workplace, and therefore must be well understood by managers designing work schedules for their employees.

The problem

Since much of people's on-the-job behavior is determined by their response to time, it is advantageous for management to take a serious look at the practices of managing time and scheduling work. It is necessary to consider what can be accomplished within a certain period of time in order to match time and task. This is important because the scheduling of staff work hours has a direct bearing on employee morale, motivation, and productivity. Thus the rearrangement of work hours, as an element of an organization's internal environment, can affect the job context either positively or negatively. Naturally, any change from a previously established norm can create unforeseen problems. Such problems arise when the scheduling of work hours does not match the characteristics of the people in the workplace to the nature of the jobs they must perform.

Reprinted with permission from *The Bureaucrat,* summer 1980.

Background

One of management's tasks has always been to motivate the people working in the organization in order to increase productivity. During the late nineteenth and early twentieth centuries workers were required to work 12 or more hours per day, six or seven days per week. The reduction of work to an eight-hour day, 48-hour week during the early part of this century was aimed at improving the workers' situation and production, and reducing organizational losses due to employee fatigue.

Although the reorganization of work hours has become common as a stimulus for employees, it motivates every individual differently. Each person has different wants, needs, and purposes in doing whatever he or she does. The question of work schedules is thus directly tied to social and economic issues, labor productivity, quality of working life, and employment opportunity.

Framework

Managers of organizations can evaluate their employees' current and future work schedules by means of five work hour models whose assumptions subsume specific management theories. These models (theories) are as follows: the standard workweek (the rational-legal), the extended workweek (human resources), staggered work hours (scientific), flextime (human relations), and the compressed workweek (systems).

The work hour models

The standard workweek The standard workweek consists of a five day, 40-hour week commencing conventionally at either 8:30 a.m. or 9:00 a.m. each day and ending eight work hours later.

The rational-legal theory implies that any innovation in the organization should have demonstrated its utility in fulfilling the requirements of the organization. The organization's procedures and hours of work must be specified in formal laws, contracts, and informal codes in order to prevent the breakdown of the organizational relationships and the power structure.

Through government legislation the standard week is now embedded within Western society, as outlined in all formal agreements. Therefore implementation of this model presents relatively few problems since these agreements contain the necessary details to the satisfaction of all parties.

Evaluation of this model's effectiveness is based to a large extent on worker motivation issues centered around the adherence to work hours. When problems arise in an organization, they appear as increases in lateness to the point of regularity, absenteeism sustained at a high level, and high rates of staff turnover. Further measurable factors concern social and personal goal satisfaction as well as individual adaptability.

The extended workweek   Such a week is comprised of five and a half to seven days of work surpassing the 40 hours of a standard week. Jobs in industries using this system often require overtime, staff to be on call, shifts that run workweeks together, or involve self-employed workers. Numerous managerial, professional, and sales workers tend to work long hours either because of personal necessity or the need for greater income and status.

Human beings are motivated by a complex set of interrelated factors such as income requirements, need for affiliation, need for achievement, and the desire for meaningful work. Employees all seek quite different goals in a job and have a diversity of talent to offer the organization. This model assumes that workers want to contribute to meaningful goals and can exercise far more responsible and creative role-direction than they may normally be required to do in many work situations. Consequently work is not inherently distasteful as workers are often self-motivated and tend to enjoy their work. Thus they may desire to work longer hours in order to contribute to the organizational goals they see as worthwhile.

For the management level employees there must exist an environment enabling them to contribute freely within the limits of their abilities. The organization must encourage full participation on important matters by continually broadening employee self-direction and control in order to create the desire within managers to work long hours.

At lower levels within organizations workers tend to be moonlighters who receive insufficient economic returns for their full-time jobs. Control over the length of this style of workday may be impossible under these circumstances.

Longer workweeks due to workers' expanding self-direction, self-control, and perceived prestige will lead to direct improvements in their behavior, productivity, and effectiveness. Management quality will increase while the management cost per unit produced should noticeably decrease. This is due to managers and workers making full use of their abilities and resources as they become more satisfied with their work. Generally, the more enjoyable the work and the greater the number of needs satisfied, the less employees will feel stress and fatigue.

Staggered work hours   This model is the same as the standard workweek except for one modification, the staggering of starting and quitting times of employees. Staff work the same number of hours per day and days per week as usual but the employer designates specific groups to start a certain number of hours earlier in the day and finish the same number of hours earlier, or vice versa.

This model assumes that staggering the 40 hours of work per week is the one best way of scheduling work for all workers. Further in this argument, employees are employees only because they need to support themselves and their families; otherwise they would not be working due to an inherent distaste for work. Therefore, the scheduling of work hours is unimportant as workers would prefer not to be at work at any time of the day.

Although workers and their jobs are the essential building blocks of an organization, the workers are only extensions of machines. Few of them want or can handle work which requires creativity, self-direction, or self-control. Thus every act of each worker must be preceded by one or more preparatory acts by management, including the regulation of the hours he or she spends on the job.

Management has complete freedom to use any available social and environmental mechanisms to enforce compliance with its decisions and to ensure its own stability. In general, work can be done faster and production assured by means of enforced standarization of methods, enforced adoption of the best implements, enforced working conditions, and enforced cooperation.

As the manager's basic task is close supervision and control of subordinates, the ease with which he or she can do so is increased with this model. Within this model the detailed work routines and procedures established by the manager may have varying degrees of success, depending on how and when work hours are staggered. However, if the work hours are straightforward and fixed, the tasks simple, and the workers closely controlled, production will meet the organization's set standards.

Flexible work hours (flextime)   This approach emphasizes the employees' privilege to choose and manage a portion of their work time. One method divides each workday into a core period, when all employees must be at work, with flexible bands at each end of the core period. Another method allows employees to come and go when they please during the flexible bands as long as they work a prescribed number of hours per day and meet daily work requirements.

This model stresses the importance of the human factor in an organization. Workers are only superficially controllable by the carrot and stick approach. Truly effective control must therefore emanate from within each individual worker. The developing of flextime schedules represents a nonauthoritarian style of leadership emphasizing group participation in the decision process in order to capture the workers' interest. Thus, a flexible work hours model permits individual autonomy leading to maximum task involvement by motivating the individual from within. As a result employees have greater freedom and self-determination at work.

A manager's basic task is to make each worker feel useful and important by keeping subordinates informed and by listening to their assessments of proposed innovations. This procedure requires that subordinates exercise some self-direction and self-control over their work environment by sharing information with other workers and involving them in decisions concerning their situation. Workers often show a greater willingness to work and cooperate in this kind of environment. A work commitment inspired in this manner will give management the support it needs to implement any new procedures or programs.

Worker satisfaction and commitment to a new program or procedure will determine its effect on the organization. Success rests with the workers rather than with management and it can be measured by decreases in absenteeism rates, decreases in lateness, and increases in overall organizational productivity.

The compressed workweek   A compressed workweek requires working in excess of eight hours per day for less than five days a week. The total hours per week equal the same number of weekly hours as the standard workweek. This model is actually a condensed version of the latter model. Examples of work hour schedules in the compressed week range from four 10-hour days to three 12-hour days, or from a four day 35-hour week to a 70-hour two week schedule. Such schedules allow for one or even two additional days off per week.

The total environment of the organization specifies certain activities and interactions for all people involved in its social system. As a result of a compressed workweek, certain feelings and sentiments are aroused among the workers toward each other and their environment. The increased daily length of worker contact achieved by this model emphasizes that the higher the rate of interaction between two or more workers, the more positive will be their sentiments towards each other.

The implementation of the compressed workweek requires a fairly broad base of support within the organization. This must develop as a result of coordination and control becoming more laterally oriented. Thus as the emphasis on the hierarchy decreases, the strong opposition to an innovation will become less formidable. In the long run implementation will progress smoothly due to the emergence of a generally open, organic, and flexible organization that is capable of adapting to change.

Organizational effectiveness is based on multiple criteria involving adaptability, a sense of identity, capacity to test reality, and internal integration. The test of an organization engaged in a compressed workweek is its openness and ability to react to further environmental changes. An innovation in the organization must not impede productivity, increase costs of production, minimize interaction in the democratic processes of control, or hinder the employees' willingness to relate to their jobs.

Strengths and limitations of the models

Environmental characteristics such as the structure of an organization, the implicit theories held by its management, the economic condition of the industry, and the work hour schedules of the staff all influence an individual in his work role.

The manager who desires to initiate a new work schedule model must consider the various strengths and limitations of each model. He must carefully evaluate alternative models with respect to his organization in order to determine the best possible work schedule or schedules that match the needs of his organization. This may be by adjusting the flow of staff hours to peak workloads, increasing the utilization of plant and equipment, or improving customer service. However, the basic evaluative criteria are generally worker attitude and behavior, organizational capabilities and productivity, and favorable public relations to the organization.

The standard workweek   The regularity of a five day workweek promotes a normative behavior in workers. Their sense of security grows through the establishment of daily routines because a permanent specified work schedule makes it easier for employees to organize their daily activities. This aids the organization in maintaining steady production rates with a satisfied staff.

On the other hand the routinized working conditions created by this schedule may create a feeling of boredom and dullness within each worker. Consequently, numerous habits may develop that are detrimental to the organization. Such habits may appear as increased lateness, absenteeism, or high rates of staff turnover. Behavior of this nature affects the whole organization by causing losses in production.

The extended workweek   The most obvious advantage of this model is the greater production possibilities per worker. An increase in production will in turn accrue direct economic benefits to the organization and also create a savings in wages paid at regular rates, especially at the managerial and professional levels.

This model often creates more jobs for moonlighters, thus benefitting the employer by enabling longer hours of operation with no overtime wages. The organization can increase productivity with minimum cost.

However, primary concern is centered around worker fatigue and stress. Long work hours often take their toll on the physical condition of workers. Without adequate rest and relaxation workers will tend to be sick more often. This in itself may be the largest drawback of this model as the organization expands resources to pay sick workers and aid the workers' recovery.

Staggered work hours   Staggered work hours represent the most direct approach to lengthening business hours, increasing customer service and alleviating traffic congestion. The first two benefits favor the organization while the latter favors both the employees and the general public. Longer business hours and increased service presuppose increased production and profits while decreased traffic congestion lowers worker frustrations and tensions.

Many organizations may find this concept impractical due to the number of employees involved or the complexity of the organization. It is certain that management's implementation of such a model will create a number of disgruntled workers whose reaction may be detrimental to the organization. Workers will resist being told to start and quit work earlier or later.

Flexible work hours   This model enhances employees' sense of control and responsibility for integrating personal lifestyles with the demands of work. It gives greater commitment to the job and allows individuals to tailor workloads to the time available. Other advantages of flextime are: savings on employee commuting time, lower absenteeism and turnover; easier recruitment; increased employee motivation; satisfaction and performance; improved handling of fluctuating workloads; and increased customer service.

The limited number of core hours may necessitate a rise in the cost of support service and increase the amount of supervisory time necessary to cover the flexible bands. Difficulties may arise in systems of highly interdependent jobs such as assembly lines, security, quality control, and continuous operations. In all of these situations there is a need for continuity from one worker to the next. Further disadvantages are: utility costs rise with longer hours of operation; recording employee working time becomes more difficult; staff may become upset over the reduction in overtime; safety and security become weaker and more costly; and restrictions may occur on contact, delivery and collection of goods from the public.

The compressed workweek   The four-day week depends upon planning that anticipates potential problems and ways to deal with them. Companies tending to adopt this system seem to emphasize purported improvements in production and morale, reduction in absenteeism rates, and the convenience employees receive from having an extra day off. Generally productivity increases over time, especially in situations where the work process requires significant startup and shutdown periods, even though the efficiency of labor remains unchanged. Work assignments, once started, are thus more likely to be completed the same day.

Cost savings also accrue due to the removal of at least two rest periods a week, one lunch period, and a start and stop phase, as compared to the standard workweek. Other advantages of the four day workweek range from reduced employee turnover and lower operating costs to providing greater production-scheduling flexibility and better utilization of equipment.

This model may be impractical in situations where employees must meet and work in groups; where customer service is provided five days a week; or where supervisors feel the need to be available during all work hours. Problems can develop in these areas because of poor planning, fatigue, monotony, commuting difficulties, coordination, and family adjustment. However, the main disadvantage arises from the need for more involved work schedules.

Analysis

The five work hour models presented above may not be appropriate for all organizations. However, by using the preceding criteria each of the jobs below can be better performed within an appropriate work schedule model.

Air traffic controller   Air traffic control requires strenuous mental concentration and attention for specific periods of time. In this situation the standard workweek is considered a stabilizing and normative factor. Air traffic controllers should not be subjected to any unnecessary complications that may reduce their attention on the job. Work schedule peace of mind can be achieved by this model's guaranteed routine. The other models would increase distraction of one kind or another and/or create a lack of shift continuity.

Manager   At the managerial level employees are often expected to work long hours because of the responsibilities connected with their positions. These workers often tend to seek greater prestige and learn to enjoy their work in order to become the best in their chosen field of endeavor. In this situation the extended workweek provides the maximum benefits to the organization and facilitates the employee's fulfillment of his needs and desires. The organization's maximum use of the manager's talents often results in improved effective management and greater organizational capabilities.

Although the other four work hour models could be justified for managerial workers, none would provide as great a benefit to the organization or as much worker satisfaction.

Assembly line   Continuous operation assembly lines have highly interdependent job functions and require workers to relieve each other without interruption of the system. The interdependencies and required continuity rule out the use of flextime. The monotony, fatigue, and stress factors of the job that currently exist within the standard workweek preclude the use of the extended and compressed workweeks. These models would also cause decreases in production and profits while increasing worker health problems.

In the final analysis the staggered work hours model is considered more desirable than the other models for the simple reasons that it alleviates traffic congestion and worker commuting problems, and increases the hours of operation. The first two reasons are a boon in regulating the large number of employees involved while the last reason positively affects production and profits.

Miner   For mine workers the hours of work underground should be strictly limited due to the nature of the work. The only model providing for daily or weekly work hours less than the standard week currently worked by most miners is the flextime model. In this occupation of physically strenuous, dirty, and dangerous activity, workers should have a great part in the decisionmaking process. The limitations of the other work models present a strong case against their use in this work situation.

Museum guard   This job requires 24-hour effectiveness with more intensive surveillance during the time the institution is open to the public, usually between 10 and 12 hours per seven day week. Given this organizational situation and the fact that the job does not require strenuous mental concentration, high levels of physical activity, or supervision, the compressed workweek could yield the best results.

The standard model would only increase boredom in an already potentially boring job while promoting a normative behavior that can also be achieved with the compressed workweek. The extended model would increase fatigue and stress, decreasing worker alertness in an occupation unsuitable for part time moonlighters. The staggered hours model can be discarded for the same reason as the standard model as well as the impracticality of constant management supervision. Finally the flextime model with its increased individual autonomy of work time is not feasible in a situation that requires a continuity of service.

Conclusions

Every manager should consider that future changes in favor of employees must attempt to accommodate the organization as well as the employees. Ideally, both should be able to attain their goals and fulfill all of their needs within a framework that will enable the organization to remain viable and cohesive. The development and implementation of a practical, effective work hour schedule would be a major step in this direction.

Before implementing a new work hour schedule the manager must carefully study its implications on variables such as the following:

1. The type of task being done;
2. Productivity (quantity and quality);
3. Worker satisfaction;
4. Capabilities to produce (cost per unit, continuity, fatigue, absenteeism, worker stress);
5. Specialization and interdependencies; and
6. Commitment of the workers.

Since each specific job is maximized within one certain work hour model, it may be necessary for the organization to implement more than one model at a time. New work hour models developed in this manner must also allow for greater worker autonomy in the hours spent at work. Such models will benefit the employee directly and benefit the organization indirectly through heightened worker motivation.

It is apparent that the five work hour models discussed in this paper do not represent a totally satisfactory answer to the autonomous distribution of workers' time while maintaining organizational goals and productivity. Also they do not take into account the environments and requirements of numerous other jobs such as those encountered by academics at universities.

Obviously research in this field of work schedules must continue but the development of a panacea work schedule or workweek may be impossible.

Flexible Benefits: A Key to Better Employee Relations

— Albert Cole, Jr.

In today's society, one challenge most human resources professionals face is the need or demand to treat employees as individuals. The emergence of flexible benefits comes as a natural result of employees' desire for recognition as individuals.

Employers have begun to realize that employee satisfaction and morale may rise when employees are allowed to select benefits most appropriate to their individual needs and lifestyles. Flexible benefit plans permit this kind of choice. (These plans have also been called "cafeteria plans" because they provide a "menu," or choice, of benefits, from which employees select those benefits they want or need.)

The freedom to choose

A key distinguishing feature of flexible benefit plans is the opportunity for each employee to spend employer contributions as he or she wishes. In contrast, many plans today are fixed, providing for employer contributions to the cost of hospitalization and other medical insurance for spouse and dependent children. Such coverage for dependents might cost $60 per month. If the employee agrees to payroll deductions of $15 per month, the employer pays the balance of $45 a month. The employee who declines to pay $15 does not receive the employer's contribution of $45 in cash or in any other benefits.

The possibilities for choice within a benefit plan may be limited or may be quite extensive. Some flexible benefit plans limit choices to just a few types of coverage, such as life insurance and health insurance. Others allow employees to choose among certain forms

Benefit	Monthly cost
Dependent health insurance	$ 60
Employee dental insurance	10
Dependent dental insurance	20
One time earnings group life insurance	20
Two times earnings group life insurance	40
$100,000 accidental death insurance	5
Long term disability insurance	25

Figure 1. Typical flexible benefit choices.

of deferred compensation, additional retirement income, or other benefits such as tuition assistance, adoption expenses, financial counseling, and increased vacation. In some plans, if the employee does not use all of the flexible benefit allowances for the options available, any balance will be paid to the employee in cash.

The amount of credits allocated to each employee may be a percentage of the employee's salary. However, it might also vary depending on the employee's age, family status (to help pay for dependent health insurance or buy additional life insurance), geographic location (the cost of medical care varies widely depending on location), and length of service.

Assume an employee has a flexible benefit allowance of $100 a month, and the benefit choices are as shown in Figure 1. Without incurring any out-of-pocket monthly costs, the employee may choose any combination of benefits that costs $100. If the cost of choices adds up to more than $100, the employee pays the excess through payroll deductions.

Meaningful benefits

Employers offering flexible benefits may basically be motivated by a desire to better employee relations. If flexible benefits are to improve relations, employees should be offered choices that are meaningful to them. An employer who currently does not have a dental plan may be surprised to learn that only 20% to 25% of employees would elect dental insurance if it became an option under a flexible benefit plan. Even fewer may be likely to accept a vision plan and the other choices available.

At the other extreme, there may be a vocal minority that would like a certain benefit, such as financial counseling, adoption assistance, or dependent care benefits such as day care centers.

The best way to find out which benefit employees want is to survey employees, and, perhaps, to have a representative group of employees on the task force that develops the flexible benefits program. The form and scope of the survey depends on the employer and work force. It could be a questionnaire sent to all employees or to just a representative sample of employees. The survey might also involve in-depth interviews with some employees.

Why offer flexibility?

While a key motivation for establishing flexible benefit plans is to improve employee relations, there are other reasons why some employers adopt such plans. A flexible benefit plan may help to shift some of the cost of fringe benefits back to employees. In a time of rapidly escalating costs, particularly in the areas of health insurance and pension plans, some employers see such a shift as necessary and desirable. Other employers may adopt flexible benefits to secure a leadership position and to attract or retain qualified personnel.

In addition, flexible benefits work particularly well as a vehicle to introduce new benefits at little or minimum cost to the employer. It may be that a company now has a group insurance plan with liberal amounts of group life insurance and comprehensive hospital/medical benefits. The company has no dental plan, and the cost of the existing benefit program does not permit the additional expenditure for dental benefits.

By adopting a flexible benefit plan, the company can offer dental expense coverage. Employees who want dental benefits pay the cost by reducing either their group life insurance and hospital/medical benefits, or both. Thus, the employer could establish a flexible benefits program by allocating employee allowances based on the cost of the existing plans.

Part of a flexible benefits plan could include benefits not now in the employer's plan, such as dental, vision, adoption, and financial counseling. Employees might opt out of part of the existing program to use their benefit allocations for some or all of the new benefits. On the other hand, the employees could retain all existing benefits and buy the new benefits through payroll deduction.

Obviously, the potential for this arrangement depends on how rich the present program is: how many different benefits are now in the program and who is paying for them. If the current plan includes a wide spectrum of benefits, and virtually all of them are paid for in full by the employer, it would be difficult to introduce new benefits to be paid for by the employees.

Administration challenges

An employer that offers flexible benefits must have the capability to administer what may be a complex program. Administration of flexible benefits normally requires a computer program for record-keeping and reporting. Determining the amount of employee allocations, recording and reconciling employee benefit choices, and calculating the amount of credits spent on each choice must be done in a timely and accurate way.

The type of plan selected by each employee and the basis of calculation of employee benefit allocations are factors affecting the complexity of the administration. If the allocations are a straight percentage of salary, or if there are few choices for the employees, administration is relatively simple.

It is important to note that employee choices must be recertified every year. Employees must confirm their prior choices or make new ones to reflect changes in lifestyle, marital status, income, or other factors. If employees do not have the opportunity to change choices periodically, they may end up with benefits that do not meet their needs. This can create serious employee morale problems. In extreme instances, it could lead to employee complaints, grievances, or possible legal action.

Choosing a plan

The next step is to pick a flexible benefits plan. Of the possible plan designs, I shall discuss three: core cafeteria, buffet, and alternative dinners.

Figure 2 represents an example of the core cafeteria plan. Under this concept, all employees have identical minimum levels of benefits in each of several areas. These benefit levels are the lowest the employer will allow each employee to accept. Coverage might

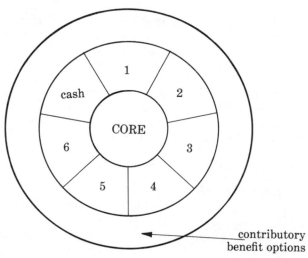

Figure 2. The core cafeteria plan.

consist of $5,000 of group life insurance, a short-term disability income plan, a one-week vacation, and a minimum level of hospital and medical coverage for the employee only.

The concept of a minimum level of any benefit represents a balance between giving the employee free choice for each benefit, and the employer's sense of responsibility for employees who might be left without a minimum benefit. For example, most employers require that employees take a minimum period of vacation each year to refresh themselves—to recharge their batteries. The employer will not want to permit employees to waive all vacation year after year.

As another example, some employees may want to decline all hospital/medical insurance because they believe they have adequate insurance through a spouse's plan. However, the spouse's employment may terminate, leaving both the employee and spouse without any hospital/medical coverage. Most employers who offer group health insurance plans would not want to permit a situation in which employees have to pay the full cost of a major health care expense because they left themselves without any health insurance.

Similarly, if an employee who took no group life insurance died and left no other funds, an employer could find itself in an awkward situation.

Beyond the core of minimum coverage, employees have a choice of additional life insurance, more vacation, better health insurance for themselves, dependent health insurance, long-term disability, dental coverage, or any other plan options within their flexible benefit allowances. They "buy" these benefits with the flexible benefit allowances and, if necessary, through payroll deductions.

The core cafeteria plan offers employees a wide range of choices, thus enabling them to tailor their benefits to suit their needs. However, because it offers many choices, the administrative requirements of the core cafeteria plan can be complex.

The buffet plan

Under the buffet plan (represented in Figure 3), employees have the option of retaining exactly the same coverage they had prior to the introduction of flexible benefits. In fact, this is a fundamental principle accepted by most employers who offer a flexible benefits plan. The starting point might be the existing level of life, disability, hospital/medical, and vacation benefits.

However, in the buffet plan, employees may choose lower benefits, such as less vacation, a lower amount of life insurance, or a higher deductible in the hospital/medical plan. By choosing lower benefits, an employee accumulates credits that may be used toward the purchase of other benefits, such as dental, long term disability, etc.

As under the core cafeteria plan, there is a minimum benefit level below which the employees may not go. The buffet also offers many choices to employees and gives them the opportunity to individualize their benefit coverage. Again, disadvantages of this approach involve administrative and pricing complications.

The alternative dinners plan

The alternative dinners plan (Figure 4) represents a degree of choice for the employee but does not provide a wide-open selection. Rather, the employer designs a set of benefit packages that are aimed at target groups of employees. One package might be aimed at the employee with a nonworking spouse and children; another might be aimed at the single employee; a third at the single parent; and a fourth at the employee with a working spouse and no children. The employee chooses one, and only one, of the packages.

The advantage of the alternative dinners plan approach is simpler administration and communications. The disadvantage is a limitation of choice and possible adverse reaction by employees who cannot get the specific benefits they want. Note that under the alternative dinners approach, no allocation is required. Each plan is designed to be of equivalent value. The cost of each dinner is roughly equal, and any employee contributions required are also equal.

Clear communications

The introduction of a flexible benefits plan creates a greater need for clear communication with employees. If a plan is to succeed and

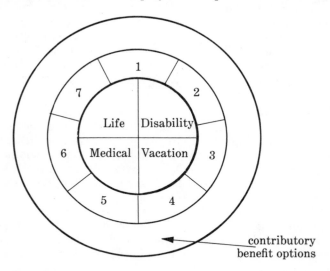

Figure 3. The buffet plan.

receive the desired acceptance, employees must understand the options, know how to select the desired benefits, and make correct choices that meet their needs. Meetings, videotapes, slide/talk presentations, availability of a telephone answering service, and carefully designed printed media may all be used in a good communications effort.

Also, it is important to confirm to employees the choices they have made. Typically, employee choices, once made, cannot be changed during the plan year unless there is a significant change in the employee's situation—such as marriage or birth of a child.

Discussed above are some of the major issues that should be considered when developing a flexible benefits plan. Other areas of concern are:

Financial commitment   What financial commitment will be required for the implementation of the flexible benefits program?

Management support   What kind of management support is needed to get the program started and keep it going?

Manpower needs   How many and what kinds of personnel are needed for the planning, implementation, and ongoing maintenance of the program?

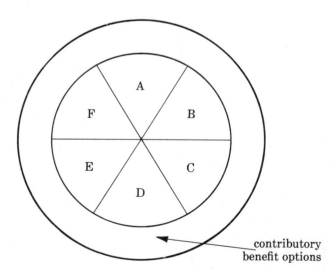

contributory
benefit options

Figure 4. The alternative dinners plan.

Underwriter support   What kind of support is expected from the insurance carriers who will underwrite the different parts of the program? They may be concerned about the impact on their premium income, and they may claim experience based on the choices employees will have.

Employee eligiblility   Which employees will be eligible: all employees, just those at a specific location, or those with a minimum period of service with the company?

Collective bargaining issues   Most unions have not shown interest in flexible benefit plans. Indeed, most plans installed to date have limited flexible benefits to nonunion employees.

Tax implications   Consider the tax implications of the benefits offered to, and selected by, the employees.

Developing a flexible benefits program involves careful planning and review. Decisions must be made in the areas of administration, benefits to be offered, determination of the employee allocations, and communication of the program to employees.

Building a Workable Participative Management System

—Philip A. Davis

Participative management systems can work. But will they do so for you?

In some instances, participative systems have yielded sustained increases in productivity, while in many other cases, improvements have been short-lived or nonexistent. Although no conclusive explanation has been developed, the differences in outcome seem to be related to the work environment and the scope with which management views participative systems. A narrow view in a poor environment inevitably invites failure. Conversely, a broad view in a cultivated environment offers the best chance of success.

Learning to detect and evaluate the differences in the work environment and the depth of management's understanding and commitment is a prerequisite to successful implementation of participative systems. Understanding the long-term dynamics of participative systems is essential for sustaining them.

Participative management implies employee involvement. Participative systems, however, connote a great deal more—they exist where there are interlocking approaches to people management that reinforce and sustain each other in a participative climate. In this sense, then, building a participative system is like building a house, and its construction consists of three reinforcing structural features:

1. A *foundation* constructed with the building blocks of group dynamics and designed to focus the energy and talent of employees working as groups.

2. A *frame* designed around the individual employee and his job with the goal of making the work as meaningful and flexible as possible.
3. A *floor plan* that, along with determining how the internal walls relate to one another, makes the house as livable and efficient as possible while promoting a sense of belonging and an identification with the goals of the larger organization.

Laying the foundation

The foundation of a participative system is the involvement of employee work groups in making decisions that traditionally have been handled solely by management. Involving employees through work groups (or teams) in these decisions focuses the energy of the group toward achieving the task. Once this focus is achieved, the decision-making process is enhanced, and the implementation phase is freed of many of the usual forms of resistance experienced during change. Although the decisions appropriate for work-group involvement vary according to the situation, they generally fall into three areas:

Personnel practices not in conflict with those of the larger organization or management's right to apply resources and specify performance criteria   For example, management might specify that three members of a 12-member work group work overtime on Saturday, but the decision on which three is left to the group. Or the work group may be assigned the responsibility for getting the work done, but the decision as to who does what task is left to the group.

Developing alternatives within parameters defined by management   Here management learns to define problems in terms of areas of acceptable and unacceptable outcomes. Once the acceptable area has been isolated by knowing what is unacceptable, the group is asked to develop and/or choose an acceptable course of action. This is done in the belief that the group can best achieve an optimum outcome when it implements an idea of its own making, even if that decision is not based on a foundation as strictly technical as an expert could have developed.

Planning for change or ease of transition between old and new   Involving the work group in planning the introduction of a new machine, process, or method can pay great dividends in terms of minimizing resistance and maximizing the productive application of technological improvement.

Erecting the frame

The framework of a participative system is constructed from the tenets of job enrichment and enlargement, which, when combined, deliver both employee motivation and job flexibility. Job enrichment consists of designing into the job wholeness of task, control over the process, and performance feedback. Job enlargement consists of increasing the range of tasks available for each employee to perform. Both concepts usually lead to fewer job classifications, thus facilitating wholeness of task and increasing the range of tasks available to a given employee. Also, the flexibility derived from these concepts should be optimized, not maximized. As jobs become too encompassing, the time required to learn the job and stay current in its many aspects becomes prohibitive.

Designing the floor plan

The floor plan should be laid out with the goals of (1) decreasing social distance between management and employees through progressive personnel policies and (2) increasing employee understanding through improved communications. If the plan is well designed, employees learn to identify with the larger organization and to feel and think as active business partners.

Decreasing social distance is a matter of eliminating class distinctions where possible. This can be achieved in many ways, such as giving employees salary status, minimizing differences in benefits and privileges, establishing an open-floor policy (where management goes out on the floor regularly to talk to employees), establishing self-supervision wherever possible, promulgating positive disciplinary programs, and eliminating probationary periods, time clocks, and set break periods.

In essence, personnel policies and practices should be rethought to bring out the best in employees and not just repress their worst. This approach is not one of letting everyone run wild; discipline must be maintained. However, in exchange for the effort required to keep social barriers down, management increases its ability to communicate business needs effectively and to gain employee cooperation. To capitalize on such rapport, one-on-one floor contact and regular management meetings with employees are an essential part of the overall communications aimed at keeping employees knowledgeable about their jobs, the products they make, and the overall business picture.

A complete participative system requires quality construction throughout. A complete system is not necessary, however, to secure value from each structural feature independently. For instance, having work groups involved in decision making does not necessarily require a job enrichment program or progressive personnel policies.

A total system offers two distinct advantages, however. First, it has an impact greater than the sum of its parts—each feature amplifies the next. And, perhaps more importantly, a total system has less tendency to decay through time because participation becomes the basic management approach within the organization, which learns to deal with people within the broader context of a system of relationships.

The most effective level of approach for a given organization depends on its circumstances. A successful implementation strategy should therefore include a review of as many relevant factors as can be identified. Because there is no exact formula, each program must be tailored to fit the needs of the local situation and the larger company environment.

Getting started

The first step is to decide which work group(s) will be targeted for introduction of the program. The participative unit should be a distinct operation with a definable "product" and control over its own material and work flow. These conditions will facilitate independent self-adjustments without having to coordinate and integrate each step of change with the larger organization.

If possible, the unit should also be physically separated from other units, having either its own building or its own work area. Separation is desirable because (1) frequent interface with fellow participative work group members helps promote unity and common purpose, and (2) frequent interface with members of nonparticipating units can create misunderstandings and jealousy.

Since participative systems are not widely understood and are long-term strategies with associated costs, the commitment of key managers within the larger organization is essential. A useful rule of thumb is to seek public support of line management at least two levels above the participative unit. Unless this level of support is widely recognized, the resolve of those closer to the unit may falter as unanticipated problems arise. Furthermore, since the system must be implemented by managers within the participative unit itself, it is imperative that they consider the system a reasonable response to a perceived need. If local management sees the system as a passing fad or someone's pet project, there will be little support, and perhaps even resistance. The best strategy to avoid this pitfall is to introduce the system to meet a specific need and to involve local management in the design of the program. In this way, a fundamental participative principle will be used in planning a specific system's application—work group involvement in the development of alternatives and the planning of change.

High-level management should also be committed to expand application of the system to other appropriate units. Unless the original participative unit is completely separate from the larger organization, there is a tendency to absorb the "deviant" back into the mainstream. The best defense against this is a conscious strategy to educate the rest of the organization about the system and to expand its application in a measured fashion either as perceived needs surface or according to a predetermined schedule.

Appropriate design

Because a participative system's chances of success are enhanced if

---

Take the long-term view

Perhaps the most important single thing for management to understand is that participation is a long-run performance strategy. It is not a panacea, nor should it be seen as a stop-gap measure. Setting up and maintaining a functioning system is an investment in the future. And, like any investment, there are associated costs.

One such cost might be the addition of a staff specialist during the implementation period to help design the system and familiarize managers and employees with the concept. Also, since participative systems are, by definition, change oriented, the process of designing the system will never fully end; there will always be a need for flexibility within the larger organization.

It also should be understood that performance measurements may not improve immediately. In some situations, performance may even decline until the new procedures become familiar and participants in the program develop the required skills.

Along with management backing, a supportive labor climate is vitally important in the implementation of a participative system. Management can support the system 100 percent, but if employees are not willing to be involved, the chances of a successful implementation are tenuous at best.

Some employees simply want to do their jobs and be left alone. They have no real desire to participate in business decisions and, in fact, are frightened, or at least suspicious, of the whole idea. But where management crediblity is high, employees will be more willing to listen to proposed changes. Where credibility is low, they will be suspicious and will resist involvement.

Although nonunion operations will usually provide the best climate for a participatory system, a union is not necessarily a barrier. Management can influence the employee opinion leaders through the bargaining committee. And once the system is in and functioning, the operation itself will serve to build management credibility.

A strong traditional employee relations program is also desirable because such activities directly affect employee perceptions of job security, safety, fairness of treatment, and related concerns. Unless these basic needs are satisfied, there will be difficulty in building enthusiasm among employees for programs designed to satisfy higher-level needs such as participatory involvement and self expression.

it is seen as a reasonable response to a perceived need, the elements designed into a particular system should be functional—and have the appearance of being functional. The design of a successful system, therefore, requires an understanding of the needs and attitudes of the people involved as well as of the technology required.

Understanding the people entails asking questions and observing group norms. What do the people who must implement the system want it to do? Has anyone had personal experience in a participative system? How do the proposed participants see themselves within the organization? Are they conservative or risk oriented? Participative systems are people systems; like a good suit, a quality system will feel good and fit its wearer well. Of course, the greatest flexiblity with regard to fit exists in a new organization where the people can to some degree be selected to fit the system.

Designing quality into the system requires an understanding of how work is accomplished in a technical sense. What is the product and how are the units of production defined—for example, service calls or light bulbs? How does the material move through the work unit? Is the process best visualized as progressive assembly, batch process, or continuous operations? Are the group members spread out or concentrated? Is the technology simple or complex? How interdependent are the various work groups in achieving routine production? At what points do individuals and groups interface? The purpose of these and related questions is to promote understanding of how things happen as contrasted with how people feel about what's happening. Knowledge of both is important. To work properly, a participative system must fit in terms of how people feel about the system and of how well the system fits the work process.

Implementation

A participative system should be introduced with the same planning and attention to detail that would be used to introduce a new computer-controlled production system. In a sense, both are new technologies requiring technical expertise and the earliest possible involvement of those who will use it.

As part of the involvement of persons within the unit, an education program should be arranged to give management and employees alike a brief overview of the theory of the system and appropriate skills training. The latter is particularly important for building successful teams and designing enriched jobs.

The implementation phase may require only two months to complete or may last as long as two years. Although the change set in motion to implement the system will never really end, the implementation period can be considered finished when the services of the technical expert are no longer required on an ongoing basis and the elements of the system are viewed by those in the organization as the normal way things are done.

Keys to sustained performance

Once a system is successfully implemented, the next challenge is to sustain its operation and performance level. Even with the initial advantages of good design and implementation, a system must endure its own novelty and the disadvantages of being different. Because it is different, forces within the larger organization will work to compel compliance with more established methods. Because most job applicants will have little if any participative experience, finding and training new employees and supervisors present special problems. In facing these and other issues, five central factors must be considered:

Realistic management expectations Participative systems are an aid to good management, not a substitute for it. To perform well, such units must be managed well; they are no less susceptible than traditional units to the damaging effects of poor financial control, inadequate inventory management, and related inadequacies.

Participative systems will also deteriorate unless they are periodically rejuvenated. Work groups need periodic help to sustain teamwork, and enriched jobs must be redesigned to accommodate changes in products and work flow. And management must remind employees to use their freedom and flexibility responsibly. In short, participative systems are not the management equivalent of perpetual motion. Like all management systems, participative operations need new energy from time to time, but since the levels of expectation and performance are generally higher in participative units, their problems are usually more visible.

Work group stability and training When a group has more than 20 members, the interface required for effective group decision making becomes cumbersome. The committee approach is one way to deal with the size problem, but for a primary work group that interfaces daily on routine decisions, small is best.

Stability is also important. If the work group has high turnover, it is difficult to establish teamwork relationships. To some degree, of course, the effects of large size and high turnover can be lessened by conducting periodic team-building exercises to promote effective interpersonal communications and help build group identity and commonality of purpose.

Supervisory training Supervisors or managers new to a participative system may feel disoriented or threatened at the start. In their previous experience, they probably learned to equate success with knowing the right answers and to associate control with specifying exactly what would be done and how—a technique that can become counterproductive in a participative situation. In contrast, the participative supervisor must involve subordinate employees in coming up with the answers and making decisions. Instead of specifying exact outcomes, the supervisor must establish what is unacceptable, leaving as much latitude as possible for the acceptable response—a technique calling for new attitudes and skills. For example, supervisors must learn that well-defined parameters provide as much or more control than specified outcomes. They must also learn to recognize the difference between decisions that should be made by management and decisions appropriate for employee involvement. To work effectively with groups on this basis, supervisors will need coaching in group problem-solving techniques and in listening and feedback skills.

Supervisors and managers must also learn to appreciate the continuous interplay and trade-offs between social and technical considerations. Technically, one person performing one repetitive task free of contact with other workers should be the ideal work unit. But however true this concept may have been in the past, today's employees usually expect more from their jobs. We now live in an age of growing alternatives in types of work and even choices between working and not working.

A "humanization" of the workplace is occurring at all levels, but what most employees will experience will come from their supervisors. Recognizing the social-technical interplay goes beyond good supervisory practices and encompasses an awareness of how changes in products, job design, and work flow can affect employees' perceptions of their jobs. Involvement in job enrichment programs or supervising a participative unit will provide repeated exposure to these interdependencies. Although instruction in theory is helpful, as in the group training situations, the best learning will take place in a program that heavily emphasizes counseling from those who already know how—that is, through modeling and coaching through real-life situations.

Institutionalization of the system   Formally documenting as much of the system as possible increases its perceived legitimacy. Discussion of the system and its various elements creates expectations of follow-through. The likelihood that the system will drift from its original purpose declines. By definition, the system will evolve through time; yet it is this very evolution that makes systematic evaluation and documentation an essential ongoing process. Institutionalizing the system means that the system defines how things are done.

Controlled growth   Unless the participative unit functions independently of the larger organization, the growth of the system becomes the only real alternative to its eventual absorption back into the broader, more traditional management system. Since lack of growth is unacceptable, the question becomes how much growth, how fast?

Ideally, the system should eventually spread in some appropriate form to all parts of the organization. This growth should be planned, if possible, and controlled. Overly rapid expansion may overextend the resources required for implementation. The exact application in each situation must be tailor-made.

Problems cropping up as a result of unmanaged growth can serve as object lessons for the doomsayers. And since each implementation period is basically independent of previous ones, all reasonable effort should be made to minimize the stress of each unit's transition.

For the long term

Participative management is a long-term performance strategy. Where attempts at participation fail, it is usually due to the absence of a systems approach, inadequate environmental analysis, faulty systems design, poor implementation, and/or lack of follow-through. Participation attempts having the greatest likelihood of success are those that are grass-roots oriented (that is, requested and largely designed by those who live with them). Such systems are operationally simple (although they may reflect the best of many sophisticated theories) and integrated in approach.

Although there are no exact formulas, there are patterns. Learning to recognize and apply these patterns to develop reinforcing systems appropriate to the specific needs of each environment is the key to successfully introducing and sustaining participative management systems.

How to Avoid Quality Circle Failure

Sud Ingle

Recent articles on quality circles have shown that the quality circle concept has not worked in many U.S. companies, thus creating doubt about circle success.

Mercury Marine, a leading outboard motor manufacturer, has experienced much success with quality circles during the last three years.[1] Starting in 1978, the program carried the following objectives:

1. Improve quality;
2. Reduce waste;
3. Better communication;
4. Learn group problem-solving;
5. Work satisfaction.

The Mercury Marine quality circles program began on a pilot basis in two of its plants, in Wisconsin and Florida, with five circles implemented at each location. The program now includes 1,200 trained circle members conducting more than 100 circles. It is also open to union employees. *MERC employee recognition circles* were set up to add expertise to the complex process of manufacturing high-quality products at reasonable prices.

Participation in a circle is voluntary, with discussion geared strictly toward solving production problems in a given work area. At the main MERC assembly plant in Fond Du Lac, Wisconsin, quality circle members tackled a list of production snags and came up with a series of workable solutions.

As a concept, quality circles have also had wide application at Brunswick Corp., following Mercury's lead.[2] The Lancer division facility in Bridgeton, Missouri, uses a program called "Circles 80." Bridgeton's circles tackled two major projects: one dealing with cost savings to be generated in the scrap and molding department; the second involving increased efficiency by changing equipment in the bottling line.

Employees at the Brunswick division facility in Eminence, Kentucky, have three active circles working on a variety of problems, from making more efficient use of available floor space to correcting loose stitching on one type of bowling bag.

At the Defense division's facility in Marion, Virginia, employees launched a "Defect Reduction Program," a variation of quality circles, to involve employees who work on the General Dynamics F-16 aircraft in efforts to reduce defects. The program was successful and drew positive employee reaction.

Quality circle programs continue to grow at Mercury Marine and other Brunswick divisions, training approximately 50 employees per month. The goal of Mercury Marine is to establish at least one quality circle in each department.

Reasons for QC failures

Based on experience in implementing quality circles, I will discuss some of the reasons for quality circle failures in American industries:

Poor communication   It is important to inform everyone in the company about quality circle programs, particularly management and supervisors.

Closed policy   When this type of program is introduced, it is important to form a policy about implementation. Although it is essential that management plan and adopt the policy, it should be based on the involvement of most of the work force, as well as management.

No training   Quality circles cannot be installed overnight. Training is essential as the "heart" of the program.

No proper listening   Very few people like to listen. This is a severe problem between employees and management. We need to listen to people and then do the best for the company.

No follow-ups on projects   Quality circles present completed projects to management. Most of the time, the project shows hard work by circle members. Sometimes, however, management needs to approve solutions because of financial and other factors. Experience shows that if a company does not plan proper follow-up procedures, many circle members will lose interest.

Poor middle management support   Some management personnel feel they will lose authority if quality circles are used to solve problems. Many feel the company might relieve some management personnel and, therefore, show poor support to the program.

"Lip service" from management   Sometimes, management personnel either feel forced into the program or want to get involved but do not have time to participate. With this type of "lip service," the program may not grow at all.

No "union" involvement   It is essential that companies ask union members (employees) to get involved from the beginning. With union cooperation, the program grows faster and operates efficiently. Some companies may find it difficult to get this cooperation at the beginning. In this case, the company should keep trying and keep the program open to all employees.

No objectives for the program   Many programs start without objectives or goals. If this is the case, the program can become short-lived because no one knows what is to be accomplished. Companies should establish objectives from the start.

"Not-for-me" attitude   This type of attitude creates problems in the program. People accept new ideas, as long as they don't have to get involved and do the work. They forget, however, that the company is one team and everyone has to help make it successful.

No publicity   Once the pilot program is successful, it is of utmost importance that good publicity be given to the project to help it grow.

No recognition   People like to be recognized for their achievements. Photos, small rewards, visits to seminars or to other plants help improve communication and contribute to the healthy growth of the program. If people realize the company appreciates their work, they will feel like part of the "corporate family."

Poor understanding of the quality circle philosophy   Many companies start QC programs on a small scale, never bothering to explain the basic philosophy and details to employees. Many employees then think the program is only for the "quality control" department. The term "quality circle" itself can be confusing; hence, a suitable name should be adopted (e.g., MERC—Mercury Employee Recognition Circle).

"Not invented here"   Many company managers and employees feel this technique was invented in Japan and can only work in Japan because their customs and culture are different. The cultures are different, but the basic philosophy behind the program is *universal*; it can work anywhere at any time.

Too much expectation from management   Quality circles are not panaceas. Many companies expect too much from them. Generally, employees in the shop can solve 20 percent to 25 percent of the problems. There exists a greater proportion of problems in the management areas, such as engineering, purchasing, etc.

Too much rush to expand the program and not enough financial support   Even if a company starts the program properly and within the first six months implements 30 to 40 circles, lack of financial support from management can cause it to fail. This creates a poor image of the program.

Problems with other programs   Some companies start many other programs like suggestion systems, work simplification, etc. Due to the rush in solving "productivity" problems, none of these gets proper attention. Failure with these creates problems in starting a good quality circle program.

Failure to maintain initial enthusiasm   Many quality circle members work hard and enthusiastically in the beginning, sometimes forgetting there is no magic in quality circles. It is continuous hard work! For this reason, one has to keep up enthusiasm throughout the program.

Changes in management   Many times, quality circles start under managements which like the program. Due to management or organizational changes, however, many times a "theory X" type manager takes charge of the plant. The program is then put on the shelf indefinitely.

No interest in improving quality of work life   Quality circles improve the quality of work life. Everyone is involved in achieving company objectives or goals. Safety projects, better communication, improved morale, teamwork and harmony may not be financial benefits, but they are intangible benefits of quality circles and add to the improved quality of work life.

These are some of the circumstances that create a poor impression of quality circles. Consequently, people are apt to lose interest. Management then starts to look for something else.

Keys to success

To start a successful quality circle program, one must understand the secrets of a successful program. When *everybody* in the company understands the principles thoroughly and implements them properly, success is close at hand! Ways to achieve success include:

Establish a suitable atmosphere for the program   The company must create a proper *atmosphere* for the quality circle program. Various management levels in the organization need to accept the idea of participative management. The program chairperson has the responsibility to spread the word. Different meetings should be arranged so that people get to know the basic philosophy of the program. Top management, middle management and union leaders should be properly exposed to the program. This will help acquire necessary funding, time and space to initiate the quality circle. A pilot study can be publicized to create a warm atmosphere in the company—the key is to generate warmth and an acceptable atmosphere.

Obtain commitment from top management   Top management commitment is essential to this type of program. One should prepare reports on other companies where such programs exist and present them to top management. Once the basic concept is sold, acceptance and formal commitment can be achieved easily. Without such commitment from the top, it is not advisable to begin the program.

Select the right people and the right area   One of the slogans commonly used in this type of program is, "There is no limit to what we can do together." This reflects power, strength and cooperation. It also indicates that, in order to achieve success, one has to seek cooperation from others. The program chairperson or manager has to be enthusiastic, persistent and hardworking. A facilitator is the key to the program; he or she must be energetic and cooperative. One also has to be careful in selecting the proper areas for implementation. The first trial run should be where one can expect cooperation and enthusiasm from participants.

Select objectives   Companies have to establish clear objectives for the program. A plant at Hughes Aircraft Company decided to improve communications for the company. Mercury Marine Corporation's major thrust lies in improving quality. These are a few objectives one can choose for a program. Objectives should be made clear to avoid confusion or unreasonable expectations from the program.

Expose people to the program   Ideas such as quality circles need clear understanding by many people. The idea of participation and sharing authority is new to the American society and needs incubation before one starts this type of program. Even though there is no change in the organizational structure, there is a major change in basic philosophy. Some people feel they've lost their authority, while others don't like the idea of participation. One of the best ways to lessen this tension is to expose numerous people to quality circles through newsletters and articles and by visiting other companies who have already implemented this type of program.

Inform and communicate   Once the program is started, information must be disseminated all over the company. Timely communication is important, and if one neglects it, one might have to suffer consequences in expanding the program. Rumors fly quickly, and people get different ideas and sometimes get discouraged if they do not get involved formally. As soon as the program is accepted, try to inform as many people as possible regarding the contents and its objectives. Better communication will always result in less resistance.

Keep the program voluntary   This is one of the key elements of the quality circle program. Pressure or force will not work to motivate people. People should realize the need and should understand the advantages to be derived from such a program. The basic philosophy and operation of the circle is for the benefit of the society; once people are exposed to the concept, participation becomes easy.

Training is crucial   Training is another important feature of the program. In Japan, this type of training is formally offered in schools or by employers as a usual practice. The same is not true in the United States. Many companies do not have good formal training programs. It is of the utmost importance that workers as well as management be exposed to the program properly so that all know what is involved. Without proper training, the program will phase out quickly.

Start slow and let it grow slowly   Whenever one tries to initiate a new concept, one has to be careful that it is not too much of a burden to others. Similarly, in order to achieve success, one should proceed slowly but steadily. Slow and brief introduction helps expose people to new concepts and helps eliminate unnecessary doubts about the program. However, if one starts big—publicizes all over yet does not provide the necessary support—one may face grave consequences. There will be little chance to start something similar again in the future.

Be open and positive   Quality circle programs need to be open. Information should be available to everyone. Ups and downs always exist in this type of program, but one should keep a warm spirit and high aspirations.

Copy wisely

Lloyd Dobyns[3] commented on NBC's White Papers presentation, "If Japan Can, Why Can't We?" In his words, "copying won't work, we are two different societies." This may create doubts in people's minds about the viability of a quality circle program in the United States or in any other country.

It is important for the world to understand the basic concepts behind successful quality circle programs such as statistics, group dynamics and other aspects. One should then change and modify these aspects to suit individual needs. Moreover, the quality circle concept is based on a "people-building philosophy," and since basic motives of recognition and self-fulfillment exist in all human beings, copying should work anywhere if done properly.

It would be appropriate to mention Lloyd Dobyns' remark: "All humans think and nowhere is it chiseled in stone that those in management think best." Some form of the quality circle should work anywhere in the world.

Conclusion

It is reported that more than ten million people participate in quality circle programs in Japan, contributing 20 to 25 billion dollars of savings per year. These programs are successful for three major reasons: use of basic statistics, job satisfaction or job enrichment and group problem-solving activities.

Dr. Ishikawa, a well-known authority on quality circles from Japan, said, "Quality circle activities are rapidly growing in many countries such as Taiwan, the United States, Mexico, Brazil, Thailand, Malaysia, the Netherlands, Belgium, Denmark and the United Kingdom. Judging from the common acceptance of the quality circle concept, I am convinced that quality circle activities have no socio-economic or cultural limitations. Human beings are human beings wherever they live, and quality circle activities can be disseminated and implemented anywhere in the world for human benefit."

1. Mercury Marine, Fond Du Lac, Wisc.
2. The 1980 Employee Annual Report, Brunswick Corp.
3. "If Japan Can, Why Can't We?" NBC Special Report.

An Overview of Useful Quality Circle Techniques

W. Maureen Godsey

Here is a brief overview of some techniques used by quality circle leaders and members in their efforts to analyze and solve problems. Reviewing these techniques will help you:

1. Understand better what members of a quality circle actually do during their meetings;
2. Appreciate how foreign these techniques may be at first for many circle members;
3. Be prepared when members of a quality circle make a presentation to you for your management group.

Problem solving techniques

This section discusses three problem solving techniques frequently used by quality circles: brainstorming, cause and effect analysis; and Pareto analysis.

Brainstorming Brainstorming is a technique for generating the greatest number of possible solutions to a problem for further development and evaluation. The technique involves a group of people using their collective thinking power to create ideas. It works because each person's ideas stimulate the others, which may stimulate even more ideas. Brainstorming isn't a "bull" session, mindless free-for-all, or waste of time. It is one important step in a systematic approach to problem solving. Brainstorming is most effective when individual thinking has not or does not seem likely to produce

Reprinted with permission from: W. Maureen Godsey, *Employee Involvement: A Local Government Approach to Quality Circles* (Washington, D.C.: International City Management Association, 1982), appendix A.

satisfactory results on a problem which has not been resolved through existing methods.

An effective brainstorming session requires that everyone clearly understands the problem, feels comfortable and relaxed, and is given an equal chance to participate. There are four basic ground rules for brainstorming:

1. Criticism and evaluation of ideas isn't allowed until all possible approaches have been generated. It is difficult to be creative and critical simultaneously.
2. Free wheeling, far-out thinking is welcomed—the wilder the ideas, the better. Unusual, seemingly impractical suggestions may lead to a solid practical solution which otherwise might not have occurred to anyone.
3. Quantity of potential solutions is encouraged—the more suggestions, the better. Creative quantity increases the likelihood of developing workable solutions.
4. Improvement and expansion of ideas is encouraged—to change, improve on, expand, or combine ideas already listed in order to lead to more ideas.

All ideas generated by the group should be recorded—again without any criticism or evaluation. One way to encourage participation in a brainstorming session is to ask members to take turns contributing one idea each. If nothing comes to mind, individuals can pass on one or more rounds. When members run out of ideas, ideally, the group should wait some time (a week or two if possible) before analyzing all the possibilities. This allows an "incubation" period to give members a chance to think of a few more ideas before beginning the analysis.

Cause and effect analysis   Cause and effect analysis is used to find out what specifically is responsible for a problem the circle is trying to solve. It is also called "fishbone diagramming," or "4-M analysis." Cause and effect analysis allows the circle to review all possible causes of a problem in a systematic and analytical manner. Figure 1 divides all contributing causes of the problem into simple categories and then shows their relationship to the problem. There are four major causes of most problems—machines, methods, manpower, and materials—but others can be examined if they seem to fit the problem.

After deciding what are the major causal areas affecting the problem, circle members begin to brainstorm on *specific causes* within these categories. For example, under the manpower category, specific problems might be lack of adequate training or high absenteeism. The rules for brainstorming described in the previous section should be followed to make sure no ideas are criticized, elim-

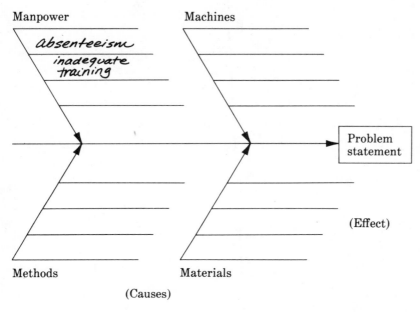

Manpower   Machines

absenteeism

inadequate training

Problem statement

(Effect)

Methods   Materials

(Causes)

Figure 1. Cause and effect analysis.

inated, or selected as the "right" one until all possible alternatives have been generated.

After the brainstorming process is completed, circle members should vote on which cause(s) seem most likely or most significant. The circle should then test the selected idea(s) to see if it is actually causing the problem.

Pareto analysis   Pareto analysis is a method for helping group members make decisions. Also known as the "80-20 rule," it is a decision making process that attempts to eliminate the "major few from the trivial many." Pareto analysis is based on the assumption that 80 per cent of all problems in the work place are caused by 20 per cent of the work. By focusing on the 20 per cent, the greatest gains can be made in eliminating what troubles work places.

Pareto analysis uses a charting system to record data on the frequencies of problems (e.g., how often patrol cars come in for repairs), or recurring equipment malfunctions (e.g., copying machines that don't work). In order to use this method effectively, circle members will have to decide what type of data they need to collect for what time period. This information is collected on a check sheet. For example, if circle members are examining why patrol cars are

Month:						
	Week 1	Week 2	Week 3	Week 4	Week 5	Total
Cause 1	𝈗𝈗	//	/	///	//	13
Cause 2	///	𝈗𝈗 𝈗𝈗	𝈗𝈗 ///	𝈗𝈗 ////	////	34
Cause 3	//	///	//	//	/	10
Cause 4	𝈗𝈗	/	///	/	//	12
Cause 5	//	/	/		//	6
TOTAL	17	17	15	15	//	75

Figure 2. Sample check sheet.

breaking down, they would first brainstorm on possible causes and then select the five most likely culprits. Using a check sheet like the one shown in Figure 2, circle members would collect data on patrol car breakdowns for an established time period—in this case, for one month. The information from the check sheet is used to construct a Pareto chart, shown in Figure 3. The chart shows the columns in descending order. This kind of systematic analysis gives clear guidance to circle members on which causes seem to warrant follow-up study first. A second Pareto chart should be constructed after the circle implements a step to reduce the cause of the problem to make sure there is a noticeable improvement.

While these three techniques are the building blocks of quality circles problem solving activities, there are many other more advanced approaches that can be drawn from the fields of statistics and industrial engineering. Once circle members become comfortable with and adept at using these basic approaches, the circle leader might want to learn about and introduce some more advanced approaches.

Group presentation techniques

Another important type of technique quality circles will need to learn about and practice using are methods for making presentations to management. Members can work together to learn how to

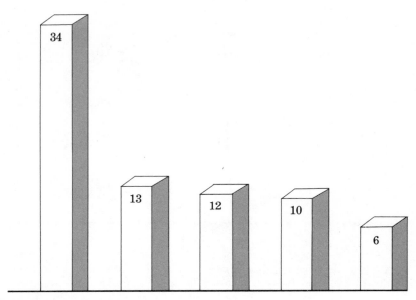

Figure 3. Pareto chart.

use flip charts to present ideas, how to develop other appropriate and simple audio visual aids (overhead transparencies, graphs, slides), and handouts. Circle members will also need help organizing material, speaking clearly, handling questions on the spot, and generally feeling (and looking) comfortable in what can be a new and often scary situation.

Group dynamics techniques

Training in group dynamics should also be strongly considered for circle leaders. Leading a group through a variety of group activities to reach some end is difficult without some coaching or training in situations like:

1. Handling strong differences of opinion;
2. Managing domination by one or two group members;
3. Encouraging contributions from the less dominant, quiet members;
4. Keeping on track despite frequent arguing among group members.

There are many group process techniques for handling situations like these without hurting feelings or discouraging participation. And it's important for the success of a quality circle that the group leader be familiar with these techniques *before* the leader is standing up in front of the group for the first time.

Case Studies of Employee Involvement Programs

The following case studies illustrate how quality circles have been utilized in Dallas, Texas, and Fort Collins, Colorado. Both are from reports published by the cities involved.

Quality circles in Dallas

The 1981-82 management plan prepared by Dallas, Texas, city manager Charles S. Anderson describes four objectives for providing efficient and quality services at a low cost and for utilizing the creativity and resourcefulness of the city's employees. These are: (1) to improve productivity, effectiveness, and responsiveness in the delivery of city services, (2) to improve the affirmative action and equal employment opportunities for minorities and women in recruitment and employment, (3) to improve the long-range planning process, and (4) to increase employee participation in the development and achievement of organizational goals.

One of the methods that the city of Dallas has used to accomplish these objectives is the development of a comprehensive quality circle program. According to productivity/management analysis supervisor Bob Winslow and quality circle facilitator James Mongaras, "quality circles, a method of utilizing worker brainpower" are prospering in Dallas.

Dallas began investigating the quality circle concept in November 1980. By March 1981, an outside consultant had been selected to assist the city in the development of a quality circle program. By May 1981, ten team leaders had received training in quality circle

Reprinted with permission from: W. Maureen Godsey, *Employee Involvement: A Local Government Approach to Quality Circles* (Washington, D.C.: International City Management Association, 1982), appendix B.

techniques and by June 1981, quality circle teams began meeting throughout the city.

The program has now expanded and there are plans to open the program to all city departments shortly. Currently, the departments in Dallas that have ongoing quality circles are the convention center, data services, equipment services, housing and urban rehabilitation, management services, parks and recreation, police, and water.

The quality circle teams in Dallas meet once a week for one hour. With one exception, the circles meet during regular working hours. For the exception, the participants receive one hour of overtime pay.

Quality circles provide an avenue of communication from the people who have actually performed the job to management of the city. The employees have the opportunity to describe those obstacles that get in the way of their performing their jobs and that make their jobs more difficult. The next step is to analyze those problems, find out what is the cause of them, and make recommendations to management about how best to solve the problems. If management approves, the employees do the actual implementation and monitoring of their recommended solutions.

Some of the problems that have been identified and solved by the quality circle teams in Dallas include:

Housing and urban rehabilitation   This quality circle decided to tackle the procedural problem of rewriting notices of violation for each individual unit in apartment complexes. The team recommended that a cover letter be developed that eliminates the rewriting of the notices. The new procedure costs far less and will accomplish the same goal.

Convention center operations   This quality circle decided to work on the problem of misplaced or lost supplies. When supplies such as mops, brooms, and dustpans were issued to contract laborers from the storerooms there were no procedures established to keep track of these items once they were checked out. This resulted in an inadequate supply of necessary supplies and high replacement costs. The quality circle decided to develop a check-out and follow-up procedure for these supplies. To date, the system has worked flawlessly.

Police: Southwest Patrol   Police officers at Southwest Patrol realized that when they had to cover another officer's beat, they were not familiar with the beat and didn't know who the at-large criminals were, the buildings and alarm systems, and other things. To aid the officers, the Southwest Patrol developed a comprehensive crime and information book that is used to identify the criminals on a particular beat, to describe buildings, alarms, hot-spots, and the like. The officers see this as a tremendous aid in the prevention of crime and the apprehension of criminals.

Although Dallas' quality circle program has only been operational since June 1981, it has proved that quality circles can and do work in a municipal government environment. Not only is the cost of producing city services being reduced by operating in a more efficient manner, but other aspects of job functions are being analyzed as well. Factors such as machine down-time, absenteeism, tardiness, and sick leave are beginning to be reduced as a result of the action of the quality circle teams. This also increases morale of the work group because people now know that they do participate in the decisions being made about how their jobs are done, and they are responsible for making their solutions work. In addition, communication between workers and management has been enhanced and strengthened. Employees are given access to more information, thereby allowing them to learn more about the total operation of the department. Management has the opportunity to learn from the employees exactly what is occurring on a day-to-day basis, which can and does influence their managerial decisions.

Quality circles in Fort Collins

Fort Collins, Colorado, city manager John Arnold and his staff formed their first quality circle with the city's automotive mechanics in October 1978.

At the beginning of the project, the equipment superintendent and service manager identified several concerns as follows:

1. Mechanics were not accounting for eight hours on their daily time cards.
2. When one job was complete, mechanics would not always ask for the next job.
3. Mechanics were wary of management attempts to discuss their productivity.
4. The shop workload was difficult to predict and was uneven.
5. Mechanics were not held immediately accountable for "unfixed problems."
6. Mechanic position classifications no longer reflected actual work responsibility.

In addition, other city departments had been expressing concerns about the seemingly poor service and high cost of the equipment operation.

The mechanics also listed a number of factors they would require to be more productive.

1. Faster parts delivery and better work scheduling.
2. Better explanations of mechanical problems by user departments.
3. More information sharing with management and better relations with other departments.
4. Better and more specialized tools and better training.
5. Monetary and nonmonetary incentives.

The advantages and disadvantages of utilizing quality circles were believed to be:

Advantages
1. Mechanics would have a commitment to any changes.
2. The incentive program would be meaningful to the mechanics.
3. Mechanics would have a better understanding of the equipment operation.
4. Productivity potential and willingness on the part of mechanics to implement measurement systems.
5. Establishment of a system for researching future problems.
6. Formation of a more cohesive work group.

Disadvantage   The main disadvantage was the commitment of two hours per week for all mechanics and parts employees for a period of three to six months. In addition, management was required to assist mechanics by providing direction and by sharing information. Management was also reminded that they would need to commit to listening to and giving serious consideration to group suggestions.

The initial quality circle was formed and began operations with training on problem solving, group dynamics, and data analysis plus additional information, and division goals and objectives. This training lasted for a period of four weeks. The mechanics were now ready to apply their training to solving the previously identified problems. To assure that they had accurately identified the problems, they collected data from work requests and repair records, and surveyed user departments. Improvements were then made in various equipment repair and maintenance operations. As a result of the quality circles efforts, savings documented through April 15, 1981, were in excess of $33,000, half of which will be available in monetary incentives for the members of the quality circle. Other efficiency improvements were also made.

Internal changes
1. Mechanics have been assigned to perform work for specific departments.

2. A new service request form is being used to improve communication and to track specific repairs.
3. Departments are receiving copies of work orders with related costs identified.
4. The Service Writer position has been formally identified as a contact for mechanics to receive work assignments.
5. Needed tools for equipment have been ordered.
6. One auto service worker and one mechanic position have been eliminated through attrition.

External changes
1. Some departments have begun to assign operators to specific pieces of equipment, thereby increasing the operator's sense of ownership and reducing repair time.
2. Departments now know who to contact for scheduling work, for emergency repairs, complaints, or praise.
3. Departments can now decide on repair priorities for their equipment when they have multiple pieces of equipment in the shop.
4. Mechanics make recommendations to departments on ways to reduce fuel consumption, maintenance, overall equipment conditions, minor repairs that operators could make, etc.

Work environment changes
1. Mechanics' morale has improved. They now feel free to make suggestions and provide backup data.
2. Management support is perceived by the mechanics.
3. Mechanics have a better understanding of equipment fund revenues and expenditures and how their work affects both.
4. Communication with other city departments has improved.
5. A methodology for measuring productivity and effectiveness has been implemented.
6. An incentive pay plan for the mechanics was developed, approved by the management and implemented.

When the quality circle operation began, one mechanic said that this was the first time he had been asked to "use his brain" instead of being "just two hands on the end of a wrench." At this point, all members of the quality circle are using analytical skills and making sound recommendations regarding improving the shop operations.

As a result of the success achieved in the mechanics' quality circle, the city has now begun quality circles in parks, streets, traffic maintenance, and with clerical support groups.

Assisting Employees with Personal Problems

William G. Wagner

Helping employees with personal problems can bring about incredible success in improving productivity and reducing costs. This bonanza can be mined at pennies on the dollar through an employee assistance program. And whether they work for the ABC Corp. or City of Utopia, with today's emphasis on increased production as a means of survival for government as well as the private sector, employee assistance programs (EAPs) deserve a closer look. One such program, Project Concern, has been operated by the City of Phoenix since 1974.

What are the savings?

In 1980 Project Concern counselled about 1,130 of the city's approximately 8,700 employees. The program has a 50 percent success ratio, resulting in returning about 565 of the participants to full productivity. It has been said that a troubled employee costs at least 25 percent of his salary and the average annual salary of City of Phoenix employees is $17,322. Thus, the worth of the EAP program to Phoenix is equal to 565 × 25 percent of $17,322, which comes to $2,447,000 annually.

Without the program, troubled employees could have cost the taxpayers an estimated $6.4 million last year. The $2.4 million saved represents a handsome return on an annual investment of $58,200 to operate Project Concern.

No attempt has been made to place a dollar amount on the improvement in work output that has resulted. However, those who

Reprinted from the November 1982 issue of *Personnel Administrator*, copyright, 1982, The American Society for Personnel Administration, 30 Park Drive, Berea, Ohio 44017, $30 per year.

are involved in the EAP can look back with satisfaction upon improved merit reviews and promotions which tell the story. These were people whose personal problems had degraded job performance to the point where their jobs were on the line.

You can apply the formula to estimate the costs due to troubled employees and the potential cost savings of an EAP for your organization. Simply divide the average total number of employees into your annual payroll to derive the average employee wage. Multiply the average annual wage by 17 percent of your total employees (statistical average of troubled employees) to obtain the payroll for troubled employees.

Next, take 25 percent of the troubled employee payroll to obtain your present loss due to troubled employees. Finally, take 50 percent of this loss to identify the amount you could save through an EAP.

Beginning the program

The city of Phoenix was fortunate in having personnel staff in the training division with big ears and small mouths for many years. This included an analyst with a background in counseling and more than 15 years of experience in employee problems. Employees learned they could air their problems in confidence and management learned to take corrective action before work problems became serious. With growth of the employee family from 1,500 in 1956 to 6,333 in 1973 came the need to expand the use of counseling and use a more formal approach.

As a beginning, the city council contracted a human resource group to provide free counseling for city employees and their dependents. The training division, however, continued in parallel to provide its "big ears" to clients who were more at ease with the internal staff. Statistics collected during the ensuing year indicated employees sought help from the in-house staff persons more often than they chose to contact the outside group. It cost $62 per employee to visit the consultants and only $37 to use the in-house staff as counselors.

For these reasons, the consultant contract was terminated in June 1974 and the city formalized its in-house counseling program. Project Concern was introduced by a letter, which announced the availability of counseling assistance to the employees and their dependents, sent to the homes of full-time city employees. The personnel analyst who provided the service in the past was not titled personnel counselor and his emphasis shifted from training to counseling.

Housing the counseling program in the training division provides several assets to the counseling program. A large number of employees visit the training division for a variety of reasons, thus providing counselees with a certain amount of anonymity. Also, the counselor is somewhat protected from the negative aspect of counseling—burnout. The burnout syndrome, created by continuous work with depressed and troubled employees, is lessened by providing the counselor with an opportunity for some change of pace in the form of training assignments.

How the Phoenix program is different

The primary difference between the City of Phoenix EAP and most others is that it offers in-depth, one-to-one counseling and is not predominantly a referral service. Though this requires a greater counselor expertise over a broad span of areas, i.e., job, marital, family, financial, consumerism, health, alcoholism, drug, preretirement and career, it provides a sense of security in that the employee-client is not given a quick diagnosis only to be sent to an outside community source. In addition, it permits follow-up counseling sessions, which are imperative to successful therapy, and it's the counselor who schedules these sessions.

The follow-up sessions can be more easily controlled and the client is more apt to feel his employer is showing a greater concern when the attention to the problem is addressed in-house. The exceptions are serious substance abuse and medical problems. In these cases Alcoholics Anonymous, health maintenance organizations and city physicians serve as the referral sources.

Who seeks help?

Employee use of Project Concern is shown in Figure 1. Approximately 60 percent of the employees aided by Project Concern are referred by supervisors. These referrals are generally related to some change in employee work output. The other 40 percent are em-

Fiscal year	Counseling sessions (includes repeat sesions)
1974-75	654
75-76	877
76-77	1,087
77-78	1,222
78-79	1,187[1]
79-80	2,121[2]
80-81	1,432[3]
81-82	1,232

[1]Decreased due to the retirement of the division head who did part-time counseling.
[2]A second full-time counselor was hired.
[3]Staff reduced to one counselor due to economic conditions.

Figure 1.

Job related	42%
Alcohol-drug	21%
Marital	12%
Family	10%
Financial	4%
Health	3%
Miscellaneous	8%

Figure 2. Counseling requests.

ployees who are concerned enough about their problems to voluntarily seek the aid of Project Concern counselors.

Total use is reflected in the breakdown of counseling contacts by type of problem, as shown in Figure 2. Resolution of any of these job-related or personal problems greatly affects the production of the individual employee and frequently the production of other employees in the work group.

Each month's statistics disclose that job-related problems predominate over problems involving alcohol, drugs, marital, health, family or financial concerns.

Referrals are made as the result of an employee's excessive absenteeism and use of sick leave, poor production, inability to work with others or negative attitudes. Typically, those seeking counseling on their own are experiencing job dissatisfaction. The boss is prejudiced or too autocratic or it's a dead-end position.

The advantages

Counseling provides employees the opportunity to: "be heard," "get it off their chest," "have someone who will listen." The counselor frequently pursues a non-directive tack in helping the employee gain insight into his problem and come up with alternative solutions. However, depending on individual circumstances the counselor must be more direct and spell out alternative courses of action at times.

If the employee wants the counselor to relay information or to act as a third person in settling a disagreement, he signs a release which gives the counselor the right to disclose information gained through a confidential interview. Often job troubles can be traced to a domestic problem and once that's addressed, the work situation clears up.

Project Concern did not evolve from an alcoholism counseling program. Therefore, it hasn't suffered the negative stigma that is often associated with alcohol counseling programs. Project Concern is more of a broad-brush approach to employee assistance. This is not to downgrade the importance of alcoholism rehabilitation, but to emphasize that many different problems affect the employee on the job.

Alcoholism

The higher degree of success attained by EAPs in the field of alcoholic rehabilitation as compared to community alcohol treatment sources is the "clout of the job." This belief is substantiated in Project Concern statistics. Seventy-five percent of those employees who are in jeopardy of losing their jobs due to alcoholism, but who agree to and follow through on the City of Phoenix program for rehabilitation, are still employed one year later. These employees are usually also the recipients of improved performance ratings.

In a typical situation an employee is referred to counseling by his supervisor because of a Friday-Monday absence pattern coupled with tardies and a poor production record (job in jeopardy). It is only after the subject of drinking surfaces in the interview as the result of selective probing that the counselor zeros in on the problem. A short 26 yes-no quiz is read to the employee and the results indicate if alcohol is a problem and to what degree. Through this test, the employee rates whether he has an alcohol problem and to what extent, not the counselor.

If the employee identifies an alcohol problem, the counselor devotes 45 minutes explaining alcoholism—a disease. During this presentation, oftentimes the employee reveals many aspects of his years of progressive drinking. Finally, the counselor confronts the alcoholic with, "Do you want to do something about your alcoholism?" If the answer is no, the employee is on his own regarding his job future; however, the counselor's door is always open if he later decides he want rehabilitation. If the answer is yes, the concept of Alcoholics Anonymous (AA) is explained.

The next step is crucial and determines the success of his rehabilitation. It is matching the employee to the most compatible AA groups. In a metropolitan area such as Phoenix, there are approximately 25 AA meetings daily. The counselor's task is to provide meetings that fit the client's social, ethnic and economic background while considering the travel time required by the client.

Attendance at five meetings per week is required. The client reports to the counselor after the first scheduled meeting to provide feedback on reaction, for evaluation and to clarify any questions as to AA's purpose and format. Soon the employee looks forward to Monday's meeting and the new friends associated with it. On Tuesday it's another meeting with more non-drinking friends substituting for old drinking buddies.

Each week the alcoholic has a counseling session and progress is closely monitored. The counselor's role is to be supportive during these first few months. As sobriety continues, attendance at AA is gradually reduced but never eliminated. In Project Concern one year's sobriety is considered a fair measure of success.

An approach similar to the AA program is very successful for rehabilitation of drug dependent persons. However, drug dependency is not as significant a problem in the Phoenix city employee population.

Sick leave and stress

Another benefit to be derived from an EAP is reduction in sick leave use. The supervisor having little success with the chronic sick leave abuser can refer him to the EAP for more in-depth counseling. At this time the employee is informed that his abnormal number of days off is of serious concern justifying the referral. The counselor is in a better position to probe and often learns that the real reason for the absences is job boredom, personality conflict with peers or supervisors or home problems. Once the cause is established, it can be dealt with through counseling with a high potential for success.

Stress management, as important as it is today, can also be addressed via EAPs. It provides an excellent vehicle to increase productivity and job satisfaction in our highly complex work and community environment. Providing employees a relief valve to vent frustrations and reduce stress is a basic concept of an employee assistance program.

Financial counseling

Inflation has increased the need for financial counseling. The incidence of overspending has risen. As a result, garnishments have greatly increased, which in turn cause harassment from creditors and result in preoccupation on the job with debt problems.

Project Concern provides an opportunity for a thorough analysis of the income-outgo of the employee with the goal of learning where the budget imbalance lies. If savings can be accomplished by more prudent grocery buying, the grocery ads are studied with the employee and spouse and loss-leader buying is explained.

Purchase of a large ticket item such as an automobile can be aided when the counselor can help clarify the automotive need and then contact the repossession departments of local banks. The savings are significant on the auto purchase compared to prices on a used car lot. The credit union interest rate that often can be arranged provides still greater savings.

In the case of a laborer referral who was continually late for work due to car trouble, Project Concern devised a unique solution. He was a good worker whom the foreman wanted to save from discharge. During counseling it became apparent that his old car was continually breaking down and was costing an inordinate amount for repairs only to have still another breakdown.

Review of his full financial picture indicated he could not purchase a better car. Since he lived only four miles from his job site and was in good health, a ten-speed bike was suggested. He couldn't afford a new one, but the classified ads yielded a good serviceable 10-speed for $40. The worker hasn't been late since he got the bike.

Marital troubles

Project Concern's approach to marital and family counseling is to provide the concerned employee and spouse an opportunity to relate their feelings individually and weigh the options of living together *vs.* divorce. Since this decision is serious, often two or three counseling sessions are required for each person to consider all of the ramifications and at the same time evaluate their true feelings. After the decision is reached, the counselor's role is to provide joint sessions on restructuring their marriage or on providing legal referral for separation.

Supervisor as counselor

A survey of supervisory training needs revealed a strong interest in counseling procedures. Project Concern counselors have developed an eight-hour course, "The Supervisor as Counselor," devoted to basic counseling skills. Topics covered are: helping relationships, interpersonal inventory, ice breaking, active listening skills and nonverbal communication. The course acquaints supervisors with what actually goes on when they refer an employee to Project Concern. They also are better able to spot dysfunctional employee behavior and make early referrals.

The question often arises as to where the counselors in an EAP go for their own counseling needs or who counsels the counselors. Employees Assistance Resources of Arizona was formed to support practitioners in the field as well as to promote the EAP concept. Presently there are 17 local organizations sharing this type of professionalism through monthly meetings with guest presenters and discussion topics.

An argument for EAPs

Any organization depletes manpower, its most valuable asset, if it chooses to ignore or terminate low or non-producing employees instead of recognizing them as human beings with problems and assisting in solving their problems as a matter of enlightened self-interest. Municipal tax dollars are coming under close scrutiny and escalating costs have forced many companies to battle to improve productivity if they are to survive. For these reasons, both government and the private sector should carefully consider an employee assistance program.

After all, you wouldn't tear down a somewhat defective, but basically sound building or throw away investment in a capital intensive machine, if you could rebuild either to greater productivity for a small portion of the replacement cost. So, why do we discard our investment in troubled personnel, when for a fraction of the recruiting and training cost we can refurbish existing good people by helping them with personal problems? An EAP is not only cost efficient, it's a humanitarian need in these troubled times.

PART 4

New
Labor-Management
Ventures

Concession Bargaining: The Time Is Now

John W. Falahee

The wage-price spiral that has plagued the American economy for decades is coming to an end. Unions and their membership are listening and yielding to economic realities. Everybody is responding —automotive original equipment manufacturers, suppliers, trucking companies, airlines, the retail food industry, etc. In light of the happenings in industry today, all employers should ask themselves these hard questions: Why not my business? Am I passing a golden opportunity?

This article examines the process of concession bargaining and its likely outcomes. This type of negotiating, though not essentially different from normal collective bargaining, has some special considerations and techniques. The process includes establishing the rationale for reopening the current agreement, timing, special proposals, union concerns and areas for mutual agreement.

Why bargain?

The essence of successful concession bargaining is the development of mutual trust and respect by the parties involved. The company has to be the moving party in the negotiations and this role reversal must be understood and appreciated to begin the process. In this instance the company makes demands and the union counterproposes. The union has to be convinced of the need to give up what it's gained through years of difficult contract negotiations. The current agreement is a living document and can be changed.

The first step in bringing about concessions is to examine carefully and realistically why the company must have concessions. The most basic reason is the survival of the business. If this is demonstrated convincingly, the bargaining task is made more simple, but it still must be done correctly to maximize gains. Proving the need for concessions takes many forms: lay-offs, personnel reductions and temporary shutdowns; documented customer pressure asking for price concessions; and/or documented loss of contracts or business because of price.

Obviously, losing money is the ultimate proof. If this is your tactic, be prepared to open your books. Fear, distrust, exposure of pricing policy and family secrets and simple reluctance always well up in any manager's mind when faced with this union demand. In reality, these concerns aren't pertinent. The usual method is to agree on an objective third-party professional accountant to verify the economic condition of the company since the union committee isn't qualified for this task and shouldn't be allowed to see the details.

Financial objectives should be kept in mind

Preparation of a complete proposal is important. The first requisite is to determine, through the financial analysis of lost bid proposals, the amount of economic relief needed to obtain profitable business and stabilize employment. Always keep this overall financial objective in mind and make it an integral part of your initial proposal. How the company and the union finally agree to arrive at the full number can vary. The company must remain flexible and open to union suggestions. The total objective must be realized and the pieces or way to get there shouldn't be controlling.

Analyze the present agreement clause by clause to generate cost saving proposals. Generally, elimination of pay for time not worked is more palatable to employees than outright wage reductions. Contract provisions to be especially studied for this type of relief are:

Vacation pay Lengthening service or work time requirements and shortening length of time off are usually acceptable.

Holiday pay Elimination of paid personal holidays or lowering the number of general days granted generates savings and more production time with fewer employees.

Break periods Eliminate or shorten rest periods and wash-up time to produce relief but not in direct ratio to minutes saved. Productive output is more often merely spread over the extra time.

Breaks are very necessary in some operations, so approach proposals in this area cautiously.

Non-productive down time and classification inflexibility   Propose work be done for all time paid so a productive effort is given even when the standard job is not operating because of irregularities. This can eliminate indirect labor costs in custodial or quality control areas.

Pension benefits   This is a complex area. There are real cash flow benefits to be realized from changing assumptions and delaying or postponing contributions. Changing from a defined benefit plan to defined contributions or, even better, a profit sharing plan, will shift the costs to more profitable times and not hold corporate assets hostage.

Insurance program   Benefit amount, timing and deductibles can be changed to save considerable costs in this area. Pay particular attention to health, medical, sickness and accident coverages, which are most costly. Pay for extended coverage on layoff, leave of absence and retirement can be eliminated or paid by employees. Preserve flexibility to change carriers to obtain premium reductions.

Seniority provisions   Streamline bidding and bumping procedures to eliminate excessive turmoil and retraining. Ensure assignment of qualified, experienced personnel to jobs to maintain peak efficiency.

Overtime assignment   Provide for only qualified people to work and eliminate unnecessary make-work assignments.

Bonus payments   Eliminate or reduce extra payments.

Wages   Consider eliminating or suspending future increases and cost-of-living allowances. If this doesn't achieve your economic objective, propose a wage reduction. Reductions of over $1 per hour have been approved in many companies.

Negotiations
The timing and length of the actual negotiations vary with the local situation; however, concession negotiations are rarely as long or arduous as normal negotiations. Usually an intense period of a week to 10 days is all that is required. Request a meeting with the union to discuss the overall economic condition of the company. During this meeting demand a reopening of the contract and present your total proposal. Give the union time to thoroughly study the proposal and

your reasons for them. Emphasize the urgency of need and welcome their ideas and approaches to solving the problems. Problem-solving, not prerogative or confrontational bargaining, must be initiated. Joint respect and cooperation are key. Both parties must keep the rank and file members informed so ratification of the new pact is assured.

The union must respond even if it declines renegotiation of the contract. It must then accept the responsibility for jobs lost or operation shutdown. Most likely, the negotiations will commence tentatively to reach an agreement. The union will look for job guarantees, equality of sacrifice by the officers and non-union employees (a reasonable request if the entire organization is to survive). Profit-sharing will be high on the union's list so the good is shared with the bad. The company negotiators must remain flexible and open to other solutions. The total economic objective is important, not the details or specific elements of the package.

Many creative and extraordinary solutions to economic recovery have been negotiated. Besides profit-sharing and specific job guarantees, new and innovative savings plans are now in place. Concessions in all areas of wages and benefits, as well as elimination of restrictive contract clauses have been won. Guard against reopeners and try to provide profit level triggers to improve or restore benefits when economically feasible.

There is no risk to concession bargaining when properly conducted. The result of failure is that your current agreement continues. Any improvement from that is a gain. The least gain is to learn the real concerns of the work force and whether there is any solution to the economic problem other than liquidation of the company. That, in itself, might be a real plus. Prepare carefully and be rewarded with a cooperative, resourceful work force building a stronger, more stable business.

Employee Bargaining in Hard Times

John Liebert

Let's start with an obvious proposition: we are in the midst of a recession. And we are in the midst of a conservative, political philosophy and atmosphere. Witness the anti-strike initiatives enacted by the voters in Los Angeles and in other jurisdictions.

This prevailing economic reality and political atmosphere also make it a period of opportunities from a bargaining point of view.

In bargaining settlements in the private sector, in the rubber, airline, auto, and trucking industries employees are making concessions and unions are making well publicized concessions. All of a sudden, after talking about 12, 14 and 10 percent increases in the consumer price index (CPI), we are now looking at increases of below 3 percent.

What does this add up to? Very realistically, there is a relatively lower factor of political power sitting on the union side of the table right now. And, whether or not an admission is made at the bargaining table, employees' level of expectation has been lowered by all this. These are the realities facing cities as they seek to contain or cut personnel costs and get the maximum mileage out of the benefit dollar.

Are you really broke?
Let's divide local governments into two categories. Category one is the cities that are broke. They really don't have any money. They are in a deficit situation. Their reserves are being depleted. They are really in bad shape, and in their case today's circumstances are not so much an opportunity as absolute necessity.

The second category applies to every other agency. They need to

Reprinted with permission from the February 1983 issue of *Western City* magazine, the official publication of the League of California Cities.

stem the tide of rapidly escalating personnel costs that have risen over the past several years.

If you think, as the financial manager of your agency, that you indeed have no money, are in a deficit situation, and absolutely must cut your personnel costs, there is one preliminary piece of advice I'd like to give you: as the chief financial manager of your agency, you had better be prepared to prove it. That kind of approach should not be used for bargaining purposes if, in fact, it is not the case.

There are two reasons for avoiding this posture. When the employer asserts he cannot provide any benefits, or if the employer's position is to cut benefits because there is no money, in labor relations parlance because of "inability to pay," a legal right is created for the union to examine your books to the extent they desire. It also creates the obvious issue of bargaining budget priorities, something that you obviously want to avoid at the bargaining table if you possibly can.

Secondly, if you assert that kind of position, but cannot reasonably convince the other side that your position is based on fact, it's very destructive of the employer-employee relationship and will hurt you more in the long run than it might help you in the short run. If your agency really is in that kind of situation, the chief financial manager should be prepared to provide some good hard data to confirm it. If you are in that situation, your objective is to reduce costs right now. You are in the position of a General Motors or a Ford, where you need to immediately effectuate savings. How do you do that?

Long before you get to the bargaining table, set the climate with your budget hearings, and by passing the word publicly and through communications to employees describing the dire financial condition of your agency. In other words, get your employees into the frame of mind where they realize how tough things are. They should realize that when they go to that "meet and confer" table, it will not be a matter of negotiating anything significant in the way of benefit increases.

At the bargaining table, you will do what some private sector employers have been doing: Seeking to balance a package that will consist of a reduction of work hours, either through attrition, layoffs or reductions of the paid work week. These approaches will be combined with at least a "hold the line" position on wages, either a zero increase in wages, a pull back, or perhaps more commonly a delay in wage adjustments. That is what has happened in private sector collective bargaining situations, where the Ford Motor Company agreement delays wage increases previously negotiated, particularly cost of living escalator increases. This could be combined with an effort to cut fringe benefit costs. This so-called "concession bargaining" with the union is the private model that will be used more and more in the public sector.

Concession bargaining

Don't be oversold about what has gone on in the private sector, however. It is true that in the auto, airline, trucking, rubber, and one or two other industries there has been concession bargaining. Adding up all collective bargaining agreements that have been negotiated during this past year, the average first year wage increase was not much more than 2 percent. But if the collective bargaining agreements in the above industries are taken out, the figure jumps to in excess of 7 percent. That figure shows how much influence those few industries have had overall.

Remember that in all cases of concession bargaining, the employer also made concessions. In return for the employees giving up wage and benefit increases, the employer gave tenure rights far beyond any that existed before, including some cases of lifetime tenure. In some agreements, what amounts to profit sharing commitments were made by the employer. It was not a total one-way street.

Schools this year have negotiated some zero percent increases. Schools, of course, are almost totally dependent on funding from the state, and the employees are aware that there simply isn't any money.

In one school district, a multi-year agreement provided for wage increases in the second and third year with a formula that tied wage increases to the increase of funding from the state. There is no increase in funding from the state, so the result is a zero agreement.

The Santa Barbara school district negotiated a 3 percent increase in wages in return for a substantial increase in the number of teaching days per year to allow the employer to reduce staffing.

Cities needing to cut costs must recognize they will get non-economic demands on the table. For example, agency shop was authorized as an allowable subject of bargaining in 1982. All employees in a unit are obligated to join the union and pay dues or a service fee for the representation services provided by the organization. It's a major item to many of the organizations, and they're going to push hard to get that kind of a concession if you cannot negotiate anything in the benefit area.

Another obvious non-economic item is binding arbitration of grievances, which they will push very hard.

More bang for the buck

Perhaps the goal of your city is not so much immediate cuts as to stem the tide, to put a lid on escalating personnel costs over the long term. How can you get more bang out of those wage bucks? How do you apply your limited dollars so they pay the greatest dividend in terms of employee morale and satisfaction?

One thing to consider is giving a wage increase that does not become part of your wage schedule—a bonus payment. Rather than increase the wage schedule, you give a wage increase without a commitment to forevermore continue to pay that higher level of salaries. The disadvantage to this approach is that your wage scales will tend to become less competitive. If you continue to do it, you can become terribly uncompetitive. You might want to consider folding a bonus into the wage schedule at the end of the term of the agreement, if at that time the financial situation allows it.

Another possibility is freezing or lowering hiring rates. For example, most cities do not need to pay the beginning rates they do to recruit firefighters. You could freeze the beginning rates and add an additional step at the bottom of the scale to keep costs down.

There are obvious advantages to multi-year agreements. You do not have to sit down every year and spend the time and create the tensions that invariably result from a bargaining operation. In a multi-year agreement, wage increases are provided on at least an annual basis.

Increases can also be staggered for a certain amount of salary movement during a given year. If we agree to 3 percent at the beginning of the year and 3 percent in the middle of the year, it's cheaper than agreeing to 6 percent at the beginning of the year. But the cumulative effect of staggered increases can be a serious hidden cost. Add 3 percent, on top of 3 percent, on top of 3 percent, and the salary will have gone up by more than 9 percent. So a negotiator might negotiate increases based on current rates, rather than the rates that would go into effect with successive 3 percent increases and would then continue to escalate. The advantage is you can talk about relatively high wage increase percentages to employees while saving that half or three-quarter percent that would result from the cumulative effect which nobody even knows about, which you don't get credit for, and which the employees aren't concerned about. It's something the unions are willing to negotiate.

In this era of uncertainty, how can you negotiate a multi-year agreement? Obviously, that is a problem. But you might consider negotiating a multi-year and have openers on the money items. Or you could negotiate a set wage increase in a multi-year contract, but reserve to the agency the right to reopen negotiations if in the judgment of the city council the financial restraints require it—a unilateral right to reopen on wages.

Perhaps the most important aspect of getting more out of the salary dollar is through retirement. Many cities have negotiated arrangements where the wage increase is not given on the salary schedule, but is given by the agency picking up all or a portion of the employees' share of Public Employees Retirement System (PERS) payments.

A few years ago, agencies were nervous and uncertain of the skyrocketing costs and obligations of retirement programs, but more and more agencies have negotiated this kind of increase and for good reason.

For example, if you negotiate an 8 percent salary increase, it would in fact cost you about 6 percent or less. At the same time it would generate for the employees something in excess of 10 percent, depending on their tax bracket. You're really generating your own little revenue sharing program, with the federal and state government funding a salary increase that benefits the local agency with lower costs and benefits the employee with an increase in spendable income. There are automatic roll up costs associated with every salary schedule increase: retirement costs, overtime, unemployment, and workers compensation increase automatically by the same percentage as the salary schedule. By paying instead the employees' share of PERS, those costs are avoided. Negotiating such a "wage increase" provision requires very careful drafting to avoid future pitfalls, but it can be done.

How about supplementary wages such as educational incentive, longevity pay, or shooting pay? Agencies don't get maximum credit for those kinds of supplementary wage benefits, so the money would be better used in a visible place like the salary schedule. A city should eliminate them, if possible, and fold that money into the salary schedule. That may be difficult to negotiate and there may be certain legal restrictions. At the very least, supplementary benefits could be eliminated for new employees, while freezing current employees at their current flat dollar amount. The result will not necessarily be significant immediate savings, but substantial long-term savings.

Another thing to consider is two-tier retirement, now authorized under the state codes [in California]. A reduced retirement program for new employees, particularly for public safety employees, can lead to substantial long-term savings.

Overtime can be paid in the form of straight-time compensation-time to avoid the cumulative effect of paying time-and-a-half.

Uniform allowances and holiday pay in the safety services can be very costly because recent court decisions say that, depending on how those items are handled, they have to be included as final compensation when retirement benefits are calculated. Instead of a uniform allowance, a city could provide uniforms. Structure the language for holiday pay so that it avoids having to include it as final compensation for retirement purposes.

Many cities have Cadillac health plans and are pressured to pick up a significant portion of the costs. Negotiating a reduction of coverages may be desirable. A $50 deductible per person and $100 per family could be changed to $100-$300. Paying 100 percent of all claims above $1,000 could be reduced to 100 percent of all claims over $5,000 and everything below that at 80 percent. Deductibles should apply to all types of claims, not just hospital claims, as in many plans.

Vision plans are common, yet employee organizations are generally not going to go to the barricades for a vision plan. Consider eliminating marginal group plans, and instead put the money where it is more visible, in the salary schedule or in the basic health plan.

Self-insurance is becoming more and more common. A city assumes the risk, rather than paying high premiums to the insurance company. Many agencies have found that joint powers arrangements can mean savings in this area.

Sick leave can be renegotiated, reduced, and possibly tied into a long-term disability plan with a tunnel, on either a self-funded or a non-self-funded basis. Look at the possibility of getting at a sick leave problem by tying it into issues that are of concern to the employees. For example, Phoenix, Arizona, negotiated to pay time-and-a-half for overtime during any six month period when the employees in the unit had sick leave experience at or below the city wide level. The formula was so structured that the reduction in sick leave would fund the 50 percent premium on overtime, and also offered an incentive to bring down sick leave use.

Another interesting idea: instead of crediting your sick leave banks with eight hours a month, twelve months a year, take the eight hours, convert it to the then current salary for the employees and credit the pool based on money. Charge the pool based on the then current pay. To the extent that the pay has risen, sick leave will be charged at that higher rate.

Contracting out services is held to be a bargainable subject, so be warned that the union can request to bargain it. If a city is looking at contracting out as a potential area for savings, plan well ahead and talk to the employee organization. Talk to them, consult with them, discuss with them, let them be tuned in early, and you will find that in many cases, contracting out need not be a bargaining operation.

Finally, agencies must minimize their legal liability in the personnel area. Every day cities get new court decisions or new legislation that exposes them to ever increasing liability, be it on the basis of employment discrimination laws or expansion of court decisions determining due process rights of employees. As employee organizations have become increasingly aggressive in representing employees, cities are increasingly exposed to these areas. The courts have also expanded the kinds of damages that agencies and officials can be exposed to. Compensatory damages that an employee claims for emotional suffering are now allowed in most of these actions. Punitive damages can be claimed against officials acting in their official capacity for depriving somebody of their due process or other constitutional rights. The courts have also expanded authorizations for collection of attorneys' fees on behalf of employees.

Agencies must be sensitive to these potential liabilities and engage in aggressive training of personnel to avoid as many of those situations as possible.

A Practical Approach to Productivity Bargaining

—————————————————— John Matzer, Jr.

Local governments are taking a new look at productivity bargaining as a tool for improving productivity and reducing costs. Productivity bargaining involves the use of collective bargaining to increase productivity by negotiating changes in work rules and practices exchange for reciprocal employee benefits and incentives. Employee representatives agree to trade off inefficient work practices and restrictive contractual provisions either for a share of the savings resulting from increased productivity or for other pay or benefit increases or greater involvement in management decision making. While traditional collective bargaining concentrates on wages, hours, and working conditions, productivity bargaining expands the number and nature of issues negotiated and focuses on efficiency and effectiveness.

This article examines the current status of productivity bargaining, the reasons for renewed interest in the technique, and the kinds of contract clauses affected by it. It then suggests ways to overcome the barriers to productivity bargaining and use it successfully.

The state of the art

Interest in productivity bargaining is not new; in fact, it was particularly topical during the 1970s. Although there has been much discussion about the technique, practical application of productivity bargaining has been very limited. A 1975 survey of 772 cities and counties by the National Commission on Productivity and Work Quality identified only 5 percent of the sample as using or planning to use productivity bargaining.

There are few examples of formalized productivity bargaining that have resulted in specific productivity clauses in the contract.

Bargaining over productivity has in many instances been a pretext for justifying pay increases but has not always resulted in improved productivity. There has been a tendency to view productivity bargaining in narrow terms and to become enmeshed in debates over terminology and philosophical issues. Therefore, alleged success stories relating to the application of productivity bargaining must be carefully evaluated to separate fact from fiction. The limited use of productivity bargaining is probably due to the complexities involved in its application and to the lack of understanding of how to use it.

Renewed interest in productivity bargaining

Interest in public-sector productivity bargaining is on the rise for several reasons. First, public employers are searching for ways to respond to the public concern for improved government performance, and productivity bargaining offers an alternative to tax increases to close the budget gap resulting from declining fiscal resources. Second, public managers are recognizing the need and obligation to involve employees in considering productivity problems. A cooperative, positive attitude on the part of employees is critical to the successful implementation of productivity improvements. Third, negotiating obligations arise out of governments' efforts to initiate productivity improvements, and these obligations have created a need to establish a framework for joint labor–management determination of productivity issues. In some respects productivity bargaining is employed to overcome the negative impact of collective bargaining as demonstrated by contract clauses that result in work practices that decrease productivity.

Public managers have recognized the practical restrictions on managerial control and their inability to initiate certain desirable productivity improvements. Public-sector unions resist any management effort to take unilateral action and are reluctant to accept increased managerial intervention without consultation and agreement. Unilateral employer action can result in work disruptions by employees' strictly following work rules. Many states' collective bargaining laws impose an obligation to give notice to unions and to bargain on management actions that significantly affect the terms and conditions of employment. Courts have given broad interpretation to the duty to bargain over wages, hours, and working conditions, including contracting out, scheduling, and personnel reductions. Even where management has the right to initiate change, it may have to negotiate the implementation of the change because it has a significant impact on conditions of employment. For example, management usually has the authority to initiate reorganizations but may have to discuss their implementation because of the potential impact on employees in terms of seniority, bumping rights, and possible layoffs.

Contract provisions

Burdensome and restrictive contract provisions such as minimum crew size and scheduling limitations can directly affect whether management may institute changes and whether they must be negotiated. Union concurrence is often required in the case of traditional work patterns that have become institutionalized as past practices. Management may have awarded rights and privileges through informal understandings, customs, or long-established traditions. Practices covering such matters as free parking, use of seniority, and discipline are difficult to change without union agreement even if they are not covered by the contract.

Restrictive contracts, laws, court and arbitration decisions, past practices, and motivational factors have forced managers to turn to productivity bargaining as a strategy. Employee support is necessary to effectively introduce new technology and methods, implement reorganizations and work standards, and change long-established work customs and routines, and employees expect to share in the benefits of improved productivity. Effective application of productivity bargaining involves the development of strong management rights clauses, elimination of restrictive clauses, control over past practices, and development of contract language promoting productivity such as the creation of labor–management committees.

Management rights clauses   Strong and explicit management rights provisions are an important element of productivity bargaining. Clearly stated contract clauses are valuable in supporting management's rights to implement changes that improve productivity because in signing the contract the union has agreed that such rights exist. In the absence of a strong management rights clause, a union could argue that any management decision should be subject to negotiation or challenge. In general there has been a presumption that all rights of management are reserved. The concept of inherent reserved management rights holds that all rights not bargained away are inherent rights which management can exercise unilaterally at any time without restriction. Existence of the reserved rights concept has led many collective bargaining experts to support brief or short lists of enumerated statements of management rights supplemented by a general statement such as: "All rights, powers, functions, responsibilities, and authority of the employer except those expressly abridged, deleted, delegated, granted, or modified by this agreement shall remain vested with the employer."

Administrative rulings and court decisions have weakened the inherent reserved rights doctrine. Because of these cases there is strong support for a long form of enumerated management rights. Unless management lists each and every specific right to take action, the exercise of the rights could be subject to challenge by the union. The management rights clause can help define the scope of bargaining and has considerable impact in disputes where the remainder of the agreement is otherwise silent about controversial issues such as the right to abolish jobs. Even carefully enumerated rights clauses have been limited by court decisions that have declared that the practical impact of management decisions on employees is within the scope of bargaining. Unions strive to include the language that recognizes the obligation of the employer to negotiate the impact or practical consequences of managerial prerogatives on the terms and conditions of employment. With such language, management actions relating to such matters as workload or staffing and having an adverse effect on employees can be subject to grievance and arbitration provisions of the contract.

In productivity bargaining, public managers should negotiate for long, carefully enumerated management rights clauses. These clauses should list traditional rights such as the right to determine mission; set standards of service; select, direct, and assign employees; take disciplinary action; schedule and assign workload; contract out; establish work rules; and initiate layoffs. They should also include the right to establish and modify productivity and performance standards and incentive programs, to maintain efficiency of operations, determine type and use of technology, consolidate or transfer activities, determine location of facilities, and eliminate any part of work.

Local government managers should strongly resist any attempt to subject management rights to prior consultation or grievance and arbitration procedures. Language should be included requiring strict interpretation of the contract, as this reinforces the management rights section. Management also should seek a zipper or waiver clause, which tends to limit the complete agreement to express terms for subjects that are bargained over and for all subjects that might have been bargained over. Such a clause is used to support management's unilateral decision to change certain practices during the term of the agreement. Management should carefully examine the implications of making concessions in the area of management rights in return for the union's assuming responsibility for increasing productivity. Even where management has the right to take unilateral action, it must be done in a reasonable manner and in good faith. Under no circumstances can the action be arbitrary, capricious, or discriminatory.

No matter how carefully written, however, the existence of a strong management rights clause is no assurance that management will be able to exercise those rights without some restrictions. In addition to rules of good faith and reasonableness, there may be express restrictions and procedural requirements in other parts of the contract.

Restrictive clauses   Contract language can directly affect whether management may unilaterally institute changes without negotiations. A major management objective in productivity bargaining is the elimination of restrictive contract clauses that limit improved productivity and management's ability to control change. Examples of such clauses include those that expressly place limits on work done by supervisors, mandate staffing requirements such as crew size, permit unlimited release time for union business, and impose limits on contracting and scheduling. Another category of restrictive clauses pertains to pay for not working, such as roll call time, preparation time, minimum call-back time, clean-up time, equipment waiting time, and travel time. Employee protection clauses relating to layoffs, transfers, red-circle rates, reemployment rights, and super seniority are also examples of restrictive clauses. Finally, procedural restrictions may be included in contracts requiring notification, consultation, bidding, and posting.

In productivity bargaining, management should strive to eliminate such restrictive language and gain back flexibility to manage. Increased productivity and reduced cost cannot be achieved unless management has the freedom to deploy workers, impose workload standards, and institute broad job descriptions and the right to contract out and implement new methods and technology.

Past practices   In addition to contractual restrictions, it is necessary to consider past practices—unwritten rules, customs, and traditions that have the force of contractual language and severely limit management's flexibility. Past practices are understood and accepted ways of doing things over an extended period of time. In some cases unions are successful in including past practice clauses in contracts. These past practice, prevailing rights, or maintenance of benefits clauses state that all employee privileges and benefits will be maintained. One example of such a clause is: "All practices and conditions not specified in the contract shall remain the same for the duration of the contract." Another example is: "All past practices and benefits except as modified by the agreement shall be continued for the life thereof unless changed by mutual consent." Or: "Those privileges of employees which by custom, past practices, and tradition have become an integral part of their working conditions shall remain in effect and not be abridged as a result of not being enumerated in this agreement." Obviously, such clauses make operating changes difficult. Examples of past practices may include crews leaving early for breaks and lunch, police relief pickups, use of vehicles, free parking, contracting, enforcement of time and leave rules, application of discipline, and use of seniority in the assignment of overtime. Prevailing rights clauses mean that any dispute which relates to any employer action that affects existing conditions of employment may be subject to the grievance procedure. Past practices are often difficult to change without making major concessions.

Arbitrators use past practices to interpret agreements and resolve disputes over the interpretation and application of the agreement. Third-party neutrals have held that established practices in existence during negotiations and not discussed are binding during the life of the contract. Many arbitrators hold that the agreement may assume the continuation of existing conditions. Past practices are often difficult to change without union agreement even if they are not covered by the contract. Discipline inconsistent with past practices is likely to lack "just cause" and be overturned. A manager may not be able to discipline an employee for being ten minutes tardy if the practice has been to overlook tardiness of ten minutes or less. Charging employees for parking that has been free is usually subject to negotiation.

In productivity bargaining management should strive to exclude past practice, maintenance of benefits, or prevailing rights clauses from contracts. If such clauses are included they should enumerate and specifically describe the practices and benefits protected. An effort should be·made to include zipper or entire agreement clauses. These clauses eliminate past practices and informal understandings from contract coverage. There is no obligation to continue past practices or benefits not expressly provided in the contract. An entire agreement clause states that the provisions of the agreement constitute the complete understanding of the parties on all negotiable matters. An example of such a clause is: "This agreement shall represent all employee rights, privileges, and benefits granted by the employer to its employees, and unless specifically and expressly set forth in this agreement, all rules, regulations, practices, and benefits granted are not in effect." Another is: "This agreement constitutes the sole, entire, and existing agreement, supersedes all prior agreements and undertakings, oral and written, express or implied, or practices between parties." ·

Clauses promoting productivity   Public managers can employ productivity bargaining to develop formal arrangements with unions to promote productivity. The contract can include pledges by the union to assist in achieving greater efficiency, recognizing the need for productivity, and acknowledging management's right to security. There can be a general declaration of a policy of cooperation in which management and the union agree to work together in the interest of maintaining and improving efficiency in all operations. Another approach is reflected in such language as: "Increased productivity will require good faith and a cooperative attitude on the part of both parties as well as the continuation of improvements and technological progress through new methods, processes, and equipment." Productivity is also promoted by language that gives management the right to:

1. Establish and revise performance standards developed by work measurement to determine performance levels
2. Prepare work schedules and measure employee performance
3. Lay off employees for economic or financial reasons or because a particular activity is abandoned
4. Reduce accidents
5. Develop flexible job assignments
6. Contract out
7. Diminish, subcontract, or change production operation in whole or in part, including the introduction of any or all new automated or improved methods or machines, provided it can be shown that such changes will create a demonstrable productivity increase and no layoffs occur as a result
8. Establish innovative programs such as civilianization in the police department, physical fitness standards for police and fire employees, night resurfacing crews, and programs to improve employee attendance.

In constructing such cooperative language, specific standards or measures of performance should be avoided because they may limit flexibility, may be unreasonable, and could change with experience. Provision should be made for management's right to discipline for failure to meet standards or perform the assigned work. Employee protection clauses such as those limiting transfers can inhibit productivity improvements. Moreover, unions may assert that the practical impact of management's efforts may be unduly burdensome. This could necessitate the need to negotiate on the impact of productivity improvement actions. Finally, provision should be made for decreasing rewards and benefits and ensuring that the overall level of productivity does not decrease as specific indicators show improvement. Contract language promoting productivity establishes a mutual labor–management framework that is conducive to the initiation of productivity improvement programs.

Labor–management committees

Another way to promote productivity during the process of productivity bargaining is through the establishment of labor–management committees. These committees are formal advisory bodies established by the contract. Labor–management committees complement the bargaining process. They recommend changes which may be negotiated later. The committees are separate from the bargaining process and do not consider matters subject to the grievance procedure. Labor–management committees are established to provide communication and joint determination between bargaining sessions. Single or multiple committees may be established by the agreement. In some cases a number of labor–management committees are created to deal with such subjects as safety, performance pay, productivity, and alternative work schedules. In other instances the contract language refers to the committee as a productivity study or improvement committee to research areas in which productivity systems could be implemented. Labor–management committees concerned with productivity review such matters as work programming; adequacy of materials, tools, facilities, and work space; workloads; work methods; work standards; training; incentive programs; contracting out; reorganizational efforts; and introduction of technology.

The clauses establishing labor–management productivity committees may be very general or may spell out in specific detail organizational and operational requirements for the committees. Specific requirements cover such matters as a written statement of intent, method of sharing cost, membership, structure, authority, chairperson, quorum, agenda, ground rules, and use of third-party facilitators. Labor–management committees and quality circles are an effective way of achieving productivity improvements. Results can be measured in terms of increased revenue, cost savings, and increased service level. On the negative side, labor-management committees can result in a fragmentation of decision making and can have an impact on unorganized employees. Such committees will not completely eliminate the conflict. They can, however, contribute to informed bargaining, reduce grievances, and create a sense of greater participation and employee satisfaction.

Barriers to productivity bargaining

There are several practical obstacles to productivity bargaining. Public managers may fear the loss of basic prerogatives and believe that the best productivity bargaining language is none at all. Management may be unwilling to share information, or the personnel system may not be able to supply sufficient and adequate information. Unions often mistrust productivity bargaining for fear that it will result in work speedup, longer hours, replacement by technology, and layoffs. Political pressure can place unreasonable demands or expectations on productivity bargaining, or lack of political support can mean failure. Productivity bargaining may simply become a mechanism for justifying pay and benefit increases without any commitment to achieving productivity improvements. Furthermore, the lack of skilled and knowledgeable negotiators on one or both sides is a major reason for the failure of many productivity bargaining efforts. The process requires individuals skilled in the techniques of negotiating and knowledgeable about the specific services being provided. Failure to provide sufficient time for productivity bargaining can be detrimental. Labor-management committees are often established to provide more time for both sides to discuss methods of improving productivity. Poor planning is another barrier to effective productivity bargaining. To be successful the management negotiator must thoroughly analyze the current contract, identify restrictive provisions needing changes, be aware of past practices, thoroughly understand the improvements that are desired, and be capable of drafting the necessary contract language.

There may be legal and contractual barriers to productivity bargaining as well. State and local laws may not permit gain sharing and other monetary incentives. Civil service laws and rules and other statutory requirements may limit the scope of bargaining by excluding from bargaining such matters as position classification. Competitive systems of establishing terms and conditions of employment such as prevailing wage laws and other wage comparability procedures established by charter or ordinance may reduce the effectiveness of productivity bargaining. Overly restrictive and poorly drafted contracts may be difficult and costly to change. Many times the intermixing of productivity issues and contractual terms can result in a failure to reach agreement. Labor-management committees are a good device for dealing with this problem.

Another set of barriers relates to the operational mechanics of productivity bargaining. Very often productivity savings or gains are illusionary. Productivity is difficult to measure, particularly in the area of quality. The absence of a well-designed performance measurement and cost analysis system can be a substantial obstacle to establishing gain sharing or monetary incentive programs. It is not unusual to increase productivity but find that excessive unit cost exceeds the gains. There is a further danger of equating productivity improvements with individual performance standards. Directing too much attention to particular activities can be detrimental to overall performance. Moreover, it is very difficult to maintain a continued level of productivity improvement; incentive formulas are usually not adequate to provide rewards after initial gains are achieved. Poor contract administration can destroy gains, and inconsistent and improper interpretation of contract language can prevent the benefits of productivity bargaining from being attained. The number of employees not covered by the contract can create another obstacle.

Criteria for success

The barriers to productivity bargaining are not insurmountable and can be controlled. In addition to an understanding of the barriers, there must be a stable and mature labor relations environment, an acceptance of collective bargaining, and a commitment to bilateralism. Mutual trust is critical. Both labor and management should perceive that they stand to gain from productivity bargaining. Management must be willing to give up control of some areas of decision making. Public managers cannot assume that employees are solely responsible for low productivity. Productivity is affected by the quality of supervision, adequacy of procedures and equipment, level of capital investment, and motivational factors.

Management should provide the initiative in productivity bargaining but must protect its managerial prerogatives if agreement is not reached. If productivity bargaining is to work, public managers must suggest concepts and proposals that will improve efficiency and effectiveness. A purely reactive approach to union proposals is not an adequate foundation for productivity bargaining. Both formal and informal approaches should be employed, including the use of labor–management committees, quality circles, and cost improvement teams. Both management and labor must be willing to share specialized information. Effective productivity bargaining requires sharing information on work force data, staffing levels, workload, the organization and quality of work, work environment, and costs and revenues.

Skilled and experienced negotiators should be used in productivity bargaining. They need to understand the intracacies of the process and the services affected. The negotiators should carefully review contract language, obtain information from supervisors on restrictive language and past practices, and understand employee attitudes regarding productivity. Operating officials should be consulted and kept advised of the discussions and proposals. Management must be willing to share productivity gains and benefits with employees in the form of monetary and nonmonetary incentives or greater involvement in management decision making. On the other hand, the contract should provide for a decrease in rewards if productivity declines.

Productivity bargaining requires the development of performance measurement techniques and meaningful general standards. Provision should be made for gathering and monitoring performance data and ensuring that the overall level of productivity does not decrease as specific indicators show improvement. Productivity gains must be aligned with reasonable unit costs. Supervisors must be trained in the meaning and application of the new contract language; they also should carefully monitor the contract for problems, provide close supervision, and apply sanctions for less-than-acceptable levels of performance. Training and coaching, motivational strategies, and participatory management can contribute significantly to the success of productivity bargaining. Finally, management must maintain realistic expectations. Practices and work rules to be changed must be carefully examined and should be inter-

nal to the bargaining unit. Productivity bargaining is slow and te-
dious. Patience, open communications, and a willingness to experiment are critical to its success.

Summary

Productivity bargaining will not produce miracles and is not a panacea for low productivity, high costs, poor management, and unstable
labor relations. Local government managers should review productivity bargaining as just one of many useful techniques available
to improve productivity and reduce costs. Although productivity
bargaining is time-consuming and difficult, a vigorous effort to
make it work is worthwhile.

In summary, productivity bargaining:

1. Offers a means for management and labor to accommodate
   both conflicting and compatible interests
2. Can increase productivity, reduce costs, and increase
   employee morale
3. Creates positive attitudes and relationships
4. Is slow and difficult
5. Involves risks
6. Requires a strong commitment from all sides and a climate
   of trust and cooperation
7. Requires a willingness to share authority and a shift from an
   autocratic to a participatory management style
8. Encourages the use of formal and informal approaches
9. Must be carefully planned, executed, and monitored.

Using Joint Labor-Management Committees

——— Paul J. Champagne and Mark Lincoln Chadwin

The search for answers to America's problems of declining industrial productivity, poor product quality, and employee disaffection has led us to look abroad. That search has come to focus increasingly on Japanese models of organization and management such as Theory Z, or European concepts such as codetermination. The problem is that these models often involve workers and administrators who share common values, perceptions, and interests, much like members of the same clan or family. Management and labor are not clearly separated in either roles or social status. Instead, they collaborate closely because they are bound together by a tradition of mutual trust and shared life experiences as well as by material self-interest. Tangible economic incentives are deemphasized as motivational devices in favor of the social and psychic satisfactions of identification with and self-fulfillment through the company.

Because such models derive from cultural and industrial conditions very different from our own, there are strong grounds for questioning whether they offer realistic answers to American problems of productivity and labor-management relations. Why not address these problems with solutions that have developed closer to home, such as labor-management committees?

This approach has two major advantages over Japanese or other imported management models. First, labor-management committees offer a less radical, more gradual departure from traditional American patterns of industrial relations in that they leave intact the separate perspectives, interests, and capabilities of both management and organized labor. Second, the mechanics of labor-management committees are readily available and have been utilized successfully for many years. In fact, early efforts can be traced back to the 1920s and 1930s, and during World War II joint committees were used extensively. However, following the war, interest in such cooperative ventures virtually died, and labor and management generally resumed adversary postures. Only in the past few years has there been a renewal of interest.

At any rate, labor-management committees are alive and well today. To help readers organize such committees, we'll discuss the issues associated with starting them, their structure and scope, conditions favoring success, costs and benefits, and diverse applications one should keep in mind.

Starting the committee

Labor-management committees typically involve eight to 12 members, half designated by management and half union representatives. Established by collective bargaining agreements, these joint committees do not deal with negotiable issues like wages and fringe benefits. Rather, they are advisory bodies that focus their attention on matters of mutual interest not usually covered by the union contract. Labor-management committees have been used in public-sector organizations, such as city government and defense facilities, as well as private firms. They have been credited with reducing turnover, absenteeism, and grievances and with improving operational efficiency and product quality in organizations as large as General Motors and as small as the Valspar paint plant in East Moline, Illinois (45 employees).

Before establishing a labor-management committee, the firm should assess current conditions. If the existing situation is good, creating a formal structure will be unnecessary. Conversely, if hostility and distrust are very high and there is little communication between labor and management leadership, the help of a trained facilitator may be needed. An initial assessment can also bring to light irritants or obstacles to cooperation that the labor-management committee will need to focus on early in its deliberations.

While either labor or management can take the first step, in most cases the initiative comes from management. In other instances, a third party suggests the formation of a joint committee. For example, mediators from the Federal Mediation and Conciliation Service (FMCS) sometimes propose a permanent joint committee as part of a strike settlement. Occasionally, a local official may initiate the idea. When Jamestown, New York, was suffering from labor strife and out-migration of industry, the mayor initiated a network of labor-management committees at the regional, company, and plant levels. These committees have been credited with eventually reversing the economic decline of this community. Regardless of who actually initiates the idea, it should be done in a way that encourages both labor and management to feel a sense of shared responsibility for the outcome.

Any move toward fuller cooperation between management and labor passes through a minefield. Leaders on both sides are often fearful of losing control, followers of being exploited. On the management side, there are deeply held convictions about the right to manage. Any increase in the authority of workers is an implied threat. Labor unions, on the other hand, often equate any mention of productivity with speedup or with the introduction of new technology that replaces human beings. Therefore, there is a need for an institutional framework that sanctions or legitimizes the effort and gives assurance that it will not spin out of control. A labor-management committee establishes this framework.

There is also a need to express the objectives of the committee in terms that take into account the interests and concerns of both sides—that is, the objective should include raising operational efficiency, productivity, or product quality as well as enhancing working conditions and job satisfaction for the employees. Similarly, assurances should be given that workers will not lose their jobs or be demoted as a result of the labor-management committee's actions.

Early successes are important: They build credibility for the idea of cooperation between labor and management. Hence the committee should first take on simple issues that are likely to provide tangible, visible, and noncontroversial results.

In a situation where previous hostility has been great or where labor and management have had little contact outside collective bargaining sessions or grievance procedures, it makes sense to use an outside facilitator. The FMCS may be willing to provide one who is familiar with the dynamics of such situations and can ease the passage through the early, uncomfortable stages. Other sources of assistance include labor relations experts from nearby universities or experienced labor relations lawyers. If the facilitator is paid a fee, both sides may want to share the cost in order to demonstrate that the labor-management committee is a joint venture and to allay any concerns about impartiality.

Finally, it is often a good idea to learn from someone else's experience before plunging in. The National Center for Productivity in Washington maintains a directory of labor-management committees and can identify organizations similar to one's own that have labor-management committees, and that could be called or visited before formally starting.

Committee structure and scope

Though successful labor-management committees vary greatly in design and in the issues they address, certain patterns are evident. As noted earlier, most of these committees are evenly divided between labor and management. General Motors, which has had extensive experience with labor-management committees, recommends that the committee have ten members: the president, business agent, secretary-treasurer, and two stewards from the union; and a top manager, department head, industrial relations representative, and two foremen from management.

Of course, adjustments can be made to take into account the size of the operation or other special circumstances. For instance, union representation in the joint committee at Armco's plant in Butler, Pennsylvania, was composed half of hourly workers and half of salaried employees. Similarly, the Ingalls Shipyard in Pascagoula, Mississippi, had to design a relatively large committee to accommodate the 14 different trade unions representing workers in the yard.

The General Motors experience indicates that responsibilities should be shared by rotating the chairmanship from meeting to meeting between the top union and management representatives. It also suggests preparing and circulating before meetings agendas that alternate items suggested by management with those proposed by labor.

Finally, General Motors suggests regular monthly meetings limited to one hour so as to focus deliberations and to "guard against this format becoming just a habitual gripe session." Many successful labor-management committees have been designated to meet on-site and during regular working hours. However, other approaches are sometimes necessary. The American Velvet Company, a textile firm in Stonington, Connecticut, reported using both telephone conference calls so that their sales manager in New York City could participate and bimonthly dinner meetings attended by two labor representatives from each department.

The range of topics addressed by labor-management committees varies enormously from one organization to another. A number of successful ventures began with a fairly restricted scope, especially where there was a history of distrust and noncooperation. Then, as labor and management became more confident in the process and its results, the focus broadened and in some cases became very wide-ranging. For example, within three years of their inception, the labor-management committees begun by the steel industry and the United Steelworkers of America developed the following list of possible topics for plant-level consideration:

... maximizing use of production time and facilities; reducing equipment breakdowns and delays; improving quality; reducing need for reprocessing products; eliminating waste of materials, supplies, and equipment; reducing excessive overtime; boosting employee morale; improving safety experience; and focusing employee awareness on the problems of productivity and those posed by the threat of foreign competition.

Most experts counsel against trying to develop a master plan of issues and projects when a labor-management committee is established. Instead, they suggest keeping things flexible and adapting to opportunities and problems as they arise. However, labor-management committees are generally advised to stay away from two types of issues—matters that are subject to contract negotiations (such as wage scales, fringe benefits, and retirement plans) and individual grievances that are covered by regular grievance procedures. This avoids giving the impression that the committee was created to circumvent regular negotiation or grievance processes.

Ultimately, many firms develop a network of joint subcommittees and task forces below the organizationwide or plantwide committee. The Kelly-Springfield tire plant in Cumberland, Maryland, for instance, has utilized subcommittees with three labor and three management members. One addressed problems that arose in the powerhouse when the plant converted from oil to coal. Three others worked on distribution of work gloves, operational problems in the tire fabrication unit, and maintenance issues.

In the Tarrytown General Motors plant, more informal patterns, such as those described below, were used to supplement formal structures and training programs:

... following the plant manager's regular staff meetings, the personnel director passes on critical information to the shop committee. The safety director meets weekly with each zone committeeman. Top union officials have monthly rap sessions with top management staff to discuss future developments, facility alterations, schedule changes, model changes, and other matters requiring advance planning. The chairman of Local 664 and his zone committeemen check in with the personnel director each morning at 7:00 A.M. and go over current or anticipated problems.

Conditions favoring success

It's possible to identify those factors that have led to successful implementation of the labor-management committee concept. First of all, a successful committee communicates its deliberations and actions to all interested parties. As the National Center for Productivity recommends, "... communications should be a two-way street, with reactions and concerns of the workforce and management feeding back to committee members so that future meetings will include topics of concern to both parties." Center officials suggest the following channels of communication:

1.   The union newspaper and/or company publication.
2.   Joint company-union newsletters.
3.   Reports posted on bulletin boards.
4.   Informal meetings and discussions.
5.   Reports by union representatives at local union meetings.

Second, successful committees recognize the importance of attitudes. The comments of one official of the International Brotherhood of Boiler-Makers to a group meeting makes the point:

From management's standpoint, are you willing to go back to your respective places, open up a door in a conference room, go in that conference room with labor's representatives, leave your authoritative hat at the door, and talk eyeball to eyeball and gut to gut across that table? Let them lay it out to you without feeling hostile, without . . . reprisal?

On the union side, are you willing to go in there and make suggestions to improve the quality of work and reduce the inefficiency of that plant that you and your people are walking around in, that plant you see every day? Are you willing to take the initiative in this crisis situation in which this American economy finds itself?

Labor-management cooperation must be seen as a continuous process, not as a program with a definite ending. Patience and sustained commitment over a period of years are extremely important. The pressure to change things overnight must be resisted; so must the expectation of quick and easy results.

If the effort can be sustained, positive attitudes about cooperation and communication can become so pervasive that formal processes and structures for collaboration, such as labor-management committees, are no longer necessary. In the case of Niagra of Wisconsin Paper Company, the committee itself was short-lived, but the spirit of cooperation lingered on. According to the personnel manager, it facilitated a variety of subtle improvements that may be difficult to measure but contribute importantly to the firm's effectiveness.

A third characteristic of successful committees is that they have support from the top on both sides—the CEO, division chief, or plant manager on the one hand, and the union's international vice-president, local president, or business agent on the other. Without this endorsement, the credibility of the effort is in doubt from the outset, and the committee's chances of achieving any important innovations are greatly reduced.

A fourth characteristic concerns the union hierarchy. If the leadership is internally divided or does not have the trust of large segments of the rank and file, conditions are unfavorable for an effective labor-management committee. Much the same is true if the union is not treated as an equal partner by management. In such situations, union leaders will be forced to take rigid attitudes to protect their personal positions. For political reasons, they will reject any initiatives that involve cooperating with management. On the other hand, when the union is strong and viable, chances of success are very good.

Finally, management must be perceived as being both technically and organizationally competent. If workers sense that management does not know what it is doing, they are unlikely to engage in a labor-management committee as a serious joint undertaking. Management must demonstrate that it understands competitive market conditions and the relevant technology and that it has basic administrative skills. Otherwise, the union is likely to stay aloof, simply getting what it can for its members for as long as possible. However, several cases we examined suggest that even if workers distrust the competence of top management, it is enough if they view local management at their own office as capable and reasonable.

Costs and benefits of committees

What kind of outcomes can a firm realistically expect if it takes the time and trouble to correctly establish a labor-management committee? Unfortunately, there are no easy answers because little carefully designed research and experimentation have been done with joint committees. Most of the information available is episodic and testimonial.

Bearing that caution in mind, there nevertheless appears to be a pattern of outcomes that may be anticipated. Available evidence suggests that successful labor-management committees frequently lead to decreases in the number of employee grievances, reduced absenteeism and turnover, and improved product quality or operating efficiency.

Examples of favorable outcomes abound. In the Tarrytown General Motors plant, union officials reported absenteeism fell from about 7 percent to 2 or 3 percent. In addition, the plant's product quality rose from one of the worst to one of the best in the General Motors system over a period of several years. Midland-Ross Corporation's Electrical Products Division in Athens, Tennessee, which operates a Scanlon plan, reported a 50 percent reduction in in-plant repairs of new products and a decline in grievance procedures from 80 to 15 a year. Similar declines in grievance actions have been reported by National Airlines; the Heinz plant in Muscatine, Iowa; several General Motors plants; and Coustauld's textile plant in Mobile, Alabama.

The expense of operating the actual labor-management committee is trivial for any large organization. However, the costs of projects resulting from the committee's recommendations can be substantial. For example, the Tarrytown General Motors plant developed a broad-ranging quality of worklife program that cost GM $1.6 million. Key management officials had no doubt the results were well worth the cost. Of course, any project recommended by a labor-management committee proposal (like one developed internally by management itself) can and should be evaluated in cost-benefit terms both before and during implementation.

Beyond quantifiable costs and savings, managers and labor leaders should be aware of the intangible benefits that may be even more valuable in the long run. From the union's viewpoint these include:

1. A channel of regular communication to top management.
2. An opportunity to deal with minor problems before they become major controversies.
3. A way to provide meaningful input on management plans and operating problems that affect employees' assignments, working conditions, and long-term security.
4. Recognition by management of the union as a responsible partner with a constructive role in the organization.

For management, a joint committee provides:

1. A forum to review quality problems, product development, customer requirements, and other matters that demonstrate the employee's role in the success or failure of the business.
2. An opportunity for advanced discussion of business conditions, operational problems, and plans that have a potential impact on employee work schedules, layoffs, recalls, transfers, or new job opportunities.
3. A way to be responsive to constructive suggestions or valid complaints, thereby demonstrating to the workers and the union that management values and respects the ideas and concerns of its employees.

Other uses

Clearly, labor-management committees can make an important contribution to productivity and organizational effectiveness. They can even be used to initiate a variety of activities that thereafter take on a life of their own. This was the case with Hope's Windows, a division of Roblin Industries in Jamestown, New York. In order to remain economically viable, Hope's had to develop and manufacture a new energy-saving insulated window. It used its experience with a plantwide labor-management committee to create a special joint committee that designed the new production layout. The new layout design benefitted from the employees' practical knowledge of fabrication and assembly operations, and the employees felt a sense of participation and reassurance from helping to design their own future work environment.

Labor-management committees elsewhere have served not only to involve employees in layout planning but also to sponsor a wide variety of product improvement, pay incentive, job enrichment, and organizational-development projects. The National Center for Productivity notes that they have been used in at least 19 different firms to design and manage productivity-incentive programs, such as Scanlon plans.

The labor-management committee can also be an effective mechanism for introducing participatory management strategies such as quality circles or the employee-involvement groups used by Ford Motor Company. Quality circles require voluntary worker participation. They cannot be successfully imposed by management in the face of employee resistance, especially in a union shop. However, if quality circles are sponsored by a plantwide labor-management committee, the union's desire for a role is accommodated, the idea is legitimized, and employee acceptance and participation are likely to be greater.

Unfortunately, most labor-management committees arise out of crisis situations. At Tarrytown, for example, both local management and union leaders were faced with a simple choice: either they worked together to overcome worker unrest and get the plant operating smoothly, or they faced a shutdown. Given the alternative, cooperation was the only reasonable outcome.

The question, of course, is, What will happen when economic conditions improve and resources are again available? Many experts are skeptical about the long-run possibilities. Yet if the present movement toward greater cooperation continues, mutual understanding and trust may help head off future crises.

Labor-management committees do not offer a panacea for American problems of productivity. We would suggest, however, that they are an alternative to be carefully considered and actively explored.

PART 5

Emerging Personnel Issues

"Comparable Worth" vs. "Prevailing Rates"

Gerald M. Pauly

"Comparable worth" already is well on its way to becoming the major new personnel issue of the early 1980s. The term has been added to the vocabulary of lawyers active in civil rights litigation. Former Equal Employment Opportunity Commission Chair Eleanor Holmes Norton has described comparable worth as "the only true large issue remaining in flux" under the Equal Employment Opportunity Act; "the big one left for the 1980s."

The comparable worth concept received much publicity in 1981 because of the strike by several hundred employees in the City of San Jose over the issue. Comparable worth is attractive to many people who are interested in affirmative action programs, because it promises women more money without having to change jobs.

The concern of women wanting to earn more money is real. Unfortunately, the comparable worth theory is not a very practical solution to the problem. There are at least four reasons why comparable worth is not a practical theory for public policy or organizational management:

1. No methodology exists to validly determine the comparable worth of jobs.
2. Comparable worth threatens the long-standing and sound public policy of using prevailing rates as the primary factor in setting pay.
3. When market demands force up wages for one job, wages for "comparable" jobs would also rise, even though the comparable positions experienced no recruitment or retention problems.

Reprinted with permission from the January 1982 issue of *Western City*, the official publication of the League of California Cities.

4.   Serious labor relations problems could be caused by the threat to employees in higher paying jobs, since the theory suggests many jobs are over-paid, while others are under-paid.

Premise

Until recent years, employment practices in the United States clearly had a discriminatory impact on women workers. Women often were arbitrarily refused employment in many better paying jobs. During the last decade, however, women have moved into many occupational areas in which few women were employed previously, and affirmative action efforts should continue to provide women access to better paying jobs.

The comparable worth concept starts with the premise that many jobs occupied primarily by women are grossly underpaid and that the low pay is due to sex discrimination that is institutionalized in this country's employment compensation system.

The theory is an effort to move beyond the concept of equal pay for equal work. The federal Equal Pay Act of 1963 mandates that women be paid the same as men when their jobs are equal. The Act describes equal as that requiring equal skill, effort, and responsibility being performed under similar working conditions. Many plaintiffs' attorneys have been foiled in their efforts to pursue claims under the Equal Pay Act, because the employers involved have been able to prove that the jobs in question are not equal. Comparable worth thus is a new legal theory that could provide plaintiffs' attorneys with a new avenue to the courts. The legal contention would be, "even if these jobs aren't equal, they are of comparable worth."

Evaluation

Comparable worth advocates propose that job evaluation systems be utilized to set the pay of all positions within an organization. Some even suggest a national job evaluation system. Inherent is the notion that jobs not at all similar in the tasks performed can be compared to each other. Under proposed job evaluation systems, numeric weighted factors are assigned to each job. Thus all jobs can be reduced to numbers, and the numbers become the basis for the salary level.

Job evaluation plans use points assigned to various job factors to help in determining wages, and have been used in the United States since before World War II. Job evaluation techniques, if used properly, can be helpful. However, they also can be used inappropriately. Under a typical job evaluation study, the basic job factors are prescribed and numeric weightings are assigned to each. A judgment is made as to how many points are to be assigned to each job in accordance with the degree to which each factor applies to that job.

The basic problem is the assumption that dissimilar jobs can be compared to each other by reducing all job evaluation factors to numbers. This gives the superficial appearance of objectivity to the job study, but the weightings assigned to various factors ultimately are subjective.

This problem is illustrated by the factors used in an actual job evaluation study conducted recently by a public agency in California (see Figure 1). What objective evidence, for example, can show that the factor "Job conditions" warrants a maximum of only 40 points, while "Contact with others" is worth a maximum of 108 points? The fact is that the people involved in this study simply made the *judgment* that "Job conditions" warrants less than half the points of "Contact with others."

Figure 1. Factors used in a sample job evaluation study.

Job factors	Range of weighting
Job conditions	0-40
Contact with others	12-108
Supervision	0-126
Independence of action	12-108
Consequence of action—cost	5-54
Consequence of action—welfare and safety of others	0-54
Analytical requirements	20-180
Physical requirements—moving objects	4-20
Physical requirements—other (examples: climbing, stooping, reaching, seeing)	0-80
General educational achievement	8-72
Specific vocational preparation—prior training, education, or experience requirements	0-54
Specific vocational preparation—on-the-job experience requirement	0-54

Below are detailed descriptions and weightings for three of the factors listed in the sample. Similar descriptions exist for each of the other factors. These three are typical, and help illustrate how job evaluation plans work.

Job conditions: The surroundings or physical conditions under which the job must be performed and over which the employee has no control. Includes occupational hazards. Disagreeable elements include: noise, dirt, fumes, vibrations, heat, cold, dampness.

Points	Description
(0) 0.	Good conditions with no disagreeable elements or factors.
(8) 1.	Good conditions with minor features which occasionally cause discomfort through poor ventilation, poor lighting, or uneven temperatures.
(16) 2.	Periodic disagreeable working conditions. Occasional exposure to disagreeable or irritating elements. Possible exposure to accident hazards involving lost time.

If one examines some of the point allocations within each job factor, some more interesting contrasts emerge. Note that under "Job conditions," there are 40 points for "Continuous exposure to hazards involving a high possibility of loss of life." Under "Contact with others," there are 44 points for "Contact with the public, officials, department heads, and with personnel of other departments ... " Under "Independence of action," there are 38 points for "Variety of regular assignments following standard procedures ... "

Now consider this question: What objective evidence can be presented to justify assigning 40 points for a job involving a high possibility of death and virtually the same number of points for contact with the public, or performing regular assignments following standard procedures?

Figure 1. Continued.

(24) 3. Frequent disagreeable working conditions; or exposure to disagreeable elements or factors. Exposure to lost time accidents or infrequent exposure to more serious accidents such as fractures, severe burns, or some minor permanent physical disability; i.e., loss of finger, impairment of hearing, exposure to communicable diseases causing lost time and minor permanent damage.

(32) 4. Extremely disagreeable working conditions, causing excessive discomfort to the worker. Exposure to accident hazards involving major permanent disability such as loss of limb, sight, etc., or loss of life. Exposure to serious communicable diseases causing excessive discomfort with possibility of loss of life.

(40) 5. Continuous exposure to hazards involving a high possibility of loss of life.

Contact with others:　Contact with fellow employees, the public, and officials of other governmental and private organizations. Measured by the nature and purpose of contacts, their frequency and the difficulties encountered. Consideration is given to the importance and consequences related to giving and securing information, explaining policies and persuading others to action. Excludes supervisor-subordinate contacts.

Points　　　　　　　　　　　　　**Description**

(12) 1. Very little contact with the public or personnel of other departments. Relationship with members of employee's own office limited to giving basic factual information.

(28) 2. Contact with the public or personnel of other departments giving and receiving basic factual information. Cooperate with members of own office on work requiring coordination.

(44) 3. Contact with the public, officials, department heads, and with personnel of other departments; tact, alertness to situations; ability to present rules, regulations, and procedural information. May include routine contacts with emotionally disturbed persons. Problems refused to supervisory personnel.

Proper use

Job evaluation systems do have value. They can be useful when applied to a group of jobs that have many common factors. For example, a job evaluation plan might be applied to determine pay differences among an employer's clerical and office jobs. Under that circumstance, a job evaluation system is being applied against jobs that have many factors in common. *The job evaluation system thus is being used to help clarify the differences among jobs that are very similar in many respects.* For example, the various grades of typist clerks, stenographer clerks, account clerks, and other general and specialized office employees share many job factors in common. Job evaluation can be a useful technique for making grade distinctions and to determine the relative pay among these related jobs.

Figure 1. Continued.

(60) 4. Same as No. 3, except that contacts also require the ability to work with emotionally disturbed persons; the ability to explain the application of rules and regulations.

(76) 5. Contact as above; may require insight into theory of human behavior and its application; ability to present justifications of idea; may aid in social adjustment of individuals. Requires the ability to explain need of a procedure or program or to explain interpretation of rules and regulations. Handles problem cases after the failure of others, including ability to secure information from recalcitrant or emotionally disturbed individuals in controversial or difficult situations.

(92) 6. Contact with officials of public and private agencies to explain or amplify the program of a department; ability to present ideas and alertness to situations to gain acceptance of program requirements or concepts.

(108) 7. Contact with administration officials and community leaders on policies which are controversial or on important changes of a departmental policy or procedure affecting general City policy.

Independence of action: The use of initiative as measured by the extent to which controls are imposed on the position by references such as supervision, regulations, precedents, procedural manuals, and advice of others in relation to their clarity, diversity, and relevance to the work.

Points   **Description**

(12) 1. Desired results are specified in detail. Routine and regularly assigned work is performed in planned sequence after preliminary instruction. Work may be so routine that supervision is seldom necessary. Advice and assistance from supervisor is readily available. Detailed instructions are provided for new procedures or changes in existing procedures.

(25) 2. Regular assignments of limited variety are made without instructions and performed according to established procedures. Supervisor controls flow of day-to-day work and provides and

As another example, a job evaluation study also could be helpful in comparing among related jobs such as street maintenance workers, water and sewer system workers, and other similar positions. Here again the jobs have many factors in common. *The job evaluation system again is used to help clarify the differences among jobs which are similar in many respects.*

The validity and utility of a job evaluation system has to be questioned when it is used to compare jobs which have virtually nothing in common. How can a typist clerk be compared to a tree trimmer, or a stenographer to a sewer worker?

In California, grape growers have developed finely tuned systems for grading each variety of grape. Similar grading systems are applied to varieties of apples. However, where is the system for grading apples in comparison to grapes? It does not exist. The reason it doesn't exist is that grapes and apples have too little in common. What is true of fruit is true of jobs. Jobs which are vastly different cannot be compared to each other in an objective and valid manner.

Today's leading cases cited by lawyers help show that comparisons can be made only when jobs have much in common. A public

Figure 1. Continued.

explains new instructions or changes in existing instructions. Assistance is readily available for solution of problems not covered by reference material. Work reviewed upon completion.

(38) 3. Variety of regular assignments following standard procedures are performed without instructions. Employee is regularly responsible for scheduling and completing own work. Work generally reviewed only as problems occur. Requires occasional choices in the application of a variety of standard methods or procedures to specific circumstances.

(51) 4. Variety of regular assignments following standard procedures are performed without instructions. Requires frequent choices in application of a variety of standard methods or procedures to specific circumstances. Work problems are solved through conference with supervisor or solved by employee in absence of supervisor subject to later review.

(65) 5. Work performed with assignments made giving general objective and requiring discretion in determining or developing methods and procedures to achieve objective.

(79) 6. Work performed according to general direction of assignments requiring the ability to proceed independently in defining and achieving the objectives.

(93) 7. Acts independently with responsibility for a field of work where direction consists of assignment of the responsibility to attain program or project objectives according to policy guidelines.

(108) 8. Work performed requires independent action in an executive capacity for definition of program and policy formulation and recommendations.

sector case, *County of Washington* v. *Gunther,* involved matrons and deputy sheriffs who worked in the jail in Washington County, Oregon. The jobs had in common the very significant factor that both were responsible for the custody of prisoners. A well known private sector case is *Taylor* v. *Charlie Brothers, Inc.* Charlie Brothers is a wholesale firm in Pennsylvania. This case involved female warehouse jobs and male warehouse jobs. Here again, the jobs had much in common. It is no coincidence that the leading cases involve jobs that have enough in common that they reasonably can be compared to each other.

Interestingly, both the Washington County case and the Charlie Brothers case include some degree of evidence that the employers did intentionally act in a manner which had the effect of discriminating against a group of women employees with respect to their pay. In neither of these cases did the courts need to endorse the comparable worth theory in order to agree that the plaintiff's cases had some merit.

Prevailing rates

Most organizations that have formal personnel policies use prevailing wage rates as one of the most important factors in setting wages. Even in organizations that are unionized and set salaries through collective bargaining, prevailing rates normally are a major issue considered at the bargaining table. The wages other employers pay for a particular job usually have a very significant impact on the negotiated rates agreed to by the parties. Even in smaller organizations that do not have a formal personnel system, prevailing rates as a practical manner dictate the pay rates for skilled jobs.

Thus, clerks who work for a public agency are compared to clerks who work for private industry and perhaps to clerks in other public agencies. Refuse collectors are likewise compared to refuse collectors. This is not a perfect system, but it is the most practical system thus far devised. In practice most public agencies, under this system, give primary consideration to private sector compensation, and thus the public agency merely follows the lead of the private sector.

Comparable worth advocates contend that prevailing rates are discriminatory for many lower paying jobs and thus should not be followed in setting the pay of such jobs. To drop prevailing rates as the fundamental factor in setting pay would be a public policy decision of enormous consequence. Such a change could have a major impact on the entire labor market in the United States.

A significant problem with the comparable worth concept is that once an employer ranks jobs according to job evaluation weightings, the employer becomes locked into a salary system that cannot adjust to changes in the job market.

For example, in public agencies it has been common to pay the same salary to systems analysts, budget analysts, and personnel analysts. Today the tremendous demand for systems analysts is driving up salaries for that job. It is very difficult to recruit systems analysts. Employers are finding they must pay more to hire and retain them. It is much easier to hire well qualified personnel analysts and budget analysts. If an employer had rated these three jobs as equal under a point evaluation system, that system dictates that the personnel analysts and the budget analysts get pay increases that are a result of a severe recruiting problem for systems analysts. That makes no sense.

Labor relations

The comparable worth theory presumes that all jobs can be graded in accordance with their relative value, and then paid in relation to those ratings. As a practical matter, the comparable worth theory suggests that some jobs are over-paid and others are under-paid. Considering the financial problems facing most employers today, implementation of comparable worth would force management to lower the relative pay of some jobs in order to increase the relative pay of others. Anyone who has ever been involved in pay administration knows there is nothing more inflammatory than changing internal salary relationships. Both the bargaining agent and the employer would have to contend with the disruption of employees fighting among themselves over salary rates. Harmonious labor relationships can never be fostered when a union is split internally over an issue.

What if the two groups of employees, the lower-paid and the higher-paid, are represented by two or more bargaining agents, which often is the case? How do you convince firefighters that their pay should be held down so that some other jobs can be paid more? How could an employer engage effectively in good faith bargaining with police officers, if a comparable worth policy required that the salaries of some other occupation be increased some corresponding amount? A comparable worth policy surely would have a chilling effect on pay negotiations because an increase agreed to for one job might be legally applicable to another job in another bargaining unit.

Comparable worth is an innovative concept, but it brings with it many practical problems. It is based upon the false premise that there exists a methodology for measuring the comparable value of jobs, but in fact there is no such methodology. There are job evaluation plans which can be useful under certain circumstances. All such plans involve many subjective judgments. No job evaluation plan can substitute for the practical policy of paying according to prevailing rates.

Managing Tomorrow's Workforce

Harold T. Smith

A manager comments: "Overall the biggest problem is cost justifying new technology with 'hard' dollars up front."

An employee comments: "It's very important to consider the possible long-term ill effects that office automation may have on the psyche as well as physical well-being, such as eyestrain and backaches."

These statements are typical of the two different perspectives on the future of human resources and office automation found in a recently completed Administrative Management Society (AMS) Foundation study on the future of human resources management. A major conclusion of this report, entitled *The Office Revolution: Strategies for Managing Tomorrow's Workforce,* is that while experts, managers and employees agree that maintaining a human perspective in the automated office is the most critical issue of the future, managers tend to be more concerned with the practical issues of justifying and implementing office automation, while employees focus more on the "human-related" issues.

The Office Revolution is the first of a four-part AMS Foundation research study on "Managing the Office—1990 and Beyond," funded in part by the Olsten Corporation. The purpose of the research is to provide managers with information and recommendations that will help them plan on a long-range basis for effective management of the office during the 1990s.

The first 132-page report concentrates on potential human resources problems and solutions. A variety of other factors that af-

Reprinted from *Management World*, with permission from the Administrative Management Society (AMS), Willow Grove, PA 19090. Copyright 1983 AMS.

fect the office will be covered over the next few years. These will include environmental factors, technological opportunities, and management strategies.

Problems

The Office Revolution apprises managers of the major human resources trends affecting the office environment, identifies problems arising from these trends, and offers ways to avert or solve those problems. After a review of current research, experts in human resources and office automation, along with over 4,000 managers and employees representing a cross-section of business, were surveyed. Their responses provided their perceptions of the importance of the 49 problems identified by current research as affecting the future office. There was a total of 730 responses, consisting of 352 managers, 362 employees and 16 experts.

The respondents were asked to rank each of the 49 problems as critical, important, insignificant, or solved/not likely to be a problem. Seventeen problems were identified as critical. The first six, which had the highest average ratings, are, respectively:

1. Maintaining a human perspective in an automated office setting.
2. Designing meaningful and satisfying jobs.
3. Ensuring automated systems are user oriented.
4. Changing management's orientation to long-term strategic planning.
5. Helping employees maintain job satisfaction.
6. Ensuring that computer files of key personnel are available to others in the company.

Nine more problems are considered to be critical because at least 50 percent or more of at least one group rate them as critical:

1. Ensuring office automation results in a substantial payoff.
2. Working with employees to dispel their fears about layoffs and needs for retraining.
3. Ensuring an adequate supply of intelligent, well-adjusted individuals.
4. Ensuring that top management assumes leadership in an office automation effort.
5. Helping managers deal with the process of change.
6. Eliminating future shortages of skilled technical personnel.
7. Considering possible long-term physical and mental effects of office automation on employees.
8. Ensuring that automated managerial support systems are "friendly."
9. Measuring non-repetitive managerial and professional work.

Finally, two more problems are considered critical because each most frequently received a critical rating:

10. Helping to improve graduates of public education systems.
11. Resolving power struggles among potential leaders of office automation.

These 17 problems were identified as most critical by all the groups taken together. There were, though, significant variations in the perspectives on certain problems by individual groups.

For example, the most critical problem—maintaining a human perspective in the automated office—is rated as critical by 80 percent of the employees. In comparison, 50 to 55 percent of the managers and experts rate it as critical. Similarly, 57 percent of the employees rate the problem of possible physical and mental effects of office automation as critical, while only 13 to 19 percent of the experts and managers rate it this way.

For two other critical problems—dispelling employee fears of layoffs and retraining, and maintaining employee job satisfaction—over half of the employees rate these as critical, while no experts rate them that way.

Experts rate practical issues higher than any other group. Such overall critical-rated problems as obtaining a substantial payoff from office automation, measuring non-repetitive managerial and professional work, and ensuring an adequate supply of competent personnel are rated as critical by more than 50 percent of the experts, as compared to approximately one-third of the managers and employees.

Managers indicate high concern for the critical problems of ensuring that automated office systems are user oriented, coping with the process of change, top management support of office automation, and demonstrating a payoff from office automation.

Overall, while the most critical problem remains maintaining a human perspective, employees are much more concerned about human-related issues, while managers are more concerned with the more practical issues involved in justifying and implementing office automation. Employees and managers both appear to be positive about the benefits of office automation, but each is concerned about problems specific to their roles.

Solutions

The experts provided a wide variety of solutions to and methods for averting the 49 problems identified. Among the guidelines that managers should follow to be successful in managing human resources in the 1990s are the following:

1. Formulate and identify for employees a clear set of job

responsibilities and performance expectations—cooperatively set clear, difficult, but attainable objectives.

2. Provide employees with the necessary resources, including office automation systems, and training so they may be able to perform more effectively and attain their objectives.

3. Provide prompt and frequent feedback on performance, and provide rewards based on accomplishment of objectives and results.

4. Redesign jobs where necessary to provide satisfying, meaningful work and use automation to relieve employees of repetitive tasks requiring little thought.

5. Solicit employee participation in all decision-making processes and keep them informed of developments in new and existing programs.

6. Develop organizational structures that integrate functions and decentralize the organization's authority.

7. Develop productivity programs that support the overall organization's mission. Include human resource development, automated office systems, and environmental design in these programs.

8. Take part in developing long-term strategic plans for the organization. Integrate office automation systems as a tool to facilitate these plans.

9. Balance the emphasis for technology and the environment with an overriding concern for people.

10. Keep current with trends and developments that have the potential of affecting the organization. Work to actively influence the course of events that determine organizational success.

These solutions are varied, and will require flexibility, foresight and determination on managers' part. Throughout these solutions, however, runs a common thread. Weaving its way through many of the problem areas is the need for a renewed focus on the people element of an organization. New technologies must serve users, whether they are managers or employees, enabling them to perform not only more efficiently, but more effectively in meeting the organization's overall goals and objectives.

Technology
with a
Human Touch

———————————— Sally E. Ketchum

*"The fact is, civilization requires slaves. . . . Unless there are slaves
to do the ugly, horrible, uninteresting work, culture and contempla-
tion become almost impossible. Human slavery is wrong, insecure,
and demoralizing. On mechanical slavery, on the slavery of the machine, the future of the world depends."* —Oscar Wilde

John Gould is a bitter man. As head of systems and procedures for
an east coast insurance carrier, it fell to him to try to establish a
"human" approach to office automation. "In 1976, no one here knew
what office automation meant," he says. "So I made a presentation
to our senior-management committee on its potential at this company. And they voted unanimously in favor of an approach that
stressed proper people solutions, *not* technical solutions."

But the data-processing department never gave up its search
for a technological fix. And after eight years of "intramural fighting," Gould (a pseudonym) has given up on ever establishing a uni-
fied, humanistic approach to office automation at the company.
"The company missed an opportunity to get more out of clerical
workers, managers, and executives; to develop a cohesive approach
that took in human factors. Nothing's tied together; people just keep
buying personal computers, which are expensive toys if they're not
doing anything substantive for the company. But management's not
doing anything about controlling them."

Gould's experience illustrates some of the consequences when a
company fails to consider the *users* of technology first during office-
automation implementation. Companies that ignore users' profes-

Reprinted from *Computer Decisions*, September 1983, pages 163 ff., copyright 1983,
Hayden Publishing Company.

sional needs risk not only inefficient equipment choices, but also damaged morale and decreased productivity. In some organizations, the high-handed imposition of office automation has spurred office unionization. And the underlying problem at Gould's company—a lack of consistent direction from the top—is not uncommon.

"CEOs almost never get interested in office automation," asserts John Connell, executive director of the Office Technology Research Group in Pasadena, California. "That's not good, because there are organizational and operational considerations associated with bringing in new systems that ought to be taken into account ahead of time. But, thus far, there is little or no appreciation of that in senior-management ranks."

Connell says that because many top executives think of office automation (OA) as a "machine problem," instead of a business problem, they are likely to delegate it to specialists or "techies." That's the first mistake, he says: "When you do that, you'll wind up with a system that has dazzling technical specifications but little appeal for people. To a great extent, OA specialists are machine-happy."

Gould agrees: "It's like buying an automobile for your family; you don't make the decision based on the differential ratio of the gears in the rear axle. Most dp people look at office automation in terms of networks, speed, screens, and refresh rate. And that has little to do with what the office needs." More pertinent considerations, he points out, are work patterns, information needs, and ease of use.

During his campaign at the insurance carrier, Gould had recommended and helped establish an OA steering committee that he hoped would deal with these issues. It included representatives from data processing, communications, and personnel, as well as executive users. It started out as an enthusiastic gathering, but Gould soon discovered that not everyone shared a spirit of cooperation.

"Data processing attended the meetings but did not tell us it was putting money into its own budget for mainframe terminals." This created a potential problem in integrating the terminals with the overall OA system. "When others challenged them, they said it was just experimental, but it wasn't. There are hundreds of terminals all over the dp department now, and they're not used much because the motivation for buying them was 'Gee whiz, this is a new technology; we should know about it.' That led to a lot of intramural fighting and the breakup of the committee."

After a last-ditch appeal by Gould, the same top-management committee that sanctioned his approach in the first place reaffirmed its position. But no action was taken, and even some of the committee members themselves ignored the edict. Since then, he adds, there has been no real, directed progress in office automation at the company.

Gould's explanation for the inaction? "Most dp organizations have their CEOs buffaloed. They're holding them for ransom. They'll say, 'We have enough problems without trying to modernize and revolutionize the way user departments handle information. If you also want your data processing done properly, if you want your bookkeeping done, you'll have to buy us bigger black boxes and build us new data centers to do all that work in.'"

The bottom line, Gould says, is that data processing is leading office-automation efforts at his company and others because it has the budgets and the clout. And sooner or later, he adds, "We'll find we've spent a lot of money and haven't gotten anything for it."

If a company *is* to get something out of office automation, there is homework to be done. Some planners routinely solicit the ideas of those who will use the machines in laying the groundwork for a system. But many others either ignore their suggestions or never ask them in the first place.

James Young, MIS director at Wrightline Inc. (Worcester, Massachusetts) offers an explanation: "Sometimes information planners feel they have the solution and the implementation date down pat, and don't want users to upset those plans. The users could delay the project, asking questions the planners would just as soon not have to deal with."

Avoiding those questions is a mistake, he adds. "You have to recognize that acceptance by the people using the equipment is the number-one factor in making office automation successful."

Unfortunately, there is no quick-and-easy way to ensure users will embrace a system. Human factors differ dramatically from one employee level to another, and determining just how those factors will affect acceptance of a system takes no small amount of time and resources. But looking at the experiences of those involved in office automation at various levels is a good place to start.

Typically, the approaches to implementing OA are strikingly different at the management and clerical levels. Where managers or executives may be given personal computers or executive workstations as perks or status symbols to use as they wish, clerical workers will likely have word processors foisted upon them with little or no warning, and then be told they must change their work patterns to accommodate the new technology. And there are more emotional issues.

"Systems brought in for clericals, even though we deny it, are aimed at least partly at eliminating jobs," says Connell. "Systems brought in for managers are never meant to eliminate jobs; they are tools to help them do their jobs better."

Connell believes that companies that began as smokestack enterprises are more likely to consider the impact of automation on workers. "In industries where unions helped to establish ground rules for automation, some form of those rules crept from the plant to the office."

Corning Glass in Corning, New York, has shown sensitivity to employees in automating its offices. "You have to involve users," says John Parker, director of Corning's information services division. "Not to involve users is suicide—in any aspect of systems design. You have to work with the professional group. Otherwise, they won't use the system, or they'll sabotage it!"

Corning's office-automation program excels in four important ways: personnel and information services work together to coordinate human needs and technological requirements; they emphasize training; user departments, considered customers, pay for services from their own budgets under a chargeback arrangement; and "involvement teams" serve as a buffer between users and technicians.

Parker's division and Corning's personnel department decided to join forces on office automation after discovering, while serving on the same corporate task force on productivity, that they were proceeding in two different directions—one technical and the other humanistic. In late 1980, the two started work on OA in earnest. They were brought even closer together in late 1981, when Parker began temporarily reporting to personnel after a corporate reorganization. Part of the reason for that, says Parker, "was to foster the relationship between information services and personnel."

Experts agree that a senior staffer from personnel—or human resources—must be involved from the very beginning in any office-automation project. No machine effort should proceed without strong consideration for employees, and, in most companies, responsibility for lobbying for that concern resides with the personnel department.

At Corning, one result of the partnership between personnel and information services is an information center containing "lots of user-friendly software." Here, teams from Parker's division solve technical problems and teach and consult with business professionals. "We spend 500 worker-days per year on education," he says.

Also, involvement teams have been formed to ensure that the important technical *and* human factors are taken into consideration in the implementation of office systems. Sandwiched between the user and the technician are an office-systems consulting group and an office-systems development group. The former, whose members have backgrounds in personnel management, organizational psychology, and the like, is concerned with human factors; the office-systems development group is made up of systems and technical personnel and serves as a hybrid human factors/technology group that determines the custom hardware and software needs of users. Parker calls this a "self-management process," and compares the groups to the Japanese concept of quality circles.

The fact that Parker's division, which encompasses data processing, office automation, and telecommunications, operates on a chargeback basis puts users in the driver's seat. Users can decide whether or not to "buy" aspects of the system. While this process has advantages and disadvantages for budgeting, it does establish that the needs of users are paramount.

Finally, Parker's background is eclectic—he has experience in finance with a manufacturing operation, a degree in math, and for 18 months he reported to Corning's personnel vice president. This variety may account in part for Parker's orientation toward assisting users. "Technical people often underestimate the need for support of and concern for the user," he says. "They get overly enamored of the technology and often fail to see the need for extensive training."

Because the need for training is not as great among clericals (who are generally better trained than managers and executives to operate keyboards) and because the organizational discipline is already in place, the clerical function is often the first targeted for automation. Connell contends that companies should be setting their sights higher. "The big opportunity lies with the rest of the workforce," he says. "Seventy-five percent of all office costs are attributable to middle managers and professionals. So the big question is, Why concentrate on clerical jobs?"

The answer may be that it's easier to start at the bottom. Middle managers, and certainly executives, won't stand for a system that doesn't suit their needs. Without a directive from the top that stresses user involvement in OA planning, all the sophisticated computers in the world won't help improve performance at this level. You can lead executives to computers, but you can't make them compute.

No one completely understands or agrees on the intellectual, emotional, and psychological needs of workers whose jobs are being automated. But on the critical need for training and support—especially at the management level—there is a consensus.

"It takes more time than anyone will admit to become proficient in the use of this equipment," says Gordon Davis, professor of management information systems at the University of Minnesota in Minneapolis. "User-friendliness and adequate training time are important at the professional level."

An organized training program will help middle managers, and especially executives, overcome computer phobia and computer illiteracy. These are more likely to be encountered in management ranks than among clericals, who are generally more familiar with keyboards and electronic office equipment. The same executive who blithely hops a plane to negotiate a tough business deal in the Middle East one day may turn to jelly in front of a computer terminal the next.

Bill Sadtler, division telecommunications analyst for IBM's Federal Systems Division (Bethesda, Maryland), cites computer phobia as one of the reasons users resisted training on the division's internal messaging system. Users, he says, weren't taking full advantage of the system's capabilities.

To learn how use of the system could be increased, Sadtler headed up a task force that interviewed users. One question in particular evoked a telling response. "We asked users whether they needed additional training to learn all the system's features," explains Sadtler. "Almost every one of them said yes. But when asked whether they would attend training sessions, they replied no."

The explanation, says Sadtler, is that most of the high-level users felt they had mastered the features they *needed*. They didn't want to invest more time learning the finer points, which they saw as being of marginal value. And, he admits, "Even at IBM, there is a great deal of computer fright among nontechnical executives." The solution, he says, is to "make our messaging system require little, if any, training."

Because time is so precious to managers, tailoring office automation to users, as Sadtler points out, is paramount at this level. Says author Ben Shneiderman, "The goal is not to create a computerized system, but to serve the user."

Even subtleties like the wording of system messages make a difference in how a user responds. Faced with enigmatic messages, an initially enthusiastic manager may lose patience with a computer and, perhaps, never return to it. As one east-coast executive observed after his first encounter with a personal computer: "It's like something out of a Kafka novel. It doesn't tell you what you did wrong; if just says, *You're wrong!*" He hasn't powered up his computer once since "ERROR 92" flashed accusingly on his screen.

In his book, *Software Psychology, Human Factors in Computer and Information Systems* (Little, Brown, 1980), Shneiderman stresses the need for interactive—that is, conversational—systems, whose design takes into consideration, among other things:

1. The time it takes to learn specific functions;
2. The speed required to perform a task;
3. The rate of errors that can be tolerated; and
4. The extent of human retention of functions necessary over time.

"Well-designed diagnostic facilities and error messages can make a system appealing," writes Shneiderman. "When user entries do not conform to expectations, diagnostic messages should guide the user in entering correct commands. Messages should be brief, without negative tones, and constructive. Avoid ringing bells and bold messages which may embarrass the user. Instead of meaningless messages like 'ILLEGAL SYNTAX,' try to indicate where the error occurred and what may be done to set it right. . . ."

Shneiderman adds that the computer should present itself as a servant rather than a know-it-all authority. A prompt might read, "READY FOR NEXT COMMAND" rather than "ENTER NEXT COMMAND," for example. Experienced users, especially those at upper levels, will "resent messages which suggest that the computer is in charge," he says.

But Gordon Davis at the University of Minnesota cautions: "I get turned off by those cutesy, anthropomorphic messages like 'That's a good answer.' These tend to help people relax, but systems must have beginner *and* expert modes. This way, once you become proficient, you can take shortcuts around prompts you no longer need." Shneiderman concurs, saying that only children appreciate praise from a computer.

Shneiderman, who is also an associate professor at the University of Maryland's Department of Computer Science and head of the university's new Laboratory for Human-Computer Interaction, says that senior managers can have a positive influence on office automation by creating a position for a "human engineer," whose duties would include organizing a system design team, interviewing users, preparing schedules, and estimating costs.

"Management support begins with the creation of the human-engineering role, which will be the center of responsibility for the human-computer interface," he says.

Shneiderman also suggests that a mechanism for feedback from users be established, such as electronic mail or online questionnaires. But most of all, he says, the CEO should simply promote the human side of OA. "That will get second-level people to jump," he says.

But for all the problems managers might encounter in automating some of their tasks, most who have learned to use computers will admit the machines can in fact help them to do their jobs better. At the clerical level, though, the widely held notion that office automation necessarily increases productivity, improves job satisfaction, and creates new jobs is being challenged almost as vigorously as the "trickle-down" theory of economics. Though the technology itself may make these gains possible, misguided management practices, based on those prevalent in factories during the Industrial Revolution, theaten to dilute and, in some cases, negate the benefits of office automation.

The Babbage principle is one concept used, perhaps unwittingly, as the basis for destructive management. One of the tenets of that principle is described by Harry Braverman in his 1974 book, *Labor and Monopoly Capital: The Degradation of Work in the Twentieth Century:* "[According to the Babbage principle], those of little or no special training are superior in the performance of routine work . . . because they can always be purchased at 'an easy rate,' and . . . because, undistracted by too much in their brains, they will perform routine work more correctly and faithfully."

This sort of management outlook jibes with automation of clerical work, which is, by nature, somewhat standardized and repetitive. But, according to 9 to 5, National Association of Working Women (Cleveland, Ohio), this view depends on invalid assumptions about human nature that can actually lower productivity.

High on the list of invalid assumptions is that clerical workers are stupid. This leads to underestimation of what clerical workers can offer—and to unnecessarily dull jobs. *Computer Decisions'* Western Editor, Martin Lasden, quoted an insurance-claims approver in his article, "Unrest in the data-entry department" (May 1983): "I hate not being able to use my intelligence. I hate the monotony. Your mind stagnates."

On the same list is the belief that computerized monitoring of workers, in combination with established work quotas, increases productivity. But according to Karen Nussbaum, executive director of 9 to 5, there is a Jekyll and Hyde potential in such close scrutiny of performance. The positive side of computerized monitoring is that good workers benefit from the irrefutable work record it provides. But, she says, "Error rates increase 40 to 400 percent when a machine monitors work."

Perhaps the most widely debated issue among data entry operators is the concern—or lack of concern—for their health. Those who presume that input operators can, like robots, manipulate a keyboard day after day, hour after hour, without consequence may be setting themselves up for a fall.

"Someday there will be hell to pay," says Nussbaum, "because health problems will begin to appear among these workers. User companies should demand that manufacturers supply hardware that, to the best of their knowledge, eases the eyestrain, backstrain, and stress" that can afflict data-entry operators.

The bottom line, Nussbaum says, is that it is in the best interests of a company to be concerned about the welfare of all its employees. "When people have more control over their work and more input into it, they tend to do better work, resulting in higher productivity. Unfortunately, we are seeing a lot more regimentation in the workplace."

As a result, lower-level office workers, through such organizations as the Service Employees International Union (SEIU) and the

AFL-CIO, are fervently seeking government regulations and union contracts that would limit the health and social costs of office automation.

District 925 of the SEIU organized claims processors at Equitable Life Assurance Society of America in Syracuse. The union subsequently filed a charge with the National Labor Relations Board because Equitable refused to negotiate with, or even recognize, District 925 as the claims processors' bargaining representative. The NLRB, in a summary judgment, ruled that Equitable's refusal to bargain with District 925 constituted disobedience of federal law. The NLRB made plans to take the insurance carrier to court.

Action is also being taken through state governments. At least seven states, including Maine, Massachusetts, New York, and Oregon, have considered legislation that would require, among other things, free eye examinations, lighting and ergonomic guidelines, and rest breaks approximately every two hours for terminal operators.

Regulations and unions—two words that send chills down the corporate spine. To business, they connote outside interference and inflated wages. To workers, they represent humane working conditions and job security.

But there are reasons beyond countering outside pressures for management to attend to human needs when automating offices. Sums up Shneiderman, "Human factors are often viewed as the final coat of paint, but they are actually the steel foundation of an office-automation implementation. The future will go to those who have a superior management-user interface."

The Human Resources Management System

———————————————————— Vincent R. Ceriello

It is becoming increasingly difficult to perform most staff jobs to-day without timely, accurate and relevant information. This fact is especially true in the personnel department.

Consequently, a human resources management system (HRMS) is becoming an absolute necessity in most organizations. Personnel professionals can use the system to properly manage employees, comply with government regulations, monitor costs and program results, and administer a variety of human resources programs.

At the same time, it is amazing how many organizations rush to automate without even having an idea of what they will do with the information the system will generate. This haste has caused some firms to rush into automation before they are really ready.

The effects of haste

Many organizations currently have some type of computer-based system. However, in many cases, these systems are mostly skeleton records added to an existing payroll system, sometimes as an after-thought. In cases like this, it is generally accepted that instead of solving a problem, this kind of system adds one more task to the already difficult job of maintaining personnel records.

The result of such add-on systems will be a computerized manual system that will inefficiently collect data that will be difficult and time consuming to retrieve on demand.

Many systems in use today are inefficient and, therefore, ineffective. Worse, they may be technical masterpieces that do not satisfy the user: the personnel professional.

The planning process

A systematic and disciplined approach should be used to plan for the development and implementation of an information system which ultimately will collect, store, maintain and report human resources data. The master database that will result from the HRMS planning process will make it practical, at reasonable cost, to accomplish the following:

1. Forecast human resources requirements;
2. Analyze historical information and trends;
3. Project manpower needs consistent with the company's strategic plans;
4. Act upon these needs through career planning, training and management development;
5. Establish long-range recruitment objectives;
6. Match individuals and positions more effectively;
7. Better utilize the capabilities of available resources.

A major reason for system failure is that most personnel departments generally have not participated in the planning of new computer applications, or have been denied the budgetary allocations to create or acquire information systems. Management often considers personnel a nonrevenue function and, therefore, generally ignores pleas to fund such "frills" as a computer-based HRMS to any significant degree.

Fortunately, this trend is changing. Management is becoming much more sensitive to the need for information about its prime resource: employees. This increased concern is certainly justified by the fact that the cost of salaries, benefits and other compensation may be as much as 25-50% of total operating expenses.

Furthermore, because of increasing government reporting requirements, it is now necessary to make efficient, expedient and accurate decisions. Decisions cannot be made with limited data.

It is obvious that any system is only as valuable as the data it maintains. These data must be readily converted into decision-making information. Ultimately, the test of the HRMS lies in the answer to the question: Does the HRMS give me more and better information than current systems—whether manual or automated?

The next step is to determine what information is needed for decision-making. This question can be answered through careful data-gathering, fact-finding and analysis. Avoid the temptation to short-circuit this phase, even though everyone wants the system to be both operational and productive as soon as possible. A review of the current system's capacity is usually a good starting point.

Where do the data come from? Where do the data go? Who handles the data? How are errors made?

It is then necessary to identify valid applications and distinguish between real needs and unrealistic demands. This may require input from nonpersonnel functions. Priorities must be established.

The HRMS should, ideally, be self-supporting and contribute to the organization's profits, or it should help control and contain costs. Maintenance of unnecessary data will greatly contribute to high operational costs, so data control is a desirable and realistic goal of planning.

An important consideration is the source and flow of employee data. Most organizations house this type of data in several places. Hiring and terminating employees can be a highly redundant exercise since numerous forms are used to process a new employee or to handle his or her termination.

By analyzing this process, and using the HRMS to consolidate or eliminate forms, it will be easier to more effectively manage human resources. Information can also be supplied through a common source with much less manual effort.

Generic guidelines

The concepts which follow are provided to assist in the development and implementation of an HRMS. These concepts are the building blocks that will foster the proper environment for development of a system that will make personnel operations more effective.

By the way, not all of the points presented pertain equally to any given organization. They are, however, mostly generic and should be applicable in most cases. Select or modify those that are most relevant to your situation and reject those that are not. These concepts are not in any particular sequence or order of importance. Therefore, you can arrange them to suit your needs.

Priorities and checkpoints

Establish priorities and allocate available resources on a priority basis; then develop an HRMS implementation schedule. The establishment of realistic timetables is critical to the success of the project. This timetable can help monitor progress, provide incentives to stay on target, and give early warning of impending problems.

Decide how frequently you need to update the HRMS so that you establish and maintain a credible database. Confidence in the data you store will lead to confidence in the decisions that are based upon that data. Remember that data is not useful unless it is timely, accurate and responsive. Maintenance of the data is extremely important.

Consider the establishment of a human resources information center as a control point for all HRMS transactions. The creation of this control point will eliminate duplicate record storage and help assure that all information is consistent.

Training requirements

Determine the need for staff training. Most organizations underestimate the amount of training required to orient employees to work with the new HRMS. Input of data to a computer system is generally a new discipline for most personnel clerks, and usually requires special training.

Discipline in control, accuracy and scheduling is necessary. Input must be available on schedule to assure validity of reports, and neatness counts. Other employees will be converting the data to a computer-format input. Improper transcription will create bad data, which, in turn, will become inaccurate reports.

It is easy to see why training should begin early in HRMS development. Training employees in basic HRMS concepts, and communicating the need for new work patterns and accuracy will prove highly beneficial in the long run.

Security and access control

In the beginning, develop a framework for system security and develop plans for limiting access. With the volume of data to be retained, policies and procedures should be established to control data. Certain data are more sensitive than others and must be more rigorously controlled. Determine who should have access to the system, to what parts of the system, and on what basis.

Next, determine which HRMS data elements to retain and how long to retain them. This, of course, adds additional requirements for security of the system since you must now be sure that record retention policies are established.

The final analysis

Don't neglect to establish a certification and audit procedure. Having the ability to evaluate and validate the data, foresee possible problem areas, and take corrective action is a frequently overlooked and underestimated concept.

Auditing can be performed by analyzing transaction edit and validation reports periodically. One easy way to do so is to run tests on specific data elements, looking for reasonableness of employee data relative to other data.

For example, employees with a college degree must have a major beyond a high school diploma, and must have graduated from an institution beyond high school. If the system has codes for education levels, majors and schools, these data can be validated.

Interfacing with payroll

If you are considering a combined personnel/payroll system, analyze carefully the interface requirements. Determine who should input the necessary data elements, and who is responsible for maintaining that data. What procedures and forms will be necessary to
maintain input control and who will use them?

Also consider processing cycles and operating costs. In many
instances, the personnel system, unlike the payroll system, is not
run under specific cycles. It may be more efficient to have the payroll system be the front end of the entire HRMS. It may also be
desirable to have all transactions flow through the personnel system first. This decision must, of course, be made before the system
is installed. If it isn't, future changes in documentation and forms
design could result and prove to be costly.

Personnel reporting

The HRMS should be able to generate numerous reports. Personnel
reports are, after all, the end product of what goes into the HRMS,
and they are all that most people "see" when they assess the responsiveness of the system.

At this point, a discussion of the various types of personnel reports, and how they should be used, is appropriate:

Personal profile   This profile contains basic employee data: name,
sex, race, age, marital status, address and phone number, physical
limitations, etc.

Career profile   This profile is used to chronicle significant events
in an employee's career: performance appraisals, job title changes,
changes in job classification, salary changes, and promotions and
transfers.

Skill profile   This profile allows review of an employee's education and training background—certificates, licenses, degrees and
individual skills—to assist in considering his or her advancement
within the organization.

Benefits profile   This profile contains relevant information on
employee benefits: life, medical and dental insurance; disability provisions and other risk benefits; pension, profit sharing and thrift
plan data; and nonfinancial benefits such as vacations, holidays and
sick leaves.

In addition, the system can generate detailed reports, summar-
ies, exception reports and reminders. Each serves a separate purpose, and each is available to HRMS users in a limitless variety of
formats and sequences.

Final advice

Implement the HRMS in bite-size chunks or modules if you want to achieve an effective system within an acceptable timeframe. Normally, human resources data are functionally interdependent. Some data is specific to one function, but most basic data will be required by all functions. In addition, some functions may need more specialized data that could overlap several functions.

If the HRMS database is well planned, it is possible to satisfy major information requirements in all functional areas. As additional data is added to support new functions, existing functions will benefit.

The concepts presented here are the primary ones you will have to deal with in the development and implementation of a comprehensive human resources management system. In my experience, these are the areas that have caused most of the problems in the past. However, other problems may arise due to unique characteristics of your organization.

Sex and Power in the Work Place

———— Richel Raines, Trudy Sopp, and Yvonne Williams

"Are you sure that sexual harassment goes on here? I've never seen it before."
— *Workshop participant, middle management level*

Everyone wants a productive work environment—especially management. Supervisors have the responsibility to create and keep the work place operating smoothly and efficiently. Sexual issues that interfere with employees doing their job cost organizations money.

Productivity is reduced when employees spend time and energy trying to avoid sexual approaches or trying to figure out how to handle them. Employee job satisfaction goes down when they see sexual power plays rewarded more than honest hard work and competence in the job.

There is evidence that absenteeism and job turnover can be the results of employees worn out by having to deal with daily doses of sexual harassment. Recruitment, hiring, and training translate into big dollars for the organization and extra work for the remaining employees.

These problems *can* be avoided. Sexual harassment is a violation of Title VII of the 1964 Civil Rights Act. Putting it simply—sexual harassment is against the law, and it can cost an organization time, money, and employees.

The Equal Employment Opportunity Commission's guidelines say the following conduct violates federal law:

Unwelcome sexual advances, requests for sexual favors, and other verbal and/or physical conduct of a sexual nature constitute sexual harassment

Reprinted with permission from the June 1983 issue of *Western City*, the official publication of the League of California Cities.

when (1) submission to such conduct is made either explicitly or implicitly a term or condition of an individual's employment, (2) submission to or rejection of such conduct by an individual is used as the basis for employment decisions affecting such individual, or (3) such conduct has the purpose or effect of unreasonably interfering with an individual's work performance or creating an intimidating, hostile, or offensive working environment.

Written examples of sexual harassment include suggestive or obscene letters, notes and invitations; verbal examples include derogatory comments, slurs or jokes; physical examples include assault, touching, impeding or blocking movements; and visual examples include leering, sexually-oriented gestures, or display of sexually suggestive or derogatory objects, pictures, cartoons, or posters. Other examples include the threat or insinuation that lack of sexual favors will result in reprisal; withholding support for appointments, promotion or transfer; rejection on probation; punitive actions; change of assignments; or a poor performance report.

The ways in which sex and power come into play in the work place can be broken down into several groupings suggested by Dr. Natasha Josefowitz in *Personnel Administrator*, March 1982.

Attraction
"He's always in her office, I know they're not talking business. Just wait until he dumps her. I bet she'll transfer."
—Office worker, city department

Attraction can occur in the workplace between both co-workers and supervisors and subordinates. One aspect is genuine, real attraction between two people. Another is attraction where the relationship between two people is misunderstood by others and comments are made like, "Gee, they sure spend a lot of time together. I wonder what is going on?"

An attraction which turns into an office romance between a supervisor and subordinate can carry the serious consequences of charges of favoritism, unequal work distribution, and "sleeping one's way to the top." Here the power difference between the two causes problems for both. Even if the person in the more powerful position, typically a man, tries every means to treat the employee involved even-handedly and fairly at work, others will perceive this behavior differently. Their actions, their exchanges, their warm glances will be perceived with ridicule and suspicion because they have mixed sex and power.

The perceptions of fellow employees create the "reality" of an affair at work. Perceptions are what count and they have enormous impacts. The supervisor cannot control how others will feel about a relationship with a subordinate. At the very least, this relationship can be seen as an abuse of power.

Such a relationship has serious consequences for the work group: time is wasted due to gossiping; the group could feel demoralized; and productivity could decrease as feelings of respect for the supervisor dwindle. If the relationship ends unhappily, one of the two parties involved might quit the organization, be bitter enough to purposely slow down the work pace, be transferred, demoted or not promoted, or simply lose job interest.

There are many examples where such office romances turn out well and the couple and organization adjust to the relationship. However, there are considerably more examples that show how the relationship affects the organization in unproductive ways.

Assumed attraction occurs when two people spend a great deal of time working together, and respect and admire each other and these feelings are read into as "an affair." A familiar example of assumed attraction is two co-workers or a supervisor and subordinate having lunch together frequently, and the rumors start flying

---

Some sexual harassment case law

Put up or get out cases
Tompkins v *Public Service Electric and Gas Co.* 568 F.2d 1044 (1977)
The victim claimed her supervisor made sexual requests and then threatened her with dismissal if she failed to cooperate. When she filed a grievance with the company and sought a transfer she was fired. The company supported the dismissal and was held liable.

Miller v *Bank of America* 600 F.2d 211 (1979)
The victim alleged her supervisor promised her a better job if she would cooperate sexually. She was terminated when she refused his overtures. The court found Bank of America liable on the basis that the bank was responsible for the sexually harassing behavior of the supervisor *even though it had an established policy against sexual harassment.*

Working condition cases
Bundy v *Jackson* 641 F.2d 934 (1981)
The victim was repeatedly propositioned by various higher ranking males. She suffered no direct employment consequences as a result of this harassment but her working environment became unbearable. The court ruled that sexual harassment which does not result in any negative employment related consequences may create an offensive working environment which is in violation of Title VII.

Continental Can v *State of Minnesota*, Minnesota Supreme Court (1980)
The victim was continually harassed by her co-workers. When she complained to her supervisor, he ignored her complaints, stating she

that there is something going on. Such perceptions can hurt reputations and productive working relationships.

It is important to watch for jokes, innuendo and gossip about two people who simply work intensely and well together. This assumption of attraction can cause the two, previously enthused and hardworking employees, to avoid one another, act awkwardly in each other's presence, alter once-effective working patterns and become angry and depressed about the injustice of the gossip. Assuming attraction and office romance where no attraction may exist is harmful and a morale issue that falls squarely on the shoulders of management.

Transference

"He helps me and looks out for me. I'm the first woman in this section . . . it's hard to get help from the guys so [he] has been a savior."
                                                     —Laborer, public agency

---

had to expect that kind of behavior when working with men. The company was held liable for the behavior of her co-workers.

Kyriazi v *Western Electric* 461 F. Supp. 894 (1978)
The victim's co-workers and supervisors continually ridiculed and harassed her and other female employees. The company's lack of response caused the behaviors to get worse. The company was held liable and was required to pay $8.5 million based on sex discrimination. Individual male co-workers were required to pay separate money damages directly to the victim for their participation in their harassment against her.

Tort and contract law cases
Clark v *World Airways* Federal District Court, District of Columbia (1977)
A female supervisor quit her job after six days because of sexual demands by her boss which were made a condition of employment. She received $2,500 in compensatory damages and $50,000 in punitive damages for negligence, breach of contract and emotional distress.

Seritis v *Lane* 22 C.P.D. Par. 30 757 (1980)
Waitresses who either sought employment or filed grievances with their union were sexually propositioned and solicited for prostitution by the secretary-treasurer of their local. Since the local controlled the hiring, salary and working conditions of waitresses in a large number of area bars and restaurants, the victims were afraid for their employment opportunities if they failed to comply. The court found both the local and secretary-treasurer liable for willful infliction of emotional distress.

When new employees transfer or associate the good feeling they have for people in their past onto their new mentor or boss, transference is occurring. The new employee relates and responds to the mentor in much the same way they responded to people in authority positions in the past. If new employees have a positive attitude toward people in authority positions, they will easily respond positively to new acquaintances in authority positions. Statistics show that most authority positions in the work environment are filled by men, so most examples of transference occur between the male mentor and the female employee. It is important to keep in mind that transference refers to the positive feelings about the *authority position*, not the individual.

It is important to be aware of and understand transference to prevent a productive relationship from becoming troublesome and tense. As a rule, there is no reason why men and women should not be assigned to work together, and the mentoring relationship between the two should be encouraged. This familiarity, sharing of expertise, and training can only benefit the organization's effectiveness and performance.

Transference can be prevented from turning into a troublesome situation if it is clear to all employees that individuals in authority positions are not to ask out employees in lower power positions. To do so would be an abuse of one's position and unethical. It is important to remember that subordinates depend on those higher in the organization for their promotions and paychecks, and they perceive few options when a supervisor asks for a date.

Harassment

"You know . . . I'm tired of all the dirty jokes they think are so funny. It bothers me, but if I complain they'll accuse me of not having a sense of humor. It's already hard enough to get accepted by them."
—Long-term employee, city department

The Equal Employment Opportunity Commission (EEOC) defines sexual harassment as "unwelcome sexual advances, requests for sexual favors and other verbal and physical conduct of a sexual nature." This conduct is usually connected to employment decisions, including pay, promotion, and layoffs or firing, or it may create a hostile, intimidating work environment.

Sexual harassment is illegal: It is important for supervisors to know that:

1. An employer is responsible for the actions of its employees with regard to sexual harassment when the employer knew or should have known about the conduct. The only exception is when the employer took corrective action immediately.

Are you a victim?

As soon as you, the victim, suspect a problem:

Get evidence of your good working record. Make notes about what is in your personnel file. Take a witness if possible. Get a letter in writing from past or present employees or supervisors about your good work record.

If you know who the harasser is, put that person on notice—with witnesses, if possible. Tell the harasser that a particular behavior is not appreciated. If appropriate, make your demands in writing—signed and dated. Send to harasser by certified mail. If you do not think it necessary to mail—deliver the complaint in person, with a witness if possible.

Document every incident: write down what was said or done and include date, time, witnesses, and your response.

Look for supporters. Search out possible witnesses or people who are aware of the incidents. Search out other possible victims.

Contact the harasser's supervisor. Preferably write to the harasser's supervisor requesting a meeting. At the interview, give the supervisor a written complaint letter, signed and dated. At the beginning of the interview, describe what actions you have taken and ask for additional help. Ask the supervisor what he or she is going to do about it. The supervisor may ask for more information, but if you feel the questions are too personal, remember all you have to do if you are contemplating legal action is put the supervisor on notice.

If the harasser's supervisor fails to act, use internal grievance procedures or administrative remedies. You can file a complaint with a state or federal agency, and a civil complaint. Seek an injunction prohibiting civil harassment.

2. An employer may be responsible for the acts of non-employees, such as salespeople, the public, or customers, with respect to sexual harassment when the employer knew or should have known about offensive conduct and failed to take immediate corrective action.

3. The EEOC has mandated that employers should act to prevent sexual harassment by all available means. This can be achieved through training, developing and communicating the organization's policy on this issue, discussion of the issue, expressing strong disapproval, and by enforcing sanctions for violations of acceptable conduct.

Most incidents of harassment are unreciprocated or onesided. Some of these behaviors are enjoyed and considered fun by some employees. What is important is that there will be employees who are offended by this behavior.

To deal with sexual harassment, a supervisor must identify the clues given by subordinates that indicate the behavior is unwelcome and offensive. But many employees will mask how they feel about certain behaviors to avoid "rocking the boat" or "hurting anyone else's feelings." Also, there are very subtle forms of harassment, such as commenting on the clothing of an individual in a sexual way. The subtle forms are the most difficult to identify and deal with.

Supervisors should inform all employees of the policy on sexual harassment, and make a strong statement that unprofessional behavior that creates a hostile work environment will not be tolerated. A good rule for all employees to follow to be safe and not sorry is: "When in doubt—*don't!*"

Supervisors should make it known to all employees that complaints will be heard and issues dealt with in a timely and sensitive way. They should be available for employees to discuss incidents, even when they aren't willing or ready for action on the information. They should also be prepared to help employees develop strategies to deal with the problem without getting the supervisor too involved.

When a problem arises, the victim should be thoroughly questioned regarding the incident. The victim may not want action taken on the information, but supervisors may be compelled to take action if the incident is serious, especially since the law requires "immediate corrective action." The sexual harasser must be informed of a complaint. If the victim does not want to be identified, his or her name should not be given. However, with a formal complaint the identity of the victim will be revealed.

Seduction

"The only way to get noticed around this place is to wear a tank top. Nobody cares about how hard you work."
                                        —*Female utility worker, public agency*

Seduction is the attempt to use one's sex to gain some sort of advantage at the workplace. Usually, it is used by employees who do not see a connection between hard work or ability and promotions or pay raises. They may feel that personal relationships have a better chance of affecting their work environment or careers, and try to use nonprofessional behavior to achieve objectives which may include better hours, better shift or crews, less work, a better salary, or a promotion. Women are usually associated with seduction since they are most often in the subordinate or less powerful position, but these tactics may also be used by men.

Seduction operates from the bottom up—someone with less power attempts to gain some kind of advantage from someone higher up. Sometimes employees will advertise their "availability" through dress or little side comments implying that a sexual relationship may be possible. Sometimes it's an overt proposition such as sexual favors for work favors. This kind of behavior gets attention, if nothing else, and if the person on the receiving end takes advantage of the situation, it usually leads to trouble.

Not every attempt to gain the favor of a supervisor is seduction. There must be a clear sexual overtone. Wearing see-through blouses or ultra tight slacks may be a part of a seduction ploy, but getting new clothes or a new hair style probably is not. There must be a direct connection between the seducer, the desire for some kind of advantage, the sexual behavior, and the victim, the person in a power position. If one of the elements is missing, seduction as a power issue in the workplace is not occurring.

Some people dress inappropriately for work. It does not mean they are trying to gain work-related advantages. They may be unaware of formal or informal dress codes or simply be unaware of the impression they are making. The "seducer" must be counseled. Clearly refer to the specific behavior and point out that such behavior is inappropriate in the workplace. Send clear messages that the particular behavior is not appreciated and will not achieve the desired result. Try not to humiliate the employee. She or he may be unaware of the messages being sent.

Hazing

"I hate going to work some days. They think that all the garbage they pull is so funny. Well, I have news for them, it's not funny and it never was."

—Female employee in non-traditional job

Hazing involves actions taken against or at the expense of new employees when they first enter an organization. These actions can include physical acts, pranks, jokes, and teasing. The purported outcome of these actions is membership in the work group. Although not every action is sexual in nature, hazing becomes a more difficult problem as more women enter the work force in nontraditional jobs. There are more opportunities for sexual harassment to occur, especially when it's disguised as hazing. When the hazing act includes sexual overtones, it may be moved beyond hazing into sexual harassment.

Hazing occurs when new members of an organization are subject to certain behaviors as a kind of initiation rite. Not all kinds of hazing are discriminatory or harassing. However, hazing is usually used as an excuse for behavior which is clearly inappropriate in a work setting.

Are you a harasser?

What should you do if you think that you might fit into the description of a sexual harasser?

Immediately stop any behaviors which you even remotely suspect may be interpreted as harassing. Stop telling off-color jokes or stories; stop touching colleagues or subordinates, except for a neutral handshake. Stop any sexually-oriented kidding around, or any sexual remarks or propositions, even if everyone "knows" you are kidding.

Check out how others view you in the work environment. Do people feel comfortable being honest with you? Do your subordinates or colleagues tell you about behaviors which they find oppressive or inappropriate?

Ask yourself the following questions, and be honest with your answers.

1.   Do you treat people of both sexes equally?
2.   Do you care if you offend people?
3.   Do you ever use negative behavior to get attention?
4.   Do you ever feel a sense of power when you make other uncomfortable?
5.   Do you ever "flirt" for recreation?
6.   Do you ever consider the effect of your actions on how others feel about you and their job?
7.   Do you like to get "even" if someone puts you on the spot?
8.   Do you understand the fact that some people have a need for more personal space than others?
9.   Do you really listen when someone tries to tell you something that you do not want to hear?
10. Are you seriously interested in changing your behavior?

Make sure you understand the seriousness of a sexual harassment charge. You could face an internal investigation which could result in your suspension, demotion, transfer or termination; a civil lawsuit against *you* personally, as well as the agency you work for, and a civil injunction to prohibit you from being anywhere near the person you have harassed.

Current law considers the interpretation of the victim, *not* the intent of the harasser. Do not think that because no one minds your behavior and you do not intend to harass anyone that you are protected.

For example, a female carpenter apprentice has her work boots nailed to the floor or her tool box hidden. Such behavior is non-productive and leads to frustration, anger and a loss of respect for co-workers. It is usually labeled as a "joke." Is that kind of "joke" appropriate to the work setting? If the joke is repeated, there is a high probability that the employee in question may resign or transfer.

Don't confuse hazing with tradition. Some jobs are traditionally assigned to new employees. These are usually the less desirable jobs, but if they are assigned to all new employees equally, then it is not hazing.

Supervisors must decide if the "hazing" is a potential problem or just a one-time test or tradition done equally to all new employees. Has hazing ever humiliated, angered, or embarrassed an employee in the past? Have the jokes been at one person's expense? Has anyone ever been excluded from the group because she or he can't take a joke? Has anyone been transferred, demoted or terminated because of group pressure?

The issues of sex and power that arise between women and men in the workplace are complex and sometimes sticky. A supervisor's responsibility is to identify these issues and to take action in a fair and professional manner. The goal is prevention. However, when a problem does arise, it must be handled quickly.

Public Employee Physical Fitness Programs

William M. Timmins

An increasing number of jurisdictions, public and private, are providing physical fitness programs for their employees. This article describes such physical fitness programs, estimates their frequency in the public sector, and evaluates the success-to-date of such efforts.

In 1894 John H. Patterson, founder of the National Cash Register (N.C.R.) Company, appointed a health and hygiene trainer for the firm (named Palmer) who initiated an unusual corporate physical fitness program:

He prescribed early morning exercises for all executives and immediately all of the executives were required to be at the factory at five o'clock in the morning, to go through calisthenics, take a bath, and be rubbed down. They were given breakfast at the factory. A little later Palmer decided that all of these men should ride horseback in the morning. Mr. Patterson bought a great string of saddle horses, and for a long time any one who happened to be wandering about Dayton at dawn could see a cavalcade of N.C.R. executives, led by Mr. Patterson and Palmer, riding through Hills and Dales. Probably nothing like this ever happened before in an American business institution. Those of the executives who did not know how to ride and would not learn how to ride ceased forthwith to be executives. It was laid down as a maxim that no one who could not manage a horse could be expected to manage men.

The whole adventure has its funny side, but actually it was a mighty good thing for these men, shut up all day as they had been, to get out into the open. The N.C.R. people who date from this period are about as healthy a lot of individuals to-day as can anywhere be found.[1]

Reprinted with permission from *Public Personnel Management*, vol. 10, no. 2 (1981). Copyright 1981.

The N.C.R. experience is no longer singular. Corporate fitness programs are relatively widespread today—more than 400 major corporations now provide extensive exercise facilities, including large gymnasiums (e.g., Xerox in Webster, New York; Phillips Petroleum in Bartlesville, Oklahoma; and Gates Rubber in Denver). Such corporate exercise programs vary from companies that simply offer in-house facilities to those that provide full-fledged cardio-fitness centers (e.g., McGraw-Hill and Exxon Corporation of New York, Times-Mirror in Los Angeles, and others). Some corporations have sponsored extensive competitive sports programs.[2]

Kimberly-Clark Corporation spent several million dollars building health and physical fitness facilities in Neenah, Wisconsin, near the corporate headquarters. The complex was staffed by 15 full-time health personnel who "help employees maintain or improve their health instead of providing medical assistance only after they become ill." The program for the 2,100 employees was voluntary but some 60 percent of eligible workers signed up.[3]

Premature death is computed to cost American industry $25 billion annually and 132 million lost workdays. Companies are spending large sums of money to cut employee costs by sponsoring medically approved and directed cardiovascular fitness programs. For instance, employee health plans cost General Motors Corporation $825 million a year. Even small improvements in employee health can effect large savings for the company.[4] Indeed, one writer has said that "a small investment yields rich human dividends." Steven Levisohn describes some significant benefits after only the first year of a program at the National Fire Protection Association in Boston, Massachusetts.[5]

Basic action steps for companies interested in corporate physical fitness programs have been recommended by Robert Kreitner as follows:

1. Stimulate top management's interests in and, later, a firm commitment to employee physical fitness.
2. Survey employee feelings concerning proposed facilities and programs.
3. Collect relevant information and data from government and industrial sources.
4. Proceed with the definition of program policy and objectives.
5. Provide the essential facilities and equipment while retaining the option of later expansion if warranted. (Leasing or sharing of public or private facilities must not be overlooked as alternatives to construction.)
6. Adequately staff the program with qualified experts. (Some may choose to carry out this step prior to or concurrent with the preceding step to assure the compatibility of facilities and programs).

7. Provide an appealing variety of programs and employ motivational aids as necessary.
8. Maintain a cycle of diagnostic/remediation evaluation with appropriate stress testing facilities, staff, and programs.
9. Integrate the physical fitness and coronary heart disease prevention programs into daily organizational activity through promotional and educational strategies.
10. Periodically evaluate and revise programs as necessary.[6]

Public employees are not less prone to heart attacks, strokes and other forms of coronary heart disease than their private sector counterparts. Nor is the cost of premature death and loss of workdays less significant. Unfortunately, government has moved more slowly than business and industry in providing for employee fitness. But some positive gains are readily apparent.

How common are such employee physical fitness programs in the public sector? What general characteristics are there among existing programs? Can recommendations be made?

The author distributed a mailed questionnaire to a random sample of 75 public agencies selected from the IPMA *1980 Directory of Membership*. Fifty-three responses were received (or a return rate of over 70 percent) from cities, counties and school districts. Jurisdictions averaged 3,700 employees with a high of 77,000 workers and low of 80 personnel. Of the random sample, eleven (or 21 percent) *do* have some form of public employee physical fitness program. Additionally, at least three other public agencies which responded to the survey are presently considering adoption of such efforts. The balance of the survey, 36 public agencies (or some 72 percent), report no such fitness programs.

The eleven systems reporting employee fitness programs tended to be larger systems. While these eleven ranged from 77,000 employees to as few as 83, seven had more than 1,500 workers (and averaged over 22,000 because of sample skewing; the mode was slightly greater than 2,700). Five respondents were local governments in the Southeast (two in Florida, Georgia, North Carolina, South Carolina), three were local jurisdictions from the Midwest (Minnesota, Nebraska, Iowa), one was from the Rocky Mountains (Utah), and two were from the West (California, Hawaii). While responses were received from all sections of the country, of course, the eleven with employee fitness programs were more concentrated geographically. No particular importance is hypothesized for this clustering, however.

Fitness program examples

Four contrasting fitness programs are summarized below, being representative of the eleven survey respondents which do provide programs.

Typical of small jurisdictions with very restricted employee physical fitness programs was the City of Rock Hill, South Carolina. Rock Hill had 600 employees. In 1979 the city initiated a voluntary fitness program which was carried out after normal working hours. No pay or benefit incentives were linked to participation in the physical fitness program. Fewer than 10 percent of city employees participated. Participation was typically in weight lifting (the city provided a facility with such equipment to those who desired to use it), softball, tennis, bowling, and jogging. Employees averaged a half hour to one hour a day in such fitness events, with participation by some executives, middle managers, first line supervisors, and non-supervisory professional employees. The city did not provide any other facilities other than for weights and did not subsidize membership in a spa, YWCA/YMCA, or health club. Very little or no difference in efficiency was noticed in the small number who participated in fitness activities (few records were kept).

By contrast, Macon, Georgia (with 1,500 workers), reported a vigorous physical fitness program for its fire fighters (starting in 1977) and police officers (starting in 1979). The city "provides an exercise facility. We furnish exercise clothing and shoes." Macon provided worker compensation and other leave privileges for those injured while working out. Over 86 percent of police and fire personnel participated in Macon's mandatory program (the practice is mandated by ordinance). Personnel spent from 30 to 60 minutes a day in jogging, soccer, basketball, weight lifting, and other exercise routines before, during, or after normal working hours—indeed public safety personnel were "encouraged" to work out while on duty status. While no "pay or benefits" were linked to participation in the physical fitness program, continued employment was conditional upon such regular workouts. Macon's director of personnel reported that a very significant difference had been noted among participating fire fighters ("fewer on-the-job injuries, less fatigue at fires, less sickness, faster response time . . .") but added it was "too soon to tell" on police officers because of the newness of that part of the city's program.

The City and County of Honolulu (with 8,000 employees) had provided several exercise facilities (with gym equipment) for executives, middle managers, and first-line supervisors for many years. Participation was mandatory among police and fire managers and supervisors, and voluntary for supervisors/managers in the other city-county departments. It was estimated that half or less of all such personnel take part in fitness activities, usually jogging, volleyball, basketball and tennis, for periods of 16 to 30 minutes daily and mostly during regular working hours. No pay or benefits were linked to participation (other than the mandatory participation by police and fire supervisors and managers) but the city-county utilized "exercise physiologists in planning programs based on individual physical profiles" in at least some cases. A very significant improvement in efficiency was claimed for those who participated in such efforts.

The largest system responding to the survey was the County of Los Angeles with a total of 77,000 employees. The county initiated its program in 1971 for executive level administrators, middle managers, and all members of the Fire and Sheriff's Departments. For Fire and Sheriff personnel, fitness program participation was mandatory, and voluntary for executives and other managers, but no pay or other benefit incentives were linked to participation in the physical fitness program. The county estimated that approximately 10,000 personnel participated in the program (Public Safety and other executives and managers), but less than 10 percent of the nonmandatory group took part. The county furnished "stationary bicycles, wall pulley weights, and universal gyms (in some locations)" but provided no sponsorship of health club, spa, or YMCA/ YWCA memberships. The most frequent activities were "jogging, calisthenics, weights, and some ball sports," with participants spending perhaps 16-30 minutes daily. Fire Department personnel participated during regular working hours, sheriff's personnel and other executives/managers participated before and after normal working hours. The county felt it was "difficult to assess" differences in performance and efficiency for those who participated except that, "performance on periodic medical examination shows physical working capacity improved" in participants.

The Los Angeles County Sheriff's Department requires an agility test as part of an annual fitness requirement, and suggests the following exercises to assist county employees in meeting these physical fitness needs:

Cardiovascular   Activities which will involve the heart, blood vessels, and lungs are the most important type of physical fitness activities to improve and maintain good health. The target heart rate to achieve minimum cardiovascular health benefits is approximately 140 beats per minute. One's heart rate should be self monitored. This can be done by counting the pulse for 10 seconds and multiplying by 6 to get the rate for the minute. A heart rate of 140 beats per minute is a desirable *intensity* to achieve a training effect. The *duration* of this work level should be continued for 20-30 minutes. The *frequency* should be at least three times per week.

The cardiovascular type activities should be performed in a designated area, either at the station to which the deputy is assigned, by using a stationary bicycle, handball or racketball court, or jogging track around the station. Other specifically designated areas close to the station may be utilized, such as local green belts, school tracks, or playing facilities. In addition, the Academy at Eastern

Avenue or the Agility Testing Station at County Jail may be used for exercising and practice.

Muscular strength   The use of the Universal Gym at each of the stations should be able to meet the needs of muscle development for those requiring a maintenance program as well as specific improvement needs. The Universal Gym Exercise Charts (examples are provided) and film (provided) may be used to involve the major muscle groups for a general conditioning program. When poor performance on the agility test requires special training and conditioning, an exercise physiology technician will work with the deputy to suggest and supervise specific training procedures. These will be designed to improve performance and, if properly carried out, enable the deputy to pass the test. Deputies who desire to exercise in preparation for taking the agility test will find the following exercises helpful. They have been grouped by the different agility tests. The exercises are illustrated in the Universal Gym Exercise Poster which should be posted on the wall wherever the Universal Gyms are located throughout the County Sheriff Stations. In general, the exercises should be performed in 2-3 sets of 6 to 8 repetitions, 3 times per week. The amount of weight selected will, of course, be relative to the size of the person and his or her past history of using weight resistance in an exercise program to improve performance. It is somewhat of a trial and error procedure to establish the correct amount of weight that one *actually* uses. In view of this it is always better to try the lighter weight until one feels a gradual increase is possible.

Flexibility   Many athletes will attest to the fact that when they are in good physical condition and maintain their flexibility they have fewer injuries. Athletic trainers utilize this concept in the teams they work with.

In maintaining maximal range of motion through regular stretching exercises, it is possible to prevent sudden extensive movements from overstretching the muscles and connective tissue, thereby causing an injury. Back problems are the second most expensive Workers Compensation type of injury for county safety employees.

Specific stretching exercises are suggested in the hand-out materials given during Phase II of the medical examination. Additional stretching exercises will be developed as the need arises in assisting deputies to pass the battery of agility tests.

A series of exercises may be used to assist in muscular development for deputies needing to improve their ability in the respective agility tests.

In summary, the Los Angeles County Sheriff covers these exercises and related fitness programs in briefing sessions and in-service training using training films, visuals, handouts, and an "exercise chart" involving some 21 exercises. The department uses materials developed by the Los Angeles County Cardiopulmonary Laboratory of the L.A. Occupational Health Service.

Examples of the public agencies which responded to the survey which are now developing an interest in employee fitness programs are Pinellas County, Florida, which "recently joined in the formation of an employers group called the Bay Area Employers Group on Health, which will pursue employee fitness as one major area of concern in decreasing employer health costs, while simultaneously improving employee well-being and effectiveness," and the U.S. Department of Commerce (with 38,000 employees) which plans to open a "physical fitness facility" for departmental employees.

Summary

The private sector has demonstrated for many years that employee physical fitness programs pay off in reduced health care costs, reduced sick leave and disability leave, and improved morale and productivity. Our IPMA survey shows that nearly 25 percent of the public agencies which responded are now engaged in some sort of fitness program(s) or are planning to initiate some such effort.

Typically, such public agencies are larger employers—that is, with 2,700 or more employees. Usually such fitness programs are mandatory for public safety personnel and optional for others. Most such programs are modest in scope, short term in nature (half an hour or less each day, or even less frequent), offer no incentives for participation (other than job retention for public safety employees), and are most commonly carried out before or after regular working hours. Public agencies which have provided gym equipment or facilities tend to be very large employers.

Finally, little serious research is presently being carried out to document the benefits of such employee physical fitness programs. This suggests a rich opportunity for funding of several research projects and further exploration by students and researchers. Anyone who has jogged or otherwise taken part in a regular program of vigorous physical exercise knows "they feel better" and so forth. What is needed now is to apply what the private sector can teach us about employee fitness and to experiment and innovate in the public sector. We have nothing to lose but our waistlines and flab, and an opportunity to make public workers feel better, live better, and work better.

About three-fourths or more of public agencies (according to our survey) have yet to become involved in better ensuring their employees' health and well-being.

1. Samuel Crowther, *John H. Patterson: Pioneer in Industrial Welfare* (New York: Doubleday, Page & Company, 1923), p. 221.
2. "The Healthy Trend Toward Corporate Exercise Programs," *Business Week*, April 3, 1978, p. 91.
3. "Kimberly-Clark is Spending Millions to Insure Employees' Health, Well-Being," *Paper Trade Journal*, December 15, 1977, p. 40; and "The New Business Boom—Fitness," *Nation's Business*, February, 1978, pp. 68-70, 73.
4. "Keeping Managers in Good Heart," *International Management*, January, 1979, p. 40.
5. Steven R. Levisohn, "One Man's Guide to Corporate Fitness," *Harvard Medical Alumni Bulletin*, Fall 1979, pp. 23-26.
6. Robert Kreitner, "Employee Physical Fitness: Protecting an Investment in Human Resources," *Personnel Journal*, July, 1976, pp. 340-344. Kreitner's article cites more than 25 excellent references and sources of information.

For Further Reference

Part 1: Increasing Personnel System Effectiveness

Argyle, Nolan J. "Civil Service Reform: The State and Local Response." *Public Personnel Management Journal*, vol. 11, no. 2 (1982): 157-64.

Cole, John, and Udler, Allan. "Productivity and Personnel." *Civil Service Journal*, October-December 1976, pp. 23-28.

"Common Themes in Public Personnel Reform." *Personnel Management Reform*, vol. 1, no. 1 (September 1979).

Fowler, Alan. "Proving the Personnel Department Earns Its Salt." *Personnel Management*, May 1983, pp. 25-29.

Fox, Louis J., and Catherwood, Hugh R. "The Reorganization of Personnel Management in the City of San Antonio." *Public Personnel Management Journal*, vol. 11, no. 2 (1982): 104-111.

Halachmi, Arie. "Evaluating Training Policy in Local Governments." *State and Local Government Review*, January 1981, pp. 33-37.

Legislative and Regulatory Reforms in State and Local Personnel Systems. Washington, D.C.: U.S. Office of Personnel Management, 1981.

Personnel Systems Improvement in States and Local Government. Washington, D.C.: U.S. Office of Personnel Management, 1980.

Wehrenberg, Stephen. "Evaluation of Training: Part II." *Personnel Journal*, September 1983, pp. 700-702.

Part 2: Improving Employee Performance

Allenbaugh, G. Eric. "Coaching—A Management Tool for a More Effective Work Performance." *Management Review*, May 1983, pp. 21-26.

Brinkerhoff, Derick, and Kanter, Rosabeth. "Appraising the Performance of Performance Appraisal." *Sloan Management Review*, spring 1980, pp. 3-16.

Clark, Stephen. "Linking Employee Salary Adjustments to Performance: Is It Worth the Effort?" *Governmental Finance*, December 1982, pp. 15-18.

Cohen, Stephen L. "Pre-Packaged vs. Tailor-Made: The Assessment Center Debate." *Personnel Journal*, December 1980, pp. 989-91.

Gallegos, Patrick M. "Communicating Performance Results." *Journal of Systems Management*, March 1983, pp. 25-31.

Goals and Techniques for a Merit Pay. Washington, D.C.: U.S. Office of Personnel Management, 1981.

Greene, Robert J. "Which Pay Delivery System Is Best for Your Organization?" *Personnel*, May–June 1981, pp. 51–58.

Hyde, Albert C. "Performance Appraisal in the Post Reform Era." *Public Personnel Management Journal*, vol. 11, no. 4 (1982): 294–305.

"Incentive Pay PEPs up Production." *American City & County*, August 1983, pp. 38–39.

Lacho, Kenneth J.; Stearns, G. Kent; and Villere, Maurice F. "A Study of Employee Appraisal Systems of Major Cities in the United States." *Public Personnel Management*, March–April 1979, pp. 111–124.

Lawler, Edward E. "Merit Pay: Fact or Fiction?" *Management Review*, April 1981, pp. 50–53.

Nalbandean, John. "Performance Appraisal: If Only People Were Not Involved." *Public Administration Review*, May–June 1981, pp. 392–96.

Ross, Joyce D. "A Current Review of Public Sector Assessment Centers: Cause for Concern." *Public Personnel Management*, January–February 1979, pp. 41–46.

Sackett, Paul R. "A Critical Look at Some Common Beliefs about Assessment Centers." *Public Personnel Management Journal*, vol. 11, no. 2 (1982): 140–47.

Stimson, Richard A. "Performance Pay: Will It Work?" *The Bureaucrat*, summer 1980, pp. 39–47.

Wells, Ronald G. "Guidelines for Effective and Defensible Performance Appraisal Systems." *Personnel Journal*, October 1982, pp. 776–82.

Winstanley, Nathan B. "Are Merit Increases Really Effective?" *Personnel Administrator*, April 1982, pp. 37–41.

Yager, Ed. "A Critique of Performance Appraisal Systems." *Personnel Journal*, February 1981, pp. 129–33.

Part 3: Motivating Employees

Brandt, Terry. "From Japan with Quality." *Western City*, May 1981, pp. 13–22.

Clark, N. Warren. "Incentive Programs in Government: Why Aren't They Being Used?" *Public Personnel Management Journal*, summer 1983, pp. 181–85.

Cosgrove, Don J., and Dinerman, Robert L. "There Is No Motivational Magic." *Management Review*, August 1982, pp. 58–61.

Derven, Ronald. "Laying the Groundwork with Total Benefits Planning." *Pension World*, September 1981, pp. 105–106 and October 1981, pp. 23–26.

Dwortzan, Bernard. "The ABC's of Incentive Programs." *Personnel Journal*, June 1982, pp. 436–42.

"Employee Incentives." *Productivity 2*. Washington, D.C.: U.S. Office of Personnel Management, 1979.

Fonvielle, William H. "Making Employee Surveys Work for Your Organization." *Management Review*, April 1982, pp. 47–54.

Golembiewski, Robert T., and Proehl, Carl W., Jr. "Public Sector Applications of Flexible Workhours: A Review of Available Experience." *Public Administration Review*, January–February 1980, pp. 72–85.

Graf, Lee A. "Suggestion Program Failure: Causes and Remedies." *Personnel Journal*, June 1982, pp. 450–54.

Halal, William E., and Brown, Bob S. "Participative Management Myth and Reality." *California Management Review*, summer 1981, pp. 20–32.

Hamilton, Eugene K. "How to Set up Flexible Benefits." *Compensation Review*, first quarter 1982, pp. 68–74.

Hellan, Richard T., and Campbell, William J. "Contracting for EAP Services." *Personnel Administrator*, September 1981, pp. 49–51.

Hollman, Robert W., and Ullrich, Maureen P. "Participative and Flexible Decision Making." *Journal of Small Business Management*, January 1983, pp. 1–7.

Juechter, W. Matthew. "The Pros and Cons of Participative Management." *Management Review*, September 1982, pp. 44–48.

Klein, Gerald D. "Implementing Quality Circles: A Hard Look at Some of the Realities." *Personnel*, November–December 1981, pp. 11–20.

Kovach, Kenneth. "New Directions in Fringe Benefits." *S.A.M. Advanced*

Management Journal, summer 1983, pp. 55-63.

Levin, Blair. "Flextime: Major Benefits for Local Governments." *Western City,* January 1977, pp. 6-16.

Manning, George, and Curtis, R. Kent. "The Why of Quality Circles." *Transitions,* autumn 1982, pp. 1-20.

Marks, Mitchell Lee. "Conducting an Employee Attitude Survey." *Personnel Journal,* September 1982, pp. 684-91.

McConkey, Dale D. "Participative Management: What It Really Means in Practice." *Business Horizon,* October 1980, pp. 66-73.

McFillen, James M., and Podsakoff, Philip M. "A Coordinated Approach to Motivation Can Increase Productivity." *Personnel Administrator,* July 1983, pp. 45-53.

Morris, Stephen. "Cutting the Cost of Employee Benefits." *Association Management,* June 1983, pp. 75-79.

Osborne, Karen Quallo, and Shevat, Renee Scialdo. "Study Circles: Personal and Professional Fulfillment for Employees." *Management Review,* June 1982, pp. 37-42.

Ronen, Simcha, and Primps, Sophia B. "The Impact of Flextime on Performance and Attitudes in 25 Public Agencies." *Public Personnel Management Journal,* vol. 9, no. 3 (1980): 201-207.

Segalla, Ellen. *Employee Assistance Programs for Local Governments.* Management Information Service Report, vol. 14, no. 8, Washington, D.C.: International City Management Association, August 1982.

Shea, James H. "Cautions about Cafeteria-Style Benefit Plans." *Personnel Journal,* January 1981, pp. 37-58.

Thompson, Walt. "Is the Organization Ready for Quality Circles?" *Training and Development Journal,* December 1982, pp. 115-18.

Turney, John R., and Cohen, Stanley L. "Alternative Work Schedules Increase Employee Satisfaction." *Personnel Journal,* March 1983, pp. 202-207.

Wadia, Maneck S. "Participative Management: Three Common Problems." *Personnel Journal,* November 1980, pp. 927-28.

Zemke, Ron. "Should Supervisors Be Counselors?" *Training/HRD,* March 1983, pp. 44-53.

Part 4: New Labor-Management Ventures

Goldoff, Anna C., and Tatage, David C. "Joint Productivity Committees." *Public Administration Review,* March-April 1978, pp. 184-86.

Horton, Raymond D. "Productivity and Productivity Bargaining in Government: A Critical Analysis." *Public Administration Review,* July-August 1976, pp. 407-14.

Labor-Management Committees in the Public Sector. Washington, D.C.: National Commission on Productivity and Work Quality, 1975.

Layden, Dianne R. "Productivity and Productivity Bargaining: The Environmental Context." *Public Personnel Management Journal,* vol. 9, no. 4 (1980): 244-56.

Lewin, David. "Implications of Concession Bargaining: Lesson from the Public Sector." *Monthly Labor Review,* March 1983, pp. 33-35.

Mills, D. Quinn. "When Employees Make Concessions." *Harvard Business Review,* May-June 1983, pp. 103-13.

Otis, Irwin. "Rx for Improving Productivity: Labor-Management Committees." *S.A.M. Advanced Management Journal,* spring 1983, pp. 53-59.

Susman, Gerald I. *A Guide to Labor-Management Committees in State and Local Government.* Washington, D.C.: Public Technology, Inc., 1980.

Part 5: Emerging Personnel Issues

Asherman, Ira G. "The Corrective Discipline Process." *Personnel Journal,* July 1982, pp. 528-31.

Brennan, Andrew J. J. "How to Set up a Corporate Wellness Program." *Management Review,* May 1983, pp. 41-47.

Carter, Michael F. "Comparable Worth: An Idea Whose Time Has Come." *Personnel Journal,* October 1981, pp. 792-94.

Connell, John J. "The People Factor in the Office of the Future." *Administrative Management*, January 1980, pp. 36–37, 74–76.

Day, Charles R., Jr. "Comparable Worth: A Smoldering Issue Is Ready to Burn Once More." *Modern Office Procedures*, July 1983, pp. 72–80.

Fitness and Health for Employees. Management Information Service Report, vol. 14, no. 4. Washington, D.C.: International City Management Association, April 1982.

Gaul, Annette. "Burnout." *Management*, spring 1982, pp. 2–5.

Glicken, Morley D. "A Counseling Approach to Employee Burnout." *Personnel Journal*, March 1983, pp. 222–28.

Hubbartt, William S. "A Personnel Policies Primer." *Office Administration and Automation*, January 1983, pp. 40–42, 72–73.

———. "Sexual Harassment: Coping with the Controversy." *Administrative Management*, August 1980, pp. 34–35, 74–76.

James, Jennifer. "Sexual Harassment." *Public Personnel Management Journal*, vol. 10, no. 1 (1981): 402–407.

McIntyre, Douglas I., and Renick, James C. "Protecting Public Employees and Employers from Sexual Harassment." *Public Personnel Management Journal*, vol. 11, no. 3 (1982): 282–92.

McKendrick, Joseph. "The Office of 1990 Human Resources." *Management World*, January 1982, pp. 15–17.

Nardoni, Ren. "The Personnel Office of the Future Is Available Today."

Personnel Journal, February 1982, pp. 132–34.

Neugarten, Dail Ann. "Themes and Issues in Public Sector Productivity." *Public Personnel Management Journal*, vol. 9, no. 4 (1980): 229–35.

Neuse, Steven M. "A Critical Perspective on the Comparable Worth Debate." *Review of Public Personnel Administration*, fall 1982, pp. 1–20.

Pilla, Lou. "The Office of 1990 Automation." *Management World*, January 1982, pp. 18–24.

Remick, Helen. "The Comparable Worth Controversy." *Public Personnel Management Journal*, vol. 10, no. 4 (1981): 371–83.

Rowe, Mary P. "Dealing with Sexual Harassment." *Harvard Business Review*, May–June 1981, pp. 42–48.

Walker, A. J. "The 10 Most Common Mistakes in Developing Computer-Based Personnel Systems." *Personnel Administrator*, July 1980, pp. 39–42.

Waltz, Anne. "Integrating Disabled Workers into Your Workforce." *Public Personnel Management Journal*, vol. 10, no. 4 (1981): 412–17.

Werther, William B., Jr. "Out of the Productivity Box." *Business Horizons*, September–October 1982, pp. 51–59.

Whaley, George. "Controversy Swirls over Comparable Worth Issue." *Personnel Administrator*, April 1982, pp. 51–61.

Wydra, Frank T. "Why Employment Relationships Are Changing and What You Can Do about Them." *Training/HRD*, October 1981, pp. 31–35.

Practical Management Series

**Creative Personnel Practices:
New Ideas for Local Government**

Text type
Century Expanded

Composition
Unicorn Graphics
Washington, D.C.

Printing and binding
R. R. Donnelley & Sons Company
Harrisonburg, Virginia

Paper
International Bookmark, 55#

Cover design
Rebecca Geanaros